CH

RADIOMAN

ALSO BY CAROL EDGEMON HIPPERSON

The Belly Gunner

RADIOMAN

An Eyewitness Account of Pearl
Harbor and WWII in the Pacific

CAROL EDGEMON HIPPERSON

THOMAS DUNNE BOOKS
ST. MARTIN'S MINOTAUR ☙ NEW YORK

THOMAS DUNNE BOOKS.
An imprint of St. Martin's Press.

www.thomasdunnebooks.com
www.stmartins.com

Book design by Phil Mazzone

Library of Congress Cataloging-in-Publication Data

Daves, Ray.
  Radioman : an eyewitness account of Pearl Harbor and World War II in
the Pacific / [edited by] Carol Edgemon Hipperson. — 1st ed.
      p. cm.
  Includes bibliographical references
  ISBN-13: 978-0-312-38694-8 (alk. paper)
  ISBN-10: 0-312-38694-X (alk. paper)
  1. Daves, Ray.   2. World War, 1939–1945—Naval operations,
American.   3. World War, 1939–1945—Campaigns—Pacific Ocean.
4. World War, 1939–1945—Personal narratives, American.   5. United
States. Navy—Radiomen—Biography.   6. Sailors—United States—
Biography.   I. Hipperson, Carol Edgemon.   II. Title.
  D767.D37   2008
  940.54'5973092—dc22
  [B]
                                                        2008024935

First Edition: November 2008

10   9   8   7   6   5   4   3   2   1

To my father-in-law, Roy H. Hipperson, and all
other Americans who served overseas and
on the home front during World War II:

Thank you for your service and your sacrifice.

CONTENTS

CONTENTS

ACKNOWLEDGMENTS

Among the many professionals and organizations who assisted with the historical research that was required to verify and clarify an American combat veteran's memories of the war years, 1936–1945, the following were especially generous with their time and expertise: Jack A. Green, Public Affairs Officer, The Naval Historical Center; Robert Clark, Supervisory Archivist, FDR Presidential Library; staff at USO World Headquarters; Joe Leather, Docent Supervisor, Aircraft Carrier *Hornet* (CV 12); James Simard, Research Librarian, Alaska State Library; Michiko Takaoka, Director, Japanese Cultural Center, Mukogawa Fort Wright Institute; Stan Roth and Ray Riches of the future Armed Forces and Aerospace Museum in Spokane, Washington.

The following relatives and friends also helped with the historical research and/or contributed materials and photographs from their personal collections: Glenn "the Good" Edgemon; Charles "Chuck" Edgemon; the late Warren "Ike" Edgemon; Brian G. Hipperson; N. A. "Stretch" Brown; Ivan Urnovitz; Larry Elsom; Dick and Misako Egner; Nicholas Hopper; Irene Ripley;

C. E. "Ted" and Marie T. Wigton; Robert and Janet Young; the late Karl "Bill" Mote; Tina McGovern; Jerry Schneider; Tim Stromberger; Angela V. Daves Boyette. Pat Culleton, Bob Brunkow, and Jerry Gleesing proofread the manuscript, caught errors, and suggested significant improvements.

In addition to loaning photos and research materials, the following members of the Lilac City Chapter of Pearl Harbor Survivors helped to identify and select the most commonly shared memories among the men and women of the World War II generation: Charles and Irene Boyer; Debbie Fockler; Jean Flechel; John S. "Sid" and Dorothea Kennedy; Evi Kohler; the late Helen McMillan; Robert Ohnemus; William and Eleanor Paulukonis; Warren and Betty Schott; James and Millie Sinnott; Pat Stone; Joseph and Ruth Wagner; the late Irv Lissy; Pat Lissy; Denis and Vina Mikkelsen; Hoyt "Bud" and Coral Colburn.

Ray Daves is the Pearl Harbor Survivor who consented to the difficult and often painful process of remembering the war years. Had his wife, Adeline, and their daughter Rayma not encouraged him, Daves would have kept his silence and the uneasy peace that came from a lifetime of refusing to talk about the war.

I must also acknowledge the contribution of my husband, Brian G. Hipperson. Without his tolerance and forgiveness of my work habits, I would have been unable to finish a project of this magnitude. Nor can I fail to express my personal and professional gratitude to those who understood and shared my vision: my agent, Marlene Stringer, my editor, Ruth Cavin, her assistant, Toni Plummer, and the production editor, David Stanford Burr.

As a person of faith, I know that most of the praise and credit for *Radioman* belongs to God. Only a series of miracles and answered prayers could have prompted all of the above individuals to come forward and assist at precisely the moment they were needed. Luck played no part in the success of this mission.

I have seen war on land and sea. I have seen blood running from the wounded. I have seen men coughing out their gassed lungs. I have seen the dead in the mud. I have seen cities destroyed. . . . I have seen the agony of mothers and wives. I hate war. . . .

Many causes produce war. There are ancient hatreds, turbulent frontiers, the "legacy of old forgotten, far-off things, and battles long ago." There are new-born fanaticisms. Convictions on the part of certain peoples that they have become the unique depositories of ultimate truth and right.

—From the speech delivered by
President Franklin D. Roosevelt
at Chautauqua, New York,
August 14, 1936

RADIOMAN

1

THE TREE ARMY

June 1936–September 1937

They were waiting for us in North Dakota. I saw the crowd as soon as I stepped off the train in that little town. At least fifty of them—men, women, children—were all dressed in leather with feathers and beads, head to toe. And bells. I heard bells jingling when they moved toward us. I was not afraid of them. I was just curious. I didn't know what they were going to do until they began to chant and step to the beat of the drums. The first dance was very slow and swaying, with lots of arm movements. It felt like a prayer or a blessing. As the drumbeats got louder and faster, the dancers were whirling in lines and circles all around the train station. It was more than beautiful. It was amazing. How anybody could dance like that for a whole hour on such a hot, dusty afternoon was beyond me.

No one told us the name of the tribe, and I have never known why they chose to dance for us that day. Maybe the Army or the government paid them, or maybe they just did it because they wanted to. Either way, I thought it was awful nice of them. I had

1

never seen Native American ceremonial dancing before. The local townspeople must have thought it was pretty special, too, because over a hundred of them came out and watched it with us. And there was a little black and white mongrel puppy. He was just wandering through the crowd, like he was looking for somebody. We tried to find his owner; the station workers said he was a stray. So we smuggled him aboard the train and took him with us.

I had a window seat through the rest of North Dakota, into Montana, and across the Rockies. I'd never seen such high mountains and thick forests—we didn't have anything like that back home in Arkansas either—and I think that's when I knew for sure that my high school principal was right. When I told him I was planning to quit school at the end of tenth grade, he advised me to enlist in the Civilian Conservation Corps (CCC). My parents had to sign the papers, of course, because I was only sixteen. I doubt that they would have agreed to it, if not for President Franklin D. Roosevelt. The CCC was one of his ideas, so it had to be good. Mom and Dad practically worshiped FDR.[1] If they needed another reason, it was me: Of their seven children, I was the renegade. My parents probably knew I would have just run away if they hadn't let me go.

I boarded that train in Little Rock in the summer of '36, along with seventy-five other guys from Arkansas. There were a few older men in my group, like in their twenties, but everybody else was under eighteen. I don't think any of us understood that the CCC was actually run by the military until we got to Idaho. The buses that picked us up from the train station in the town of Worley had Army markings, and when they dropped us off at Camp Peone, the first man who spoke to us was a captain in the Army. He was the camp commander. The assistant camp commander was an officer in the Navy. They gave us each a couple of sets of Army-looking olive drab uniforms, and all of the camp buildings had military-sounding names: the "mess hall" was for eating, the "barracks" were for sleeping, and toilets were "latrines." But we never had to salute or march around the camp or anything like that. They even let us keep our puppy. He slept with us in the barracks that night. We called him Camp Dog.

The next morning, and every morning except Sunday for the next six months, the LEMs—"local experienced men"—took us somewhere outside the camp to work. Most of the time, they had us planting trees on the hillsides, which was supposed to stop soil erosion.[2] We also dug irrigation ditches for the farmers in northern Idaho and built roads for the loggers. I'd be lying if I said I liked that kind of work, but it was a whole lot better than farming. I didn't mind milking cows and feeding chickens, but I hated the rest. I especially hated pitching hay in the barn on a hot summer day. All those little stickery pieces go down the back of your neck and get stuck in the sweat underneath your shirt.

For me, the CCC was just a way to get out of working for my dad on the family farm. It was probably also the only way. Some

From 1933–1942, about 3 million Americans chose to live and work in CCC camps much like this one. The CCC "Tree Army" was the first organized attempt to restore and preserve the nation's natural environment. COURTESY OF NATIONAL ARCHIVES.

of the guys at Camp Peone had high school diplomas, and even they couldn't find a job anywhere else. But the CCC gave us each a five-dollar bill at the end of the month, plus a twenty-five-dollar check that we never saw because the government mailed it directly to our families. My parents could have got by without it—farmers always had something to eat, even in the worst of times—but I think a lot of families really depended on those checks every month. The older men didn't even keep their five-dollar bills. They sent those home to the wife and kids, too. I never heard anyone say this was all because of "the Depression." We just called it "hard times."[3]

Most of us at Camp Peone were just killing time until we were old enough to join the real military. I was thinking about going into the Army myself, until I heard the Army was still using mules.[4] That didn't sound very modern to me. I was afraid I might end up pitching hay for a string of mules. I didn't know there was such a thing as an Army Air Corps, and I'd never even heard of the Coast Guard or the Marines. As far as I knew, there was only one other choice. I started asking questions about the Navy.

The CCC officers told me all about the Navy's service schools, which sounded a lot like trade schools. They claimed you could learn to be a mechanic or an electrician or a baker, or just about anything in the Navy, and it only took four years. The camp commander told me I should try for radio school. "Son," he said, "the future is in communications. If you can get the Navy to teach you about radios and electronics, you'll never be out of work again." That was all I needed to hear. Right then and there, I decided to join the Navy, and patriotism had nothing to do with it. I doubt if I could have even spelled the word.

If anyone had told me America was about to go to war, it wouldn't have made a bit of difference. I didn't know the meaning of war. It was just History, something you studied in school. Oh, there were lots of World War I veterans around then, but not in my family. I'm sure my great-grandfather could have told me a thing or two—he was a Civil War veteran—but he died when I was four. I didn't even know which side he was on. I did get scared when I overheard my parents talk about an invasion somewhere.[5] I went right out, loaded my granddad's shotgun, and stashed it under my bed that night. I thought I was ready if anybody tried to invade Arkansas. I think I was about ten.

By the time I got to high school, I'd heard so much war talk, I was sick of it. I tuned it out. I didn't care which country was invading which country. They were all on the other side of the world, anyway, and Current Events class was boring. The only class discussion I really remember was when the teacher told us about the Nazis and all the crazy laws they were making against the Jews in Germany.[6] We even had to listen to one of Adolf Hitler's speeches on the radio. My classmates and I agreed that Hitler was the craziest Nazi of all. We had no idea what he was saying, of course, because none of us understood German. It wouldn't have mattered if we did. You couldn't make out the words, what with all the crowd noise in the background. It sounded like cheering, so I assumed Hitler was popular in Germany. My parents couldn't stand him. They called him "that crazy paperhanger." I guess he used to be an artist before he went into politics.[7]

Mom and Dad were just sure we would go to war with Germany again. "It'll be just like World War I," they said, "only bigger." I don't know where they got that idea—probably from listening to Kaltenborn. Of all the different news programs on the radio, they liked H. V. Kaltenborn the best.[8] I can't recall if my folks thought we might also go to war with Japan at that time, but I knew better than to tell them I'd decided to join the Navy. They still had it in their heads that I was going to come home and finish high school. So I wrote and told them what they wanted to hear, that I was taking classes at Camp Peone. Some of it was even true.

The CCC did offer a few high school–level courses. I took a couple in soil conservation, mainly to get out of digging ditches. I signed up for typing because the camp commander said it would help me get ahead in the Navy. He also advised me to visit the high school English teacher in Worley and ask her what books I should be reading. She recommended *The Canterbury Tales*. According to her, if I could read that book and pass the same test she gave her students, I would have no trouble with the Navy's technical manuals. So I read *The Canterbury Tales*. Took me weeks to get through that sucker, and I hated every minute of it. But it sure felt good to pass that test. I guess I just needed to know that I could.

The CCC took us on field trips, too, just like in school. The one I remember best is when they let us ride in the seat behind the pilot of a small airplane. That was my first plane flight, and I loved it. Couldn't wait to go again. When they told me that the Navy had planes, too, I was all the more determined to join up. Of course, I didn't put that in the letters I was writing to my parents either. I told them I was going to church. That was quite a stretch. I'd always been the family rebel that way, too. When Dad read the Bible

CCC workers who took classes sometimes wore a school sweater over their uniform. Ray Daves, 16, models his new P sweater at Camp Peone, Idaho, December 1936. Building in background is the camp administration building. COURTESY OF RAY DAVES COLLECTION.

out loud every night after supper, I usually went to bed early so I wouldn't have to listen. But there was that one Sunday at Camp Peone when the Baptist youth group from Spokane came out and conducted church services for us in the mess hall. One of the girls was pretty cute, too. You better believe I got her phone number.

Adeline Bentz was older than I—nearly seventeen when I met her—but that was all right. And even though she lived in Spokane, which was in the state of Washington, it was only an hour's drive from Camp Peone. I didn't have a car, of course, but the CCC bought most of our supplies in Spokane. Well, somebody had to go along and help load all those groceries on the trucks. I got to visit her two or three times a month that way. I met her parents, too. They didn't seem to mind that I was in the CCC, and they never made fun of the way I talked. Frankly, I thought they were the ones with an accent, but I never said so. I wanted them to like me, because I really liked that girl. She had a lot to do with my decision to reenlist for another six months in the CCC.

CCC worker Ray Daves, 17, said goodbye to "that girl" Adeline Bentz, also 17, at her home in Spokane, Washington, August 1937. COURTESY OF RAY DAVES COLLECTION.

When I passed my typing class at Camp Peone, I got promoted to company clerk. That raised my pay to thirty-six dollars a month, and I got to keep ten instead of five. The best part was, I didn't have to plant trees or dig ditches any more. I just sat in the camp office all day and listened to the radio while I did the commander's paperwork. I kept the radio tuned to the music stations at first, but I soon got hooked on the news about the king of England. He was threatening to quit if he couldn't marry Mrs. Simpson, but she was married to somebody else when she took up with the king, so she was trying to get a divorce, and it was just one thing after another, like a soap opera. Every day there was some new development. Sometimes I stayed past quitting time—typed the same report twice—just so I could keep up with the king of England's love story on the radio.[9]

I could have signed on for another hitch in the CCC after I turned seventeen, but I was anxious to go home and join the Navy. When I said goodbye to Adeline, I didn't think it was very likely that we would ever see each other again. I just promised to write and let her know if I made it in the Navy, and that's where we left it in the summer of '37.

See Time Line, page 213, and Historical Notes, page 214.

2

JOINING THE NAVY

September 1937–mid-April 1939

Okay, so I admit I lied to the Navy about my age. I thought I was old enough when I got home from the CCC, and, technically, I guess I was. But everybody in town said forget it. There were too many older guys out of work, and they were all trying to get into the military. The Navy had so few openings, they weren't even taking applications from anybody under eighteen. That's what I heard, and I was crushed. I thought about going back to the CCC for another year. My two older brothers talked me into a road trip instead. We had an aunt in Oregon; she invited us to come and stay with her until we found jobs there. So the three of us pooled our savings and bought a used Model A Ford. We packed the rumble seat with food and blankets and took turns driving.

It was about a two-week trip from Arkansas to Oregon. Some nights we slept in the car; other times we camped out on the ground by the side of the road. If we happened to be near a town, we stayed in a hotel. That cost two or three dollars a night, which was kind of expensive for three guys out of work, so we shared a single room. We never had any trouble finding a gas station—that cost around twenty cents a gallon—but there were no freeways.[1] Some of the roads weren't even paved. I saw lots of Burma Shave signs with silly jokes and sayings, but I do not recall any posted speed limits. We didn't come across any sheriff or state patrol cars either, which was good, because we didn't any of us have a driver's license.[2]

There were more jobs in Oregon, and the pay was better, too. Even the temporary, seasonal work paid twenty-five cents an hour. They called it "minimum wage."[3] First time I ever heard the term. It was great money for a potato sorter. All I had to do was stand there and pick out all the green ones on the conveyor belt. It was a lot easier than working for my dad on the family farm. Around Christmastime, I got on at the soda fountain in the drugstore. That didn't take much training either, as soon as I figured out how much cherry syrup to squirt in with the carbonated water, and I was fine with being a soda jerk until I turned eighteen. That was the plan, until my brother Velton got laid off again. My eighteenth birthday was still a couple of months away when he walked into the drugstore and said, "To heck with it. I'm going to join the Navy." No way was I going to let him go without me.

We took the bus to the nearest recruiting station, which was inside the post office in downtown Portland. I sat down on the steps and started filling out the application. When I got to the blank for "date of birth," I never thought twice. I wrote "June 1, 1919." I was afraid the Navy wouldn't take me if I told the truth: I was actually born in 1920. I knew it was wrong to lie, but I'd have done just about anything to increase my chances of getting accepted. It didn't seem like such a big deal. The recruiters did not require any proof of age.[4] They didn't even ask for a social security card, which was also good, because I didn't have one of those either. I didn't know there was such a thing at the time.[5]

After I filled out the application, I had to take a written exam. It was all essay questions, like, "What can you do for your country in the Navy?" I think the only purpose was to prove you could read and write. When I finished that, I had to go inside the post office and take the physical. I was five feet eight and weighed 128 pounds. That's all I saw on the doctor's clipboard; everything else was just checkmarks. Next came the interview. I honestly do not know what I would have said if that Navy officer had looked me straight in the eye and said, "You're not really eighteen yet, are you?" But he never did. He just thumbed through all the papers in my file and asked the same questions I'd already answered on the written exam. That's all there was to it. He said I was accepted, but there were no openings at the moment. I was told to go home and wait for a letter. I don't know why my brother got rejected. I felt sorry for Velton. He just laughed and said he was a whole lot sorrier for me. I was the one that had to go home and tell Mom and Dad I had just enlisted in the Navy.

I knew my mother would cry. What surprised me was when my dad cried, too. I'd never seen him get so emotional before. I told them I only did it for the education. The way they carried on, you'd have thought I was going off to war. Dad was worried about the Nazis taking over in Austria, and Mom was all upset about Japan invading China. Kaltenborn had them both convinced that we would be at war with either Germany or Japan tomorrow. I didn't believe it. I still thought Hitler was a harmless kook, and I couldn't see how we had a bone to pick with the Japanese.[6] We went round and round on that. Dad finally shook his head and told my mother to start praying for me. As soon as she left the room, he said, "Son, why the Navy? You can't even swim!"

I tried to avoid talking politics with my parents after that. All summer long, I ran out to the mailbox every day to see if I'd got my letter from the Navy. It didn't come. Adeline was writing to me, though, just like she promised. She sent me a picture after she graduated from high school. I had to write back and say I was still waiting on the Navy. I felt like a total loser. I quit checking the mailbox after Christmas. I thought they lost my application and forgot about me. I knew I couldn't take another summer on the family farm, so I signed on for another hitch in the CCC in the spring of '39. Wouldn't you know, that's when it came.

Nearly a year after I filled out the application in Oregon, the Navy finally had an opening for me.[7] The letter said I had two weeks to report to the recruiting station, and there was a one-way bus ticket to Portland inside. I didn't need two weeks. I was on that bus the very next day.

There were seven other guys ahead of me on the day I arrived in Portland. The recruiters swore us all into the Navy at once. After we signed our oaths, they put us on a train to California. Sure I was nervous; everybody was. We didn't know exactly where we were going or what was going to happen when we got there. So we talked about girls. I did not have a steady girlfriend back home, and Adeline was only a pen pal. I did think about her a lot, though, until I walked through the main gates at the Naval Training Station in San Diego. It was bigger than a hundred CCC camps, and it was right on the Pacific. That was the first time I'd ever seen the ocean, but I was really looking at all those warships in the bay.[8]

See Time Line, page 215, and Historical Notes, page 217.

3

BASIC TRAINING

Mid-April–August 1939

The first thing they did was cut off all our hair. Then we got our uniforms. The dress whites and dress blues were for Sundays and special occasions. Those had stripes around the collar and two stars in the back. The regular or "undress" uniform—whites or blues—were plainer, for everyday. None of the pants had zippers. Instead, they all had this square flap across the fly, and thirteen buttons. The guys issuing the uniforms told us this was for the thirteen original colonies. If you wanted bell-bottoms, which everybody did because flared legs were the style, you had to take them to a tailor and pay for the alterations yourself.

There was one piece of the uniform everybody hated, and that was the leggings. We were apprentice seamen—lowest there is in the Navy—so we had to wear them every single day. Leggings were these stupid-looking white canvas things that snapped around your pant legs. I have no idea what purpose they served, except to show we were the scum of the base for the next sixteen weeks.[1] Oh, we had a lot of choice words for those leggings. Some guys called them "boots." Maybe that's why it was called "boot camp."[2]

We couldn't go to bed at night until we scrubbed our leggings with a brush in a bucket full of soap and water. And every morning before breakfast we had to do the same with our hammocks. We hated those, too. I never understood why we had to sleep in hammocks.[3] Maybe it was to teach us discipline, but they were torture. It was like sleeping on a banana. If you heard a big thump in the night, it was some poor guy that made the mistake of turning over in his sleep. You had to stay on your back or the hammock would flip upside down and dump you on the floor.

There were about a hundred of us in Company Nine; our barracks were located in what they called the John Paul Jones section. I didn't know who John Paul Jones was.[4] I thought he was the guy that invented marching drills, because that's what we

U.S. Navy recruits (also called apprentice seamen) in Company Nine, Naval Training Station, San Diego, California, with John Paul Jones barracks in background, April 1939. Seaman Third Class Ray Daves, 18, is seated, front row, second from right. "Dress blue" uniforms have white markings. The "seaman's stripe" around right shoulder seam indicates sailor is "unrated," not yet trained in any Navy specialty. [This is a portion of the original 8" x 39" print that shows the entire company.] COURTESY OF RAY DAVES COLLECTION.

did, every day, for hours at a time. The marching field was called "the grinder." Maybe it was supposed to grind the civilian out of you. The Navy had a lot of weird terms for ordinary things like that. Stairs were not stairs; they were "ladders." Floors were "decks," and right is "starboard," and left is "port," and it just goes on and on. I felt like I was learning a foreign language. There was no sense trying to figure it out. After a while you just get used to speaking "Navy"; you follow orders, and you don't ask questions anymore.

Marksmanship was pretty fun. I'd done a fair amount of squirrel and quail hunting with my grandpa's shotgun, but the Navy issued rifles. Ours were Springfields, thirty-ought-sixes. The shells were about as long as your index finger and as big around as your thumb. It was not an automatic, or even a semiautomatic weapon. Everybody said it was probably left over from World War I. I liked it for target practice, though.[5] It even had a bayonet attachment, which was kind of cool. The blade was about twelve inches long and sharp as a razor. We kept that in a leather sheath, clipped onto our ammunition belts.

I only remember one time when we actually used our bayonets, and that was on the dummies—gunny sacks stuffed with straw. When we went out to the shooting range that day, I saw them hanging like a bunch of scarecrows on a line about chest high. The instructor told us to snap the bayonet on the end of our rifle and take turns running up and stabbing the dummies. We had to fire one round before we pulled the blade out. He said that would shatter the enemy's bones and make it easier to withdraw your bayonet from the "body." So we all did that, several times apiece, but there was a lot of mumbling up and down the lines. Finally, one of the guys in my company spoke up. He actually had the nerve to ask the question all of us were thinking, which was, "Why do we have to learn all this Army stuff?" The instructor said, "Sailor, if this country goes to war and your ship gets sunk, you might find yourself on a beach in enemy territory." End of discussion. Well, we didn't think there was ever going to be a war, and we still thought the bayonet drill with the dummies was lame.[6]

There was also a swimming pool. It looked Olympic-sized to me—about fifty meters long—and we couldn't graduate from basic until we could swim the length of that pool three times, without stopping. Well, my dad was right. I really was a rotten swimmer. Would you believe it, I was the only one in my company who did not qualify on the first try. So, every day after that I had orders to report for swimming lessons. The guy in charge of the pool was a boatswain. It's pronounced *bo-sun*. Don't ask me. That's another one of those Navy words. Anyway, this boatswain was a chief petty officer, which is like a master sergeant in the Army, and he was really old, like in his forties. Every time I showed up for another session with him, he said, "Boy, I'm gonna teach you to swim if it kills you." He had this long pole with a net on the end, and whenever he caught me dog-paddling, he would reach out with that pole and push my head under the water. I really think he would have liked to drown me if he thought he could get away with it. That chief boatswain was the second meanest guy I ever met in the Navy.

The first meanest was our company commander. He was a chief petty officer, too, but his specialty was torpedoes. You could tell by the insignia on his sleeve. Now, why the Navy would put a chief torpedoman in charge of training a hundred new recruits, I have no idea. I just remember swearing to myself, if I ever got to be a chief of anything in the Navy, I would never be as mean as he was. The man never spoke to us in a normal tone of voice. He just yelled, all the time. One morning, we were all lined up on the grinder, and the chief hollered out, "Davis! Step forward!" Well, we did have a guy named Davis in my company, but the chief wasn't looking at him. He was looking at me. So I stepped forward. He got right up in my face and started chewing me out for something I had not done. One of the older guys finally spoke up and told him I was "Daves," not "Davis." That chief petty officer never once admitted that he'd made a mistake, and he never told me he was sorry. But he did call me into his office a few days later and told me I was now one of his four apprentice petty officers. Maybe that was his way of making it up to me.

Apprentice petty officer was sort of like squad leader in the Army, I think. We got no extra pay, and the title did not exist outside of boot camp. All I got was a square knot insignia on my sleeve and a whole lot of teasing. Everyone called us "the square knot admirals." It was now my job to enforce lights-out in the barracks by ten o'clock. Real big deal. I was also supposed to report anybody who broke the rules. I never did, and neither did the other apprentice petty officers, as far as I know. Oh, I suppose if a guy came back from a night on the town with his trousers on backward, he might have been reported, but nobody in my company ever stepped that far out of line. We didn't have much free time to begin with, and there was very little horsing around, because we were all so serious about being in the Navy. Most of us saw it as our one and only chance to learn a trade. We were always talking about what great jobs we were going to get when we got out of the Navy.

The only times I remember just hanging out with the guys in my company was on Sunday afternoons, after church. Church attendance was required in boot camp. I didn't go around checking everybody else's dog tag, but if they were anything but Christian, they were out of luck. The only choice we had was Catholic or Protestant. The same Navy chaplain conducted both, one right after the other. I always went to the Protestant service. We had to march to the chapel on Sunday, the same as everywhere else in boot camp. After church, I usually walked over to the channel and watched the ships coming and going in the harbor. I'd never been on anything bigger than a rowboat, so I was just fascinated with the idea of going to sea on a warship.

On the way back to the barracks, my friends and I would stop for a Coke or an ice cream cone at the "gedunk." This was what they called the little convenience store on the base. It was where you went for stuff like newspapers and shaving cream and snacks. What caught my eye were all the photos of the ships on the walls. Some were just postcards, but they had bigger sizes, too, and they were all for sale. That's what I was staring at the first time the guy at the gedunk counter asked me if I'd come for my "pogey bait." I didn't know how to answer that until he told me it meant "candy."

Pogey bait was not one of the Navy words listed in *The Blue-jackets' Manual*. Almost everything else was. We each got one of those books, and we were supposed to read it on our own in our spare time. It was like going through the Bible; I read a few pages every night. It was mostly rules and regulations. The classroom lessons were a lot more interesting. We got those every day, for about an hour after lunch. That's where they taught us stuff like the definition of a man-o'-war. That's a warship; it carries offensive weapons. All the other types of ships, like minelayers and repair ships—they carried weapons, too—but only for defense, like antiaircraft guns.

I also remember learning the Navy's system for naming all the different types of ships. Some kinds of ships were named after birds, some were rivers, and some were stars. There were about a dozen different name categories like that. If you memorized them all, you could tell what kind of ship it was, just by the name. The only name categories I ever learned were the five types of warships: destroyers, cruisers, aircraft carriers, submarines, and battleships. Battleships were states, cruisers were cities, and submarines were fish. Aircraft carriers were named after famous battles or ships in American history, and destroyers were people. The instructor said the Navy might even name a destroyer after one of us. All we had to do was die like a hero in battle. That got a laugh. Nobody in my company believed that was very likely.

The only other classroom lesson I really remember was the VD movies, and, man, was that ever an eye-opener. Me, a dumb farm kid from Arkansas, I didn't even know what a venereal disease was, much less how you caught one. But, you know what, it was news to a lot of the city boys, too. I could tell by the expressions on their faces. Most of the guys in my company were under twenty-one. They didn't know any more about gonorrhea and syphilis than I did. The Navy had a very strict rule about that stuff: If you had any reason to believe you were exposed to an STD, you were supposed to report to the nearest sick bay, sign your name in the doctor's book, and get this medicine that you spread on your private parts. If you showed up with any symptoms after that, you were in the clear. The Navy doctors would just treat you and send you on your way. But if you came down with any of those diseases and your name was not in the book, you were in big trouble.

A week or two before we graduated from boot camp, an officer came into our classroom and read off the list of trade schools. After each one, he asked for a show of hands. Most of the guys in my company wanted to be mechanics or electricians. Nobody— I mean *nobody*—asked for torpedo school. No use for that skill outside of the Navy. I was one of five or six that raised our hands for communications. After that, you had to say which kind: flags or radios. Of course, I picked radios. I had to take the aptitude test, which was to put on headphones and listen to a series of tones. The object was to see if you could tell which tones sounded shorter, like the dots in Morse code, and which were a fraction of a second longer, like dashes. This was easy for me, because I already knew Morse code. I learned it in Cub Scouts. That was how we sent messages back and forth between the tents when we were supposed to be asleep. We usually did it with flashlights, but you could tap it out with sounds just as well.

On graduation day in August, we all got promoted to seaman, second class. That was a huge pay increase, all the way from twenty-one to thirty-six dollars a month, just like that. And most of us also got reclassified as "strikers." I was very happy when I found out I was now a striker radioman. As it was explained to me, this meant I was accepted into radio school, all right, but, for whatever Navy reason, I had to go to sea for a while first. I was okay with that, especially when I saw the ship's name on my orders. It was a man-o'-war. I ran right over to the gedunk and bought the biggest picture they had of that ship and mailed it home to my mother. I didn't know who Flusser was, but he must have been some kind of a hero.[7] The *Flusser* was a destroyer.

See Time Line, page 218, and Historical Notes, page 219.

4

THE DESTROYER

September 1939–May 1940

I had two weeks' leave after I graduated from boot camp. I could have asked my parents to wire money for a bus ticket to Arkansas, but I didn't think it was worth it. By the time I got home, I would have just had to turn around and go back to San Diego. So I got permission to stay on base until it was time to ship out, and that's where I was when I heard the big news: The war had started in Europe. There were great big headlines in the newspapers, and everyone on the base was saying we were going to war, too. It was kind of exciting, really, until President Roosevelt gave one of his Fireside Chats on the radio. As soon as I heard him say America was staying neutral, I lost interest.[1] I paid more attention to packing my seabag than I did to the beginning of World War II.

There were several destroyers tied up to the docks in San Diego. They all looked alike to me, with nothing but numbers painted on the sides. According to my orders, the *Flusser*'s hull number was 368, which meant it was the 368th ship of the destroyer type. I knew that much from boot camp. But none of the

pictures I saw in the classroom or the gedunk could have prepared me for the real thing. If this was what the Navy considered
a small warship, I couldn't imagine the meaning of "big." Good
grief, the *Flusser* was as long as a football field.[2] I was just standing there, staring across the main deck and taking it all in, when
a boatswain's mate came over to the gangplank and told me to
follow him.

We went down all the ladders to the very lowest level of the
ship, where I saw about a hundred bunk beds. He pointed to the
last one at the end of a row and said, "That's yours." At the time,
I was just glad it wasn't a hammock. I didn't yet know how important it was to make friends with the boatswains. They were
like the ship's police and custodians all rolled into one. Among
other things, they got to decide which junior member of the crew
got the worst possible location for sleeping on the entire ship. I
think that must have been me. I was assigned to the bed that sat
directly above the ship's propeller on the port side. If you can
imagine sleeping on top of a lawnmower, that's pretty close to
what it was like when that propeller was turning. The vibration
was as bad as the noise. I soon made it my business to get on the
good side of the boatswains. I could hardly wait for the next new
guy to come aboard.

My duty station was inside this little room they called the radio shack. It was on the main deck, a few steps below the captain's bridge. I didn't know a receiver from a transmitter at the
time, but the radiomen didn't mind. They called me "Sparkie" because of the three little lightning bolts on my striker badge. They
had the same insignia, but they also had stripes on their sleeves,
which made them all very senior to me. Even the third class petty
officers with only one stripe could order me around, and, boy,
did they love that. If I wasn't making their coffee, I was delivering messages and running errands all over the ship. Until the
Navy decided to send me to radio school, I wasn't trained or
qualified for anything else.

The *Flusser* did not have a chief petty officer in the radio
gang, but we did have a couple of "old salts." These were the

guys who'd been to sea lots of times. Butch Littlefield was an Old Salt. He was also Native American—Cherokee, I believe he said—but I don't recall his hometown. I know he was from somewhere in the South, because everyone said we talked alike. I didn't think so, and neither did he, but I suppose if you were from some other part of the country, we probably did sound the same. I wanted to hear stories about all the places Littlefield had seen since he joined the Navy. Why, he'd even been to China.[3] But all that the radiomen wanted to talk about was the war. Even Littlefield thought it was just a matter of when, not if, we would end up fighting the Germans in Europe. That sounded fairly exciting, but I lost interest in that, too, when I heard them say the *Flusser* would never see any action unless the Navy transferred us over to the Atlantic Fleet. There was no talk whatsoever about us going to war in the Pacific against Japan. Not even Littlefield saw that coming. Not then.

The only other guy I really got to know on my first ship was Ensign Harris. He was the commissioned officer in charge of the radio shack on the *Flusser*. I was surprised when he spoke to me. An ensign in the Navy is about the same as a second lieutenant in the Army. I don't know how it worked in the Army, but I came out of basic training with the idea that commissioned officers of any rank in the Navy were gods. In boot camp, we couldn't even pass an officer on the sidewalk without saying, "By your leave, Sir?" We had to wait until he said, "Granted," before we could walk around him. But Ensign Harris wasn't like that. He just came in, poured himself a cup of coffee, and talked to us like a normal person.

The radiomen said Ensign Harris was different from all the other officers on the ship because he was a "mustang." That was what they called a guy who started out as an enlisted man—went through boot camp just like the rest of us—but, for some reason, got picked to be an officer. I had no idea this was possible, so I asked him. He told me he took some test, went to sea for a while, and then the Navy sent him to Annapolis.[4] Not only did he get a first-class, four-year college education for free, he graduated with the rank and pay of a commissioned officer. That gave me a brand-new goal. I didn't just want to learn a trade in the Navy—I wanted to go to college at Annapolis. Ensign Harris gave me a big stack of books and told me to start studying for that exam, and I did, for at least an hour every day.

Some of the other habits I picked up on my first ship were not so good. I didn't drink coffee before I joined the Navy, and I'd never smoked a cigarette in my life. By the time the *Flusser* put out to sea from San Diego, I was doing both. I wanted to fit in—be like the older guys in the radio gang—and I thought it made me look cool. As the ship began to pick up speed outside the harbor, I was just lighting up another Pall Mall. All of a sudden, I couldn't smell the ocean any more. I couldn't smell anything but diesel. The smoke coming out of the ship's two smokestacks was so thick, it felt like the whole inside of my mouth and nose and throat was coated with it. The very thought of breathing in more smoke on top of those diesel fumes made me nauseous. Most of the guys around me kept right on puffing, so maybe it was just me. Of course, this was years and years before anybody knew what smoking does to a person's heart and lungs, but that's when I quit.[5] I gave away my first pack of cigarettes, and I never smoked again while I was at sea.

The next thing I learned was how to walk. As big as that ship seemed to be, it still tossed quite a bit, even when the ocean was calm. I had to brace myself with the opposite leg every time I took a step. I was very proud when the radiomen commented that I was beginning to walk like a "tin-can sailor." They said destroyers were called tin cans because they had no armor. One enemy torpedo was all it would take to sink us. I didn't know if that was true, but we were not at war, so it didn't matter. The only thing that worried me was the queasy feeling in my stomach. I was afraid I might get seasick. I got a little cocky when it went away. After a week or so of cruising along the California coast, I thought I was one of the few sailors who never got seasick. Yeah, well, that was before the storm.

I did notice the ship was tossing a little more than usual when we dropped anchor in the harbor at Long Beach. By the next morning the wind was blowing so hard, I could hear it inside the radio shack. When I opened the door to see what was happening, the sky was totally black. At eight in the morning, it looked like midnight. All the buildings on shore had their lights on—the streetlights were coming on, too—which was kind of eerie, like a solar eclipse. There was no thunder or lightning—just that incredibly strong wind. I should not have gone over to the railing and looked down at the waves. Littlefield called them "big rollers," which is what you get in a really serious storm, like a typhoon.

I didn't have enough experience to be scared. I thought it was fun, like riding a roller coaster, until I got woozy. Next thing you know, I'm hanging over the side of the ship, feeding the fish. One of the cooks came up from below decks and hollered, "That's right, Sparkie! Get it all out! We're fixing pork chops for dinner!" That gave me the dry heaves, and the cook laughed even more. I stayed sick and dizzy until the storm blew over. It seemed like a lifetime, but it was only twenty-four hours. I was pretty embarrassed when I crawled back to the radio shack afterward. The radiomen were listening to the civilian weather reports. They told me this was the first storm of its kind that had ever come ashore at Long Beach. I thought they were just trying to make me feel better.[6]

A lot of the ships in the harbor at Long Beach needed repairs after that storm. *Flusser* was one of the last to get back out to sea, so we were all by ourselves for several days until we caught up with the rest of the fleet, and then it was just destroyers as far as the eye could see. We joined up with four others in what they called a "division." Each ship had its own captain, but everybody was taking orders from the same admiral. Whatever ship he was on was called the flagship because each admiral had his own personal flag. I never got close enough to see how many stars were on that particular admiral's flag, and I don't believe anyone in the radio gang ever mentioned his name.[7] I just knew the radio signal he used if he wanted all the ships to turn in the same direction at

once. Whenever I heard that one long tone, I grabbed onto something. At thirty-five knots, it felt like the *Flusser* was going to lie
down on its side in the water.[8] And all the other destroyers around
us were doing the same thing. It was awesome. I wished I could
have seen it from the air.

I'm not sure how long we were out on maneuvers with the
fleet. It must have been over a month, because I remember my
first payday at sea. The paymaster gave me a choice: I could take
it all in cash right now, or I could "leave it on the books" until
we got into port. Well, there was nothing to buy on the ship, and
I hadn't learned to play poker yet. I told him to let it ride. The
only other day I knew for sure was Friday. The cooks always
gave us scrambled eggs with cornbread and pork and beans for
breakfast on Friday. Hey, at least I remembered to take a shower
every day. A lot of guys didn't. One sailor got to smelling so ripe,
the men he worked with couldn't stand it anymore. It took four
or five of them to strip him down and manhandle him into showers. They gave him a cold one with a scrub brush and saltwater
soap. You could hear that guy cussing and hollering all over the
ship. I thought the officers would step in and put a stop to it, but
they didn't. They just looked the other way.

One morning I walked out on the main deck and saw Diamond Head. I recognized it from the pictures of Hawaii in the
geography books in school. I never thought I would ever see it
for real. Pretty soon the whole crew was buzzing about how they
were planning to spend their money in Honolulu. Some said they
were heading straight to Hotel Street. I didn't know what that
was about. The older guys told me not to go there unless I
wanted to write my name in that book in sick bay, so I guessed it
had something to do with prostitutes. But nobody was going
anywhere until we got inside Pearl Harbor, and that took most
of the day.

There was only one entrance channel to Pearl Harbor, and it
was so narrow, only one destroyer could go through it at a time.
When it was finally our turn, the *Flusser* ended up in what they
called a "dry dock." It looked like a giant bathtub. As soon as

The U.S. Navy base at Pearl Harbor, on the Hawaiian island of Oahu, as it appeared prior to America's entry into World War II: 1. Entrance channel; 2. Dry Docks; 3. Ford Island; 4. Battleship Row; 5. Pacific Fleet Head-quarters/Submarine Base; 6. Fuel Storage Tanks. COURTESY OF U.S. NAVY, PHOTO #80-G-182874.

the ship was inside, it was like somebody pulled the plug and all the water drained out. A whole bunch of dockworkers came swarming up to the sides of the ship. I was told they were scraping off the barnacles. I didn't know what that was either, so I leaned over the railing and looked down. I saw millions of those little critters, like miniature snails. Every part of the ship that was normally underwater was just covered with them.

About half of every section on the ship had to stay on board as the skeleton crew. Since I was the lowest-ranking member of the radio gang, I thought it might be a few days before I could go ashore. I was surprised when Ensign Harris gave me a card with my picture on it and said I was free to go. This was the first time I'd ever seen my liberty card. I knew I was supposed to return it to him as soon as I got back to the ship, but for the next two days that liberty card was my ticket to freedom. The older radiomen told me to bring my swim trunks, so it sounded like we were going to the beach.

There were two ways to get from the Navy's base at Pearl Harbor into the city of Honolulu. Well, three, if you count walking. It was a good six miles. We didn't want to wait for the bus, so we shared a taxi. I couldn't believe it when we stepped out in front of this big fancy hotel on Waikiki Beach. That was the Royal Hawaiian.[9] I suppose an officer could have afforded to get a room there; it looked way too expensive for me. But the older radiomen said it was okay. They said the hotel allowed us to change clothes in their restrooms, and they encouraged sailors and soldiers from all the different bases in Hawaii to come for the weekly radio show.[10] It was broadcast live from Waikiki Beach, right outside the Royal Hawaiian Hotel.

This was the first time I'd ever heard Hawaiian music. I loved the ukeleles and the local folksingers, but, truthfully, I would have to say that it was the girls in the grass skirts that drew the crowds. My friends and I were lucky to get there early that day: We had seats in the front row. I'm sure that's why one of the dancers picked me to come up on stage for a hula lesson. I thought I was special until somebody told me the girls always did that. It was so funny to embarrass a guy that way, they made it a regular part of the weekly show. We spent the rest of our first day on liberty drinking mai tais and flirting with the girls on Waikiki Beach. I even tried surfing. I decided that was like hula dancing, one of those things that's a lot harder than it looks.

The four of us shared a room at the YMCA in Honolulu that night. The next day we rented a car and drove all over the island. I had no idea there were so many beautiful beaches on Oahu. And fruit stands. Every time we stopped, there was a fruit stand. The bananas looked good, so I asked for a quarter's worth. Guy hacks off a stem with about fifty of them. We ate as many as we could and took the rest back to the ship. The *Flusser* was still in dry dock at the time, and all the barnacles had died. They were rotting in the sun, so the whole ship smelled like dead fish. It reeked so bad, I finally grabbed my bar of Palmolive soap and held it right up to my nose. I never would have got to sleep that night without it.

On my next liberty, all the stores in Honolulu had Christmas decorations in the windows. I shopped and went to the movies. They had the most amazing theater in Honolulu. The walls around the lobby were only about six feet high, and there were palm trees and flowers growing inside. I wouldn't normally pay to see a movie unless John Wayne was in it, but the theater in Honolulu was showing newsreels of the Fleet on maneuvers.[11] It was a lot of fun to go to the movies and see if you could spot your ship on the big screen. Afterward, we usually hit the taverns for sandwiches and pool. I was only nineteen, but no bar in Honolulu ever asked for my ID. I guess they figured if you were old enough to be in the Navy, you were old enough to drink. So, yeah, I had a beer or two. Coming from such a conservative family as mine, born and raised in the Bible Belt, this was the first time in my life that I felt like I was really free to do anything I wanted. And I did.

I took the Navy's entrance exam for Annapolis while the *Flusser* was still in dry dock at Pearl Harbor. There were a lot of math questions. I thought I knew most of them. Ensign Harris sent it to Washington, D.C., for scoring. He said it might take over a year to find out if I was accepted. He encouraged me to keep reading, and I did, but sometimes I just stood out on the main deck and watched all the different kinds of ships that went by. Most of them were not tied to docks on shore—they were tied to piers out in the middle of the harbor—so there were always a lot of liberty boats buzzing around. These were like water taxis, for sailors to come and go from their ships. I had a great view of the naval air station on Ford Island, too. It was basically an air base with runways and hangars for the planes from the aircraft carriers, but none of the carriers ever came into Pearl Harbor while I was there on the *Flusser*. The only planes I saw on Ford Island were the Navy's scout planes—the PBYs—and, every now and then a C-47. Those were the big cargo planes from the mainland. They brought the mail.

My mother wrote to me about once a week. It was usually just family news, but she never failed to write a Bible verse at the end. Her favorite was John 3:16.[12] She was always after me to get right with God. Adeline was writing to me, too. She told me about her friends, her brothers, all the Christmas parties she was going to. She was especially excited about getting her first job out of secretarial school. *The Spokesman-Review* newspaper hired her to type the mailing labels for all their out-of-town subscribers. I didn't really think of her as my girlfriend, but she was getting to be more than a pen pal. I hadn't seen her in over two years, and I didn't know when or if I would ever see her again. I just knew she was different from all the other girls I'd met and dated since I joined the Navy. I sent her a little Hawaiian music box for Christmas that year.

We did not have a tree or any holiday decorations on the ship, but the cooks went all-out for dinner on Christmas Day. We had turkey and cranberries and pumpkin pie, so that much was familiar to me. After New Year's, the *Flusser* went out on maneuvers again, but we usually came back to Pearl Harbor every ten days or so. Sometimes the whole fleet anchored off the coast of Maui, at a place called Lahaina Roads. I liked that anchorage, because we didn't have to wait outside the entrance channel for hours and hours before it was our ship's turn to come in and get liberty.[13] The downside was, there was no place to go on Maui.

Lahaina was nothing like Honolulu. There were no bars or restaurants or theaters. About the only thing to do was go swimming, which is what a bunch of us were doing when I saw the shark. It was at least twenty feet long. I was paddling like crazy for shore when I felt it brush against my legs, and I thought I was lunch. I couldn't understand why nobody else was trying to get away, until they finally broke down and told me it wasn't a shark. They called it a blackfish. Whatever it was, it didn't eat sailors, and it was playful. It hung around the ship and swam with us for about an hour that day.[14]

We had a lot more weapons training on the *Flusser* after the first of the year. Whenever I heard the ship's big guns firing, I went out to watch. Sometimes the gun crews got to practice on an old tugboat. Sometimes they actually hit the thing. The antiaircraft gunners had to make do with balloons for target practice. I watched the torpedomen, too. That wasn't nearly as much fun because the torpedoes did not explode on contact. All of ours had red paint on the noses, to show that they were duds. The torpedomen just aimed for a spot on a deserted beach. Hit or miss, they lowered a lifeboat, retrieved the torpedo, and launched it all over again.[15] The depth charges were way more exciting. They looked perfectly harmless, like oil drums or garbage barrels, but they were full of TNT. Whenever somebody rolled a depth charge off the fantail, which was the tail end of the ship, I always stopped and waited for the explosion. It looked like a mountain was rising up out of the ocean. There was a huge mound of spray, about fifty feet across. I was told that the underwater concussion from a depth charge explosion would rupture the hull of any submerged submarine within range. I had no doubt that this was so.

Sometimes we practiced radio silence, to prevent the "enemy" from knowing where we were and what we said to each other. When we had radio silence during the day, the signalmen used flags to communicate between the ships. I never learned to read the flag messages, but I always knew what the ships were saying to each other at night, because they flashed Morse code back and forth with lanterns, the same as we did with flashlights in Cub Scouts. One night, I was delivering a fresh pot of coffee to the bridge, and I noticed that the captain and the executive officer were both staring up at this one particular cloud. I knew they were waiting for a signal from some other ship. I saw it before they did, and I just blurted out, "They got your message." The XO whipped around and said, "How did you know that?" I was scared. I said, "Sir! They flashed Morse code for our call sign on that cloud, followed by the letter R, which means, 'Roger, message received.' Sir!" I thought he was going to tell me to keep my eyes down and my mouth shut in the future, but he didn't. The XO said, "Captain, I think this boy is ready for radio school."

See Time Line, page 220, and Historical Notes, page 221.

5

RADIO SCHOOL

May–August 30, 1940

I had orders to attend Fleet Radio School in San Diego, and the next session was starting in May. There were all kinds of ships going back and forth between Hawaii and California at that time. I was hoping to catch a ride on a cruiser, but I wasn't that lucky. I was told to board the *Whitney*. This was one of the auxiliary ships that brought supplies out to the fleet when we were on maneuvers. It looked more like a troop carrier on the day we left Pearl Harbor.

Most of the passengers on the *Whitney* were Marines. I never saw so many fancy tattoos—dragons, mainly, with lots of different colors. They said they got them in Shanghai. I guess dragons were a sign of good luck in China. I also heard the Marines speaking in Chinese. The only phrase I recognized was "*ding-how.*" Littlefield used that one a lot. He said it meant "excellent" or "wonderful." I didn't talk to the China Marines that much— they generally kept to themselves—but they sure seemed happy to be going home. As far as they were concerned, even a slow boat to California was *ding-how.*[1]

It took us nearly a week to get to San Diego. The harbor was not as crowded as I remembered from when I was there for basic training. I assumed all the warships were out on maneuvers.[2] The radio school was several miles east of boot camp, so I didn't even have to look at the stupid grinder. The barracks were another pleasant surprise: no hammocks. My classmates and I were not required to march either. We didn't even have to go to church on Sundays. All we had to do was show up for class and pay attention for about eight hours a day, Monday through Friday.

The Navy's radio school was a lot like high school, without the spitwads. There was none of that, because the instructors were chief petty officers. You didn't have to be in the Navy for very long to know those guys did not put up with any foolishness. What really got my attention on the first day of class was when the instructor said, "You boys better learn this stuff and learn it good, because you're going to need it when we go to war." We thought he was talking about the war in Europe, and maybe he was, but it still wasn't clear to me how that had anything to do with us in the Pacific.[3] I just took his word for it, because he was a chief petty officer. I doubt that any of my classmates were any better informed on current events than I was. No one in the barracks had a personal radio; the only news we got was whatever the instructors chose to tell us. A week or two into the term, they said the Germans had taken Holland and Belgium, and it looked like France was next.

There were about thirty in my class, and we all knew Morse code. We just weren't very fast. I couldn't send or receive more than twenty words a minute on the first day of radio school. The Navy expected us to do sixty words a minute, at least. I thought that was impossible, but of course it wasn't. It's really the same as typing: the more you practice, the faster you get. And practice we did, for hours and hours at a time. The main drill was called "copying code." This was where we put on headphones and typed the letters as we heard them from the instructor's transmitter. He increased the speed a little more each day. The dots and dashes came through in tones—similar to musical notes—like when you take a hearing test.

When the instructor wanted us to send Morse code back to him, we put our hand on what they called "the key." This was like clicking the mouse on a computer, and the key did make a clicking sound when you tapped out the dots and dashes for the letters and numbers. The only trick to it was that your clicks for a dot had to be a fraction of a second shorter than your clicks for a dash. If the instructor couldn't tell the differences between your dot clicks and your dash clicks, he said you had a "sloppy fist."

About midway through the three-month course, the instructors let us send a real transmission to somebody outside the classroom. The Navy must have had some kind of a deal with Western Union, because I sent one to Adeline. The next letter I got from her said she received my message in the form of a telegram. I wanted to see her, but I couldn't afford the plane fare from San Diego to Spokane. I suppose I could have gone by bus or train, but no way could I have got there and back in time for class on Monday. I only had Saturdays and Sundays off.

I spent most of my weekends in downtown San Diego with my classmate George Maybee. George sat beside me every day in class, and his bunk was right next to mine in the barracks. When we went downtown, we usually took a trolley. Sometimes we went to the movies. That cost about ten cents, the same as the trolley. Once in a while we treated ourselves to dinner at a restaurant. You could get a full-course meal with mashed potatoes and gravy at some pretty nice places for about forty cents. I met some pretty nice girls in San Diego, too, but I never dated any of them. Adeline and I weren't going steady or anything, and I knew she wasn't sitting around the house by herself on Saturday nights either. She said so in her letters. It's hard to say how I felt about her at that time. I think I was just hoping that she wouldn't meet a guy that she liked better than me before I got a chance to see her again.

My other best friend in radio school was not a classmate; he was one of the instructors' assistants. That was a little unusual, I guess, because he was a radioman and a petty officer third class—a full pay grade above me—but, for some reason, the two of us just hit it off. In my opinion, he was "four-oh." In the Navy, that meant "perfect," like straight A's on your report card.

Whenever we spoke to each other in class, I had to call him Petty Officer Webb. Outside the classroom, he was just "Spic." That was not considered an insult for a Hispanic guy at the time. I couldn't even tell you what his real first name was, because that's what he called himself, and that's what his parents called him, too. I know that because he took me home with him one weekend. His parents lived in Long Beach, but they had a vacation cabin on Big Bear Lake in the San Bernardino Mountains, and that's where we went.

The weather was much cooler in the mountains. It wasn't sunny enough to go swimming, so there were no girls to watch on the beach. Spic said we should go for a drive around the lake. He put on his dress blues and told me to do the same, in case we saw any girls on the road. He was a couple of years older than I was, and he had way more experience in that department than I did. So we were just driving along, looking for girls, when we came across a long line of cars and trucks parked by the side of the road, and there were all these bright lights shining from the forest. Spic thought it meant somebody was making a movie. He said a lot of people from Hollywood came to Big Bear Lake because of the scenery. Well, of course, we had to stop and check that out. I'd never seen a movie star in person before.

We hid behind a tree and watched for about ten minutes. All we saw were guys dragging great big lights and cameras around. There were no movie stars, no director hollering "cut," and no girls. It was just boring, so we left. The only problem was, we couldn't. Spic had parked his car a little too far off the side of the road, and the back tires were stuck in the mud and snow. I had to get out and push. Spic was yelling at me to push harder, and I was yelling at him because it was all his fault, and the tires just kept spinning deeper. I was about to tell Spic to put the darn thing in neutral and get out and get dirty with me, when all of a sudden I heard someone say, "Can I give you a hand with that?" The voice sounded familiar, but I didn't believe it was really John Wayne until I turned around and saw him. The stagehands and bodyguards were glaring at me, but he just smiled and said,

"Let's get this car back on the road." He put his shoulder to the fender, and we pushed together.

John Wayne stayed and talked with us for quite a while. He asked a lot of questions about the Navy. He wanted to know what we did and where we were stationed, whether we'd ever been to sea on a warship, and how did we like it.[4] Spic did most of the talking. I was too tongue-tied and starstruck. I'd been going to John Wayne movies since I was a little kid, even before he got really famous. It was just fortunate that Spic had the presence of mind to get his camera out of the car and ask if we could have our picture taken with him. He ordered one of the stagehands to shoot it with Spic's camera, and then he shook our hands and thanked us for serving our country in the Navy. We were still standing there in the road when he turned around and walked back toward the lights in the forest. I never even thought to ask the name of the movie he was trying to film that day at Big Bear Lake.[5]

About a month after that weekend with Spic and his parents, I filled out my "preference form." The Navy didn't guarantee anything, of course, but the instructors told us to mark down our first, second, and third choice of where we wanted to go after radio school. Annapolis was still at the top of my list. If I couldn't go there, I wanted Pensacola, Florida. That was where the Navy trained pilots.[6] I didn't have a third choice. Spic said he wrote "submarines" in that blank, so I did, too. He may have known that submarines paid more, but I didn't.[7] It just sounded like a good idea at the time. The only other preference form I saw besides mine and Spic's was George Maybee's. His first choice was to be a radioman on a battleship. He knew cruisers were faster—we all knew that—but battleships were bigger. More glamorous, I guess. George thought the battleships were the queens of the Fleet, and that was where he wanted to be.

There was no graduation ceremony on the last day of radio school. We just took our final exams, and I passed. I took another exam to get "rated." I had to pass that test to get promoted from

Seaman second class Ray Daves, left, 20, and Petty Officer Webb, 22, meet and talk with movie star John Wayne at Big Bear Lake, California, summer 1940. (The sailors' uniforms are dress blues with white markings and black ties. Seaman's stripe on Daves's right shoulder and striker badge at left shoulder indicate he has not yet completed training in any Navy specialty. Webb, at right, has left arm eagle, indicating petty officer, with radioman's rating insignia below. Webb's single red chevron showing "third class" is not visible in this black-and-white photo.) COURTESY OF RAY DAVES COLLECTION.

striker radioman to radioman third class. This gave me another huge pay increase, plus I got my first stripe to show that I was now a petty officer, like Spic. He said petty officer third class was the Navy's equivalent to the lowest rank of sergeant in the Army. I was very pleased.

My orders were to return to the *Flusser,* and that was fine, too, for the time being. I was looking forward to seeing Littlefield and Ensign Harris and all the other guys I knew in the radio gang on the destroyer. Maybe now they would let me do something besides make coffee. I was even happier when I saw my transportation back to Pearl Harbor. This was no slow-moving troop carrier. The *Richmond* was a cruiser.[8]

See Time Line, page 223, and Historical Notes, page 224.

6

THE CRUISER

September 1940 Through March 1941

I talked to a couple of cruiser sailors before I left San Diego. They said if I ever got a chance to go to sea on their kind of warship, I would never want to go back to a destroyer. I thought they were just bragging—every sailor I'd ever met thought his ship was the best in the Navy—but, I have to admit, I did like the way the *Richmond* felt at sea. It was about twice the size of a destroyer, so it didn't toss nearly as much. The cruiser had bigger guns, too, and a lot more of them, but I was fascinated by the plane. It was a small two-seater; the crew said they used it for scouting. Except for the landing gear, which was pontoons instead of wheels, it reminded me of the first plane I ever rode, when I was in the CCC. I asked the radiomen if it was possible to get a ride on this one. A half day out of San Diego, they told me I could.

The *Richmond*'s plane was an OS2U Kingfisher. It sat on the stern in this contraption they called a catapult. I didn't know how that worked, and I sure didn't know how to aim and fire the machine gun. I suppose that would have mattered if we'd been at war, but we were not. Our mission was to fly back to San Diego and pick up the mail. All the pilot cared about was whether or not I could communicate with the ship once we were out of voice range. When I told him I'd just graduated from radio school, he said, "Let's go." Somebody handed me a different kind of life jacket than what I usually wore at sea. They called it a Mae West because of the way it puffed up around your chest if you pulled the strings to inflate it.[1] Otherwise, it stayed flat like a regular cloth vest. You didn't get a Mae West–type life jacket in the Navy unless you were an aviator. I felt like one the minute I put it on.

As soon as I sat down in the seat behind the pilot, the launch crew was all over me. I never saw so many straps and buckles. They had me belted in so tight, I could hardly turn my head, and when I did, they yelled, "Don't do that! Keep your head straight! Lean back, hard as you can or it'll snap your neck off!" They were still hollering instructions—I saw their lips moving—but I couldn't hear a thing because the pilot was revving the engine. When it sounded like he had it up to full throttle, I saw him give the launch crew a thumbs-up.

I've never tried being shot out of a cannon, but I don't know how else to describe a catapult launch. That little plane shot straight up in the air above the ship. For three or four seconds, it felt like my teeth and my eyeballs were going through the back of my head. After we leveled off, at around five thousand feet, it was like any other plane flight. I had a great view of the Pacific Ocean all the way to San Diego and back. It was about a two-hour flight each way. We landed on the water next to the ship. A crane swung over, lifted the plane back up onto the catapult, and the launch crew asked me if I wanted to go again. I said no thanks. I still wanted to fly in the Navy, as much as ever, but not that way. I took off that Mae West and told them they could keep it. I guess some guys thought catapulting off a cruiser was a ton of fun. Once was enough for me.

I spent the rest of the trip hanging out in the *Richmond*'s radio shack. They drank as much coffee as we did on the destroyer, and the war talk was just as boring. I was envious when they said they were expecting orders to the Atlantic after they dropped me off in Hawaii. If it was really true that we might go to war with Germany, all of the action at sea would be in the Atlantic.[2] That's where I wanted to be. I also thought it would be fun to go through the Panama Canal to get there. But orders are orders, and mine were to return to the *Flusser* at Pearl Harbor.

When we came through the channel, I found the *Flusser* tied up next to two or three other destroyers. There were several "nests" of destroyers like that in the water around Ford Island. As usual, none of the carriers were in port; they hardly ever were. But I did see seven or eight battleships on the east side of Ford Island. That part of Pearl Harbor was always reserved for them. We called it Battleship Row. I could not tell which was which—battleships didn't have their names painted on the hull either—but I'm sure one of them was my friend George's ship.

Prior to and during World War II, most U.S. Navy cruisers and battleships carried one or two small float planes for scouting purposes. The OS2U Kingfisher shown here is prepared for catapult launch from the heavy cruiser Boston *(CA-69), 1944.* COURTESY OF U.S. NAVY, PHOTO #80-G-272781.

He was assigned to the *Arizona* after we graduated together from radio school.

The radio gang on the *Flusser* was glad to see me, probably because I still had the least seniority. They put me on the regular schedule, though. I got the midwatch.[3] That was the shift nobody else wanted, because it was so boring. There was hardly any radio traffic at that time of night. The only challenge was to stay awake. Littlefield said I needed a pet cockroach. He claimed he had this cockroach in China that was so well trained, it would bite him and wake him up whenever it heard his ship's call sign on the radio. I was almost young enough to believe him. But I didn't really mind the midwatch. I used that quiet time to study for my next promotional exam. At the end of my shift, I got eight hours off, and then it was four hours on again, and so on, just like that, around the clock, until I got liberty.

It was still a lot of fun to catch a bus or taxi into Honolulu on my days off, but the city was way more crowded than it was the year before. All of the bars and restaurants were just crammed with guys in uniform. It took hours to get a table. I even had to stand in line to get next to this girl on the sidewalk outside the YMCA. She was out there every day, charging guys a quarter to get their picture taken with her. I don't know if she was getting rich that way, but it looked like she had all the business she could handle. The prostitutes and the tattoo parlors were swamped, too. I never spent much time in that part of town myself, but there was one radioman on the *Flusser* who did. We couldn't believe it when he told us he was in love with this girl he met on Hotel Street. And, by golly, they got married. Everybody said he should have let her keep working. I'm sure she was making a lot more money than we were.

The radiomen were actually pretty tame compared to all the other gangs on the ship. A lot of sailors drank and partied way more than we did. I'd say maybe 20 percent of the *Flusser*'s crew hit the bars and stayed drunk until their liberties expired. You weren't supposed to bring any alcohol back to the ship, but there were ways to smuggle it aboard if you really wanted to. I heard the boatswains caught somebody with a hollowed-out pineapple full of rum. For most of us, going ashore was all about a change of scenery. If you didn't have any money, you could just hang out on the sidewalk and whistle at the girls when they walked by. The girls in Honolulu wore less clothes than what we were used to seeing on the mainland. We had special terms for that: "SS" was a girl in a short skirt; "VSS" was very short skirt. Our favorite was what they called a sarong. It looked more like a scarf than a skirt. The girls tied them around their waists, barely covered their backsides. You had to be fairly close to the beach to spot a girl in a sarong. I spent a lot of time at the beach.

I was entitled to a thirty-day leave after my first year in the Navy. They would have given me free transportation back to San Diego, but I would have had to pay all my own travel expenses from there. I had enough for a bus ticket from California to the state of Washington. I decided to wait until I could afford that plus a visit to my family in Arkansas. Adeline got a compact with a powder puff and mirror from Hawaii for Christmas that year. In early January, I heard the *Richmond* was back at Pearl Harbor. I talked to those guys on the radio, and they said they had an opening for another radioman.

I loved the *Flusser*—I suppose every sailor loves his first ship—but I wanted to try something different. Ensign Harris approved my request for transfer; he even showed me what he wrote in my file: "Calm and stable on the job." He told me I was one of the radiomen he wanted next to him if his ship was in combat. He probably said the same to Littlefield and the rest of the radio gang on that destroyer, but, from that day forward, I think I was always trying to live up to his opinion. Ensign Harris was the first commissioned officer I really got to know. If the Navy ever decided to make a mustang out of me, I wanted to be like him.

The *Richmond* was not a drastic change. Everything was just bigger, that's all. Instead of seven or eight guys in the destroyer's radio shack, the cruiser had about fifteen. But everybody slid down the ladders between decks, just the same: Put your hands on the rails, lift your feet, and slide. You could get from one deck to another in about two seconds that way. I felt right at home when I heard the boatswains cussing. It was a regular art form with those guys. They swore more creatively and more often than anybody. I think they went to school for it. The only real difference I noticed was that the *Richmond* was nearly always at sea. I don't think we were ever very far from Hawaii, though, because their little scout plane was flying to Pearl Harbor and back nearly every day. Sometimes they brought the mail.

My dad was writing to me nearly as often as Mom that winter. He usually enclosed a few clippings from the newspaper. I think he was trying to explain why my family was so worried about me. Based on the news I was getting on the civilian radio frequencies, plus Dad's letters, I sort of figured it out: The Japanese were mad at us because we weren't trading with them so much anymore. I guess the President thought this was the way to make them pull their troops out of China. Dad thought Japan would rather go to war with us than leave China alone. He never predicted when or where it would start. He just said it was going to happen, and I believed him, but I wasn't afraid of war with Japan or anybody else at the time. The only thing that scared me was a Dear John. That was what we called a letter from your girlfriend, where she says she's not your girlfriend any more. A lot of guys on the *Richmond* were getting them. It's hard to keep up a long-distance relationship when you can't see your girl-friend for a year or more. I think I held the record on that ship. Nobody understood how I could be falling for a girl I hadn't seen for over three years. It was a mystery to me, too.

Our workload doubled when the admiral brought his flag on board the *Richmond*.[4] He was generating a steady stream of orders to the rest of the fleet, and they were constantly reporting back to him. He never set foot inside the radio shack, and neither did the captain. The only high-ranking officer who bothered us at all was the executive officer. Every time the XO came through the door, he would reach down and grab a handful of our candy. We kept a five-gallon can full of hard candies in the radio shack. Whenever we were in port, we took up a collection to buy more. Well, the XO never gave us a cent. He didn't even say "thanks for the candy." That really ticked us off. So we gathered up a whole bunch of those chocolate-tasting laxatives and sprinkled them on the top of the candy can. Nobody got in trouble for it, and the XO never said a word. But he quit stealing our candy.

I saw way more weapons training on the cruiser than we ever had on the destroyer the year before. The *Richmond*'s guns were a major nuisance to us in the radio shack, because they were so loud. They looked like cannons and they sounded like thunder.[5] The only time I went out to watch was at night. When you have a couple of cruisers and about a dozen destroyers so close together, all firing their guns after dark, it lights up the whole sky. It was just beautiful, like roman candles on the Fourth of July. I didn't see the collision. I just heard that a couple of destroyers ran into each other in the dark and somebody got killed.[6]

Japan's Mitsubishi A6M, model 21, type 0 (thus the nickname "Zero") fighter plane is shown launching from the flight deck of the Japanese air-craft carrier Akagi, *1941.* COURTESY OF U.S. NAVY, PHOTO #80-G-182252.

Prior to World War II, the U.S. Navy's best carrier-based fighter plane was the Grumman F4F-3. (F4F-3A Wildcat pilots in this April 1942 photo are the famous Lt. Cmdr. "Jimmy" Thach and Lt. "Butch" O'Hare.) COURTESY OF U.S. NAVY, PHOTO #80-G-10613.

I never really thought of it as practicing for war, not even when the communications officer handed out the flash cards. There was a picture of a Japanese plane on one side, facts about it on the reverse. We were supposed to learn them, but nobody took it very seriously. It was just a game. I remember laughing when I saw the card with the picture of the Japanese fighter plane. They called it a "Zero." I thought the facts about it had to be a misprint. I wasn't all that familiar with our carrier planes, but I knew we didn't have anything that fast or that maneuverable.[7] I did not know that the Imperial Japanese Navy was so much bigger and more powerful than we were at that time.[8]

I took the promotional exam for radioman second class while I was on the *Richmond*. It was a written test, followed by an interview with the communications officer. A week or so later, he told me I passed and handed me a new set of orders: "Report to the administration building, Submarine Base, Pearl Harbor, immediately." I was disappointed. Submarines were my third choice on the preference form at radio school. The older radiomen on the *Richmond* couldn't believe it. They said these orders showed I was now "on the flag." According to them, I had just been assigned to the staff of some admiral at Pacific Fleet head-quarters. As far as they were concerned, this was the cushiest job a Navy radioman could get. They wanted to know who I knew and how much I had to pay for that assignment. I had no idea.

See Time Line, page 225, and Historical Notes, page 227.

7

THE SUBMARINE BASE

April 1941–7:55 A.M., December 7, 1941

There were about twenty radiomen on the staff at Pacific Fleet headquarters, and one of them was Spic. He swore he had nothing to do with it, claimed he'd only been there for a couple of weeks himself. So maybe it really was just a coincidence that I got that assignment. I suspected otherwise, but I couldn't prove it. I was even more surprised when he showed me to the barracks. It looked like a regular three-story hotel, with tennis courts and a swimming pool and a bunch of guys lounging around like tourists. Spic said these were the enlisted men from the submarine crews. We didn't either of us know why the Navy treated them so differently from all the other sailors at Pearl Harbor—everybody else had to bunk on their ships while they were in port—but it sure was nice for us. Anybody who worked at Fleet headquarters got to live in those barracks, too.[1]

The radiomen were assigned to one big room on the second floor. The mattresses were thicker, and the bunks were only two-high. Compared to the sleeping quarters on the lower deck of a destroyer or a cruiser, this was privacy. My gosh, we even had windows. I'd forgotten what it was like to sleep in a room with windows. The view was just rows and rows of fuel storage tanks, but Spic said this was a good thing. Because of all those millions of gallons of diesel behind our barracks, we never had to put up with the noise of low-flying planes from all the Army, Navy, and Marine air bases on Oahu. Too much risk of a training accident, I guess. If one of their planes happened to crash near those fuel tanks, it would have blown the whole southeast end of Pearl Harbor to kingdom come.

I'll bet I saluted at least three admirals on my first day of work at the submarine base. The administration building was just crawling with them.[2] The radio room was right in the middle of the main floor, surrounded by hallways on all four sides. It was about twice the size of the radio shack on the cruiser, and the communications officer in charge was a lieutenant commander. That's about the same rank as a major in the Army. I'd never reported to anyone that high up the chain of command before, but Lt. Commander Guenther was not hard to please. His procedures for sending and receiving messages by Morse code were no different from what I was used to on the ship. I thought I had it made until he ordered me to qualify in the dive tower by the end of the week.

The dive tower was right outside the administration building. It looked like a lighthouse, but it was for training you to escape from a submerged submarine. All the radiomen said it was easy, and I'm sure it was, if you were a strong swimmer. I tried to act casual, but I was scared to death when I stepped inside. The dive tower was hollow, like an elevator shaft. They handed me a life jacket just before they slammed the door and flooded the whole thing with saltwater. I had to hold my breath and kick until I got all the way up to the platform at the top. It was only about a hundred feet, but it seemed like a mile to me. I was relieved when the instructor said I qualified. Barely. I couldn't understand why I had to go through that whole ordeal, but the Navy required it for anybody who might go out on a submarine. I didn't think that was very likely for me.

The Sunday after that was Easter, and for some reason I decided to go to church. It might have been the dive tower, or maybe it was all the war talk in the barracks. Maybe Mom finally got to me with all those Bible verses at the end of her letters. Whatever it was that put the fear of God into me, I ended up in a pew on Easter Sunday, along with several other sailors at this church in downtown Honolulu. And when the pastor asked if anybody needed to get baptized, I raised my hand. Well, this particular church didn't believe it was good enough to sprinkle a few drops of water on your head. You had to get wet all over. They took us to the swimming pool at Roosevelt High School. The pastor thought I was kidding when I told him I'd just as soon not go in the deep end. When I got back to the base and told the guys in the barracks that I'd just been baptized, I found out that a lot of them had already been there and done that. I didn't even know they were Christians. After that, we started talking more about religion. Some thought Hitler and the war in Europe was the beginning of Armageddon, the end of the world.

Everybody at Fleet headquarters believed it was just a matter of time before America got dragged into the war with the Nazis in Europe. Toward the end of the summer, it sounded like we might go to war with Japan, too. That's when the President cut off their oil.[3] You had to leave the barracks if you didn't want to listen to another when-are-we-going-to-war discussion. My favorite escape was to rent a motorcycle in Honolulu and ride north, up the Pali Highway. The view from that cliff, looking out over Oahu, was beautiful, but I mostly went there for the peace and quiet.[4] Some guys wanted noise. I knew several radiomen who kept a set of civilian clothes in their lockers at the YMCA and changed into them before they hit the bars. I guess they had their reasons, but I never could understand why they did that. Everybody knew girls were more attracted to a guy in uniform.

I turned twenty-one in June. It was no big deal. I'd been drinking in Honolulu taverns since I was nineteen, and I knew my limits. I never had more than one or two beers at a time, which is probably why I never woke up with a headache or a tattoo the whole time I was in the Navy. I'm not going to say that every sailor with a tattoo in Hawaii was too drunk to remember how he got it, but I think that accounted for a lot of them. Most of the tattoos the guys got on Hotel Street were ugly. Some of them were so downright hideous, guys would try to have them removed. The scars looked even worse. I guess I was finally old enough to vote that summer, but no one told me how to register.[5] There was nothing to vote for anyway. The presidential election was the year before: Roosevelt was already into his third term.

Most of the older radiomen were married, and a lot of them were bringing their wives over to Hawaii that summer.[6] They rented apartments and houses in Honolulu, and they threw some great parties. I went to a few of those. The wives were always trying to fix me up with single girls they worked with, but by that time I knew I was in love with Adeline. I was just afraid to tell her. When I finally wrote and told her that I loved her, I was a nervous wreck until she wrote back and said she loved me, too. After that, we were writing back and forth all summer long about how great it would be if she could move to Hawaii and get a job and we could be together. We just couldn't seem to work out the details. It would have been easier if I could have just talked to her, but I had no access to a phone that could call the mainland. I should have asked her to marry me then, but I didn't want to put that in a letter. I thought that was something that needed to be said in person.

The only way to take my mind off of Adeline was to keep busy. Most days I stayed past my regular shift in the radio room and copied the news that came in on the civilian press frequency. We got that in Morse code, too, at about a hundred words a minute. That was a lot faster than the military frequencies, but I kind of liked the challenge. I especially liked being the first to know the baseball scores. I was a Yankees fan; Joe DiMaggio was my favorite player. He was on the most amazing hitting streak that summer. I didn't normally follow the Red Sox, but everybody wanted to know if Ted Williams was still batting over .400.[7] A lot of money changed hands when I reported the baseball scores at the end of the day. That was about the only professional sport anyone at Pearl Harbor really followed in the summer of 1941.

I never gambled on baseball myself. All my spare change was going for poker, and I was just learning to play the game. We were supposed to have lights out in the barracks by ten, but that didn't stop us. We just draped a blanket over the top bunk and made ourselves a poker tent. Four or five guys could sit on the lower bunk with flashlights and play cards all night long. "Scoop" Hoffert was by far the best player. We called him Scoop because he won more than anybody, and he had a certain way of scooping up all the money in the pot. It usually took both hands. I really liked Scoop, and so did Spic. Pretty soon, everybody at the submarine base was calling us the "Three Musketeers" because we were always together.

If we weren't playing poker in the barracks, we were hanging out at the Tin Roof. That was the name of a tavern close to Pearl Harbor, one of the first stops for sailors who came into port on the weekends. The music was loud, the girls were friendly, and there were lots of fights. It was great. One night, Spic and Scoop and I were there, playing pool, and somebody taps me on the shoulder. It was George Maybee. Next to Spic, he was my best friend from radio school. George was on liberty from the *Arizona*. We spent the rest of the night getting caught up on each other's adventures, and from then on he came over to the sub base whenever he was in port. If I was working, he spent his time off with Scoop and Spic. All three of us tried to talk him into transferring to the staff at Fleet headquarters, but George loved being a radioman on a battleship. He said he would never leave the *Arizona*.

Me, I was still holding out hope for a college education at Annapolis. It just about killed me when I got the message from Ensign Harris that I was rejected. He said I passed the entrance exam, all right, but the Navy did some checking into my background. That's when they discovered that I'd lied about my age. This was considered a sign of bad character; I was not "officer material." I was devastated. Moped around for days. Spic thought a change of scenery would do me good, so he volunteered us for the "measuring crew."

These were the guys who took the submarines out for testing, and it was our job to go down the captain's checklist and see if all the repairs he'd ordered were actually done. None of the subs could go back out on patrol until we took it out for a spin. We always stayed on the surface until we got past the entrance to Pearl Harbor. After that, the measuring crew was encouraged to dive those submarines as often and as deep as we dared. Two hundred feet was considered safe. Below that, you had to expect a leak or two. Spic and I tested all the radio equipment, and it was also our responsibility to notify every ship in the area before we submerged. I always made extra sure the destroyers knew it was us. I'd seen enough depth charges to know what would happen if they thought we were an enemy submarine.

As usual, Spic was right. I had so much fun on those joy rides in the submarines at Pearl Harbor, I forgot all about the rejection from Annapolis. By the end of November, I was looking forward to a thirty-day leave. Between my poker winnings and what I'd saved from my pay as a second class petty officer, I finally had enough for travel expenses. I had it all planned. I was going to spend the first week with Adeline in Spokane, take a bus from there, and be home with my family in Arkansas for Christmas. Well, that was my next big disappointment. My leave was canceled. I couldn't even get any sympathy, because everybody else's leave was denied or canceled, too. And we all knew why. The Navy's head office in Washington, D.C., was sending us all kinds of war warnings. They told us to expect a Japanese attack any day now.

So, yes, we were on alert at Pacific Fleet headquarters at Pearl Harbor, but all the messages I saw said that Japan was most likely to attack our base in the Philippines, or maybe Thailand.[8] In Hawaii, it seemed like everybody was more concerned about Japanese spies and terrorists. I saw extra guards posted around the docks where the submarines were tied, and I saw guys painting doors and windows on the fuel tanks behind our barracks. I guess they were trying to make them look like office buildings from the air.

I remember everything about the sixth of December. It was a Saturday night. Spic was meeting some girls at the Tin Roof, and they were all going to a party at somebody's apartment in Honolulu. Of course, he invited me to go with him, but I had to work that night, from eight to midnight. Scoop was supposed to come on after me, but I took his shift, too, so he could go party with Spic. I loaned them both a couple of bucks and told them to have a good time. After they left, I radioed George on the *Arizona*, but he'd already gone to bed. I assumed he had to work early in the morning. I also tried radioing the guys I knew on the *Flusser* and the *Richmond*. I usually talked with them whenever they came into Pearl Harbor, but I couldn't reach them either. I'm pretty sure

The submarine base complex at Pearl Harbor, October 13, 1941: (1) Barracks for sub crews and other enlisted men; (2) Fuel storage tank, camouflaged; (3) administration building and Pacific Fleet headquarters; (4) The 134-foot "dive tower" (Submarine Rescue and Training Tank); (5) Six submarines at docks are Tuna *(SS-203),* Gudgeon *(SS-211),* Argonaut *(SM-1),* Narwhal *(SS-167),* Triton *(SS-201),* Dolphin *(SS-169); (6) Battleship at upper left is* Nevada *(BB-36); Battleship Row and Ford Island are left of* Nevada, *not visible in this photo.* COURTESY OF U.S. NAVY, PHOTO #80-G-451125.

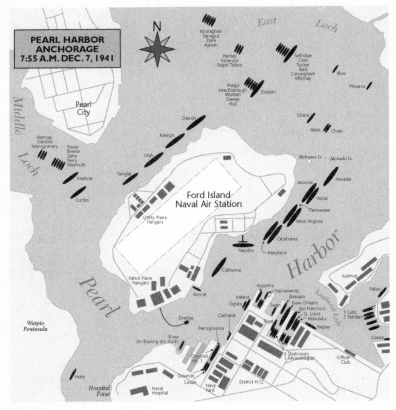

PEARL HARBOR
ANCHORAGE
7:55 A.M. DEC. 7, 1941

N

East   Loch

Monaghan
Farragut
Dale
Aylwin

Henley
Patterson
Ralph Talbot

Selfridge
Case
Tucker
Reid
Conyngham
Whitney

Blue

Phelps
MacDonough
Worden
Dewey
Hull

Dobbin

Phoenix

Pearl
City

Middle Loch

Detroit

Solace

Raleigh

Allen   Chew

Ramsay
Gamble
Montgomery

Trever
Breese
Zane
Perry
Wasmuth

Utah

Mokuumu Is.   Mokuiki Is.

Medusa

Tangier

Arizona
Vestal

Nevada

Curtiss

Ford Island
Naval Air Station

Tennessee

West Virginia

Utility Plane
Hangars

Oklahoma

Maryland

Harbor

Neosho

Patrol Plane
Hangars

California

Kuahua

Argonne

Pelias

Avocet

Sacramento
Ramapo
New Orleans
San Francisco
St. Louis
Honolulu

Pearl

Helena
Oglala

Swan

3 Subs
2 Tenders

Bagley

Dredge

Cachalot

Tangier

Castor

Waipio
Peninsula

Pennsylvania

Shaw
(In floating dry dock)

Drydock

6 Destroyers
1 Minesweeper

Officer
Club

Helm

Downes
Cassin

Navy
Yard

District H.Q.

Hospital
Point

Naval
Hospital

© maps.com

they were at sea.[9] The only radio traffic I got at headquarters that
night was weather reports from the submarines. There were several of them on patrol in the South Pacific. They always checked in
with us when they came to the surface after dark.

I was very tired after working two shifts, back to back, so I
went straight to bed. I had every intention of sleeping late, but I
forgot to pull the shade on the window above my bed. I woke up
at 6:30. The sun was shining in my face. I turned over and tried to
go back to sleep, but it was no use. I got up and showered. Spic
and Scoop weren't back yet; their bunks were empty. No surprise

there. They were probably still partying with those girls from the Tin Roof. Me, I was thinking pancakes and a big glass of cold milk. We always got pancakes on Sunday morning. I hadn't yet decided if I would go to church after breakfast or go back to bed.

The mess hall was in the same building as the barracks, but I had to go downstairs and outside to get to it. I could smell the bacon and the maple syrup from the sidewalk. My hand was on the door to the mess hall when I heard plane engines. It sounded like a lot of them, all coming from the direction of the fuel tanks behind the barracks. They were flying way too low. Whoever they were, those pilots were in serious trouble. It didn't matter if they were Army, Navy, or Marines. Every one of them was going to get chewed out and probably grounded for violating the restricted air space over the submarine base complex. I was just curious to see who they were.

I stepped back, away from the building to get a better view. I'd never seen that many planes flying over Pearl Harbor all at once. About ten of them were at such low altitude, they barely cleared the roof of the barracks. As they passed overhead, the whole formation banked in unison toward Ford Island. That's when I saw their markings. They weren't ours.

See Time Line, page 228, and Historical Notes, page 231.

8

THE ATTACK ON PEARL HARBOR

Sunday Morning, December 7, 1941

The planes were Japanese. I saw the red circle marking on their wings—the flash cards we had on the cruiser called it "the rising sun"—and my brain said, "Run!" but my legs didn't get the message. For I don't know how many seconds, I just stood there, frozen and horrified at the sight of all those enemy planes overhead. I saw the lead plane drop its bomb, and I heard the first explosion. It sounded like it came from Ford Island, or somewhere close to it. I couldn't tell where all the other planes' bombs were falling. There were so many, the explosions were blending altogether into a constant rumble, like thunder echoing in a canyon.

I had to get to my battle station. I must have run fifty yards before I realized that I actually *was* running, but it felt like I was in slow motion, like in a nightmare. I didn't look up again until I was almost across the courtyard. Another formation of planes was coming in fast and low behind me. I thought they would strafe me with their machine guns, but they did not. I was almost to the door of the administration building when I turned and looked at the sky again. I'd never seen planes fly that low to the ground. They had to divide up and fly around the building instead of over it. Each plane had a torpedo hanging from its belly, and the whole formation appeared to be headed in the direction of Ford Island and Battleship Row. I yanked open the door and ran down the hallway.

I didn't see any admirals that morning, but the communications officer was already in the radio room, along with about eight other radiomen. More came flocking in behind me. It seemed like the walls were shaking from the noise of the plane engines and the bombs exploding in the harbor. I was shaking, too. Some of the men had tears in their eyes, but Lt. Commander Guenther was calm. He ordered the older, more experienced guys to take charge of all the radio traffic. I wanted to help, but I didn't know what to do. So I asked him, "Sir! What should I be doing now?" He told me to run back outside and climb out on the roof. Japanese planes were still whizzing past the administration building on both sides. I was too afraid to turn around and look at them while I was on the ladder, so I couldn't say how many or what kind. The engine noise was deafening.

When I stepped out on the roof, I saw two sailors and a thirty-caliber machine gun. They had it all set up on a tripod at the northeast corner. I'd never seen either of those guys before, so they must have been with one of the submarine crews. Whatever their normal job was, they knew how to handle a machine gun. One man was firing at the planes; the other was feeding a belt of cartridges into the gun. When they saw me, they both hollered, "More ammunition!" The storage shed was on the opposite, south side of the roof, and the door was hanging open. They must have broken the padlock. There were stacks and stacks of ammunition canisters inside. I ripped the lid off one to see if the belts were already loaded with cartridges. They were. The ammunition belts were folded and coiled around like snakes in a five-gallon bucket. I grabbed two canisters by the handles and ran them over to the gun. I don't know how I did that—they must have weighed at least fifty pounds apiece. Adrenaline, I guess.

I dropped the canisters next to the gun and watched the planes fly past us. As soon as they were over the water, they dropped their torpedoes, and then I watched the wakes of the torpedoes—dozens of them—until they exploded against the sides of the ships on Battleship Row. I still didn't know one battleship from another, but the two sailors beside me sure did. When we saw one battleship turn over and sink upside down, they both shouted out, "There goes the *Oklahoma!*" Another battleship was exploding. I could actually feel the concussions—it was like a small earthquake—and the man next to me was yelling, "That's the *Arizona!*" I thought I was going to be sick. I doubled over and dropped to my

Torpedo wakes approach Battleship Row, during the first few minutes of the attack on Pearl Harbor, December 7, 1941. U.S. battleships shown here are: 1. Nevada *(BB-36)* 2. Arizona *(BB-39)* 3. West Virginia *(BB-48)* 4. Tennessee *(BB-43)* 5. Oklahoma *(BB-37)* 6. Maryland *(BB-46)* 7. California *(BB-44)*.

Other ships in this photo are: 8. repair ship Vestal *(AR-4); and* 9. oil tanker Neosho *(AO-23). (Smoke in distance is from bombs exploding at Army Air Force Hickam Field.)* COURTESY OF U.S. NAVY, PHOTO #NH 50931.

Five torpedoes struck the battleship Oklahoma *(BB-37), shown at left after it turned upside down (capsized) and sank.* Oklahoma *was one of the three damaged ships that never returned to service after the attack on Pearl Harbor.* COURTESY OF U.S. NAVY, PHOTO #80-G-33035.

knees, and all I could say was "No! Oh, no!" The *Arizona* was a giant fireball. I couldn't imagine how George or anyone else on that ship might have survived.[1] I wanted to stay on my knees and pray and cry for my friend, but there was no time: The gun was almost out of ammunition.

I don't know how many trips I made across the roof between the machine gun and the storage shed. Ten or twelve at least. It could have been more. We just kept firing at every plane that came within range, and I'm sure everyone else around the harbor did the same.[2] I couldn't begin to tell you how many enemy planes were in the air at any given time. It looked like hundreds in the beginning. I don't believe there were ever less than twenty. I thought the planes that dropped bombs actually did more damage than the torpedoes. I saw a lot of Japanese fighter planes, too.[3] The Zeroes didn't carry

Arizona *(BB-39), center, exploded near* Tennessee *(BB-43), left.* Arizona *was never raised from where it sank at Pearl Harbor, December 7, 1941. The memorial that was built over its remains was dedicated in 1962.* COURTESY OF U.S. NAVY, PHOTO #80-G-19942.

bombs or torpedoes, but they had machine guns, and they were flying low all around the harbor, strafing anything that moved. They were even firing on the rescue boats that were trying to pick up the sailors who got blown off their ships. And then I saw the plane that was flying straight at me.

I'm not sure if it was a torpedo plane or dive bomber or a Zero-type fighter plane. I just pointed and yelled at the gunners; they turned the gun and fired at it. There were three submarines tied up to the docks below us.[4] They had machine guns, too. They may have been firing at the same plane. It was about two hundred yards from the administration building when the engine burst into flames, but the plane did not go down. It was still coming at me. It was less than fifty yards away when I saw the canopy was thrown back, so I knew the pilot was preparing to bail out. As the plane got closer, I saw why he did not. That Japanese pilot was dead. His head was tilted at a grotesque angle, and there was a trickle of blood down the side of his mouth, but his eyes were still open, and his plane was going to crash on the roof of the building where I was standing. I don't know why it swerved away at the last possible second. Maybe the pilot's body slumped over and moved the stick. It was less than twenty feet from the edge of the roof when it exploded in the air and crashed into the water instead.[5] I thought it was probably our gun that killed that Japanese pilot. If so, it wasn't my finger on the trigger. All I did was bring the ammunition. But I still felt bad when I looked into the cockpit and saw his face. For a couple of seconds, I forgot that he was the enemy. At that moment, he was just some mother's son, same as me, and somebody was going to have to go back to Japan and tell that poor woman her boy died at Pearl Harbor. I felt sorry for her—and for him—but there was no time for that either. The machine gun was low on ammunition again, and there were still so many enemy planes in the air.

I was almost to the storage shed when I saw another plane coming toward us. I wasn't sure what that one was going to do until I looked down and saw the liberty boats—six or seven of them—in the water below me. There were about thirty sailors in each boat, all in dress white uniforms, probably on liberty in Honolulu when they heard we were under attack. Those men were unarmed, just trying to get back to their ships, when that pilot opened fire on them with his machine guns. I saw the splashes in the water all around them, like they were caught in a rainstorm, but their white uniforms were covered with red blotches, and there were pools of blood forming around their bodies in the water. Most of the liberty boats and the men in them were blown to pieces, but one boat was still intact, and I saw one sailor in that boat stand up and shake his fist at the plane that did it. Another enemy plane came along and strafed him. I watched the bullets cut his body in half, and I saw his buddies swimming through his blood to get to shore. That's when I lost it. For the first time that morning, I was more angry than I was afraid. I was ready to go to war.

The smoke over Battleship Row and Ford Island was so thick at that point, I couldn't see anything but the topmasts of the ships. Even the water around the battleships was on fire from the fuel spills, and then there was another exceptionally large explosion in the dry-dock area. I had no idea which ship or even what kind of ship it was. From where I stood, it looked like a volcano erupting. I felt the concussion from that, too. The dry docks were in flames.[6]

The three of us stayed on the roof of the administration building until there were no more planes to shoot at, and then we just stood there for a few minutes, in case more were on the way. I did hear a few plane engines in the distance, but they sounded different from the Japanese planes. I assumed they were ours. I don't

The destroyer Shaw (DD-373) *was in dry dock when it was struck by bombs from Japanese carrier planes, December 7, 1941. This ship was repaired and returned to service during World War II.* COURTESY OF U.S. NAVY, PHOTO #NH 86118.

know where they were during the attack. I never saw or heard anything but enemy planes in the air over Pearl Harbor that morning.[7]

The two sailors on the machine gun climbed down from the roof ahead of me. I didn't ask their names, and I never saw either of them again. I was about to follow them down the ladder when I noticed that my uniform was damp. I thought it was sweat until I looked at my watch. It was ten o'clock in the morning, and there was blood dripping from a big gash on my left hand. I don't know how or when that happened. I didn't feel a thing at the time. I must have caught a piece of shrapnel from the plane that exploded so close to where I was standing on the edge of the roof. I just stared at my blood and wondered why. I didn't really care why the Japanese attacked us at Pearl Harbor.[8] That hardly mattered any more. We were at war now. I was thinking about my friend George on the *Arizona*. I was sure he was dead, and if anybody had asked me how many others I thought were dead and dying all around me, I'd have guessed five thousand.[9] The only question in my mind was, why am I not one of them, and I felt so guilty because I was not.

I was still trying to figure out if I was lucky or blessed when I started down the ladder from the roof of the administration building. I was about halfway to the ground when I heard the screams in the water.

See Time Line, page 233, and Historical Notes, page 234.

9

AFTERSHOCKS

10:00 A.M., December 7–December 24, 1941

The first guy I dragged ashore was bleeding way more than I was. He'd been trying to swim with a broken arm—more like shattered, really—but he didn't seem to know it. When I waded in to get him, he was just babbling incoherently. I think he was in shock. I'd never seen a machine-gun wound in my life, but I'm pretty sure he was in one of the liberty boats that got strafed. I put his good arm over my shoulder, half-carried him to sick bay, and ran back for another. About twenty of us spent the next hour or so pulling injured men out of the water near the submarine base. There were bodies and pieces of bodies floating all around them. We had to push them aside to get to the wounded. I did not help pick up the dead.

It was close to noon when I reported back to the radio room inside the administration building. Scoop and Spic were there, along with all the other radiomen assigned to Fleet headquarters. I didn't ask how or when they made it back from Honolulu; I was just glad they were okay. Everyone looked shocked and scared, but I never saw anything like this one junior officer. He was on the floor, curled up in a fetal position, rocking back and forth and bawling like a baby. He was only an ensign, but still. I was ashamed of him. I think it was a relief to all of us when the communications officer ordered a couple of older enlisted men to "get that guy out of here." I don't know where they took him; I never saw him again. A few seconds later, Lt. Commander Guenther turned around and ordered me to leave, too. I tried to tell him it was just a shrapnel wound—and most of the blood on my uniform wasn't even mine—but he wouldn't listen. He made me go to sick bay and get stitches on my hand.

There was only one sick bay at the submarine base. It was hardly more than a first-aid station. I don't believe we ever had more than one or two doctors on staff. Most of the guys who worked there were pharmacist mates or corpsmen—sort of like paramedics, I guess. I have no doubt they had experience with treating minor injuries—sprained ankles and such—but on that Sunday morning they had men on stretchers, wall to wall and out the door.[1] They were trying to save guys from bleeding to death. The older medics applied the tourniquets; the strikers were running from stretcher to stretcher giving morphine injections. It must have been a powerful painkiller. Even the worst-injured sailors weren't screaming anymore. I was one of about a dozen with lesser injuries. We just stood back, compared our shrapnel wounds—they all looked pretty much like mine—and talked among ourselves while we waited for stitches. That's when I first heard the rumors. One guy claimed he knew somebody who saw Japanese paratroopers dropping out of planes somewhere north of us. Another sailor said he heard there were enemy ships unloading troops on Barbers Point.[2]

By the time I got out of sick bay with a bandage on my hand, I believed there were thousands of Japanese soldiers on the island, and they were all marching toward Pearl Harbor, and there was going to be one helluva battle on the ground to stop them. I fully expected my communications officer to issue me a rifle and tell me to climb out on the roof again. But Lt. Commander Guenther sent all of us running to the barracks instead. He said there was a truck on the way to pick up our clothes, for the guys that got blown off their ships. The explosions burned everything, even the hair and eyebrows, right off those sailors' bodies. If they weren't completely naked, their clothes were coated with oil. I ran to the barracks, took off my bloody uniform, changed into my dungarees, and threw everything else I had on the collection pile.

The next call for help came from the rescue teams in the dry-dock area. They wanted firefighters. I had no training in that specialty, and neither did any of the other radiomen, far as I know. They just gave us fire extinguishers and told us where to stand. I was posted on what was left of the main deck of a destroyer. The flames were out, but they needed someone to keep the sparks away from the guys who were bringing all the bodies up from the lower decks. Some of the dead died from smoke inhalation. They still looked human. The rest must have been burned to death. Their bodies were just black and brittle, like charcoal. I saw the arms and legs snap off when they stacked them in the beds of the trucks. As awful as that was to watch, the smell was worse. Burnt human flesh gives off the most sickeningly sweet odor. If I'd eaten breakfast that morning, I'm sure I would have thrown it up. A lot of guys around me did.

I caught a ride back to the submarine base at sunset. Except for the ships that were still on fire along Battleship Row, there was no other light showing from anywhere around the harbor. Even the administration building looked dark from the outside, but there was a sliver of light shining below the door to the radio room on the main floor. Maybe that's why the Navy put central communications in the center of the building—like a kiosk in a shopping mall—so the radiomen could keep their lights on during a blackout. When we were at sea on maneuvers, we called it the "darken ship" exercise. It was supposed to keep the enemy from knowing our position at night. I never thought we would ever do that drill at Pearl Harbor.

There were only five or six positions for sending and receiving radio messages. The rest of us had nothing to do. The radio room wasn't much bigger than my mother's kitchen, so we were shoulder to shoulder, but nobody wanted to leave. I don't know about everybody else, but I was too nervous to sleep, and I was afraid to be alone. I sat on the floor between Scoop and Spic. I wanted to be with my friends when the enemy attacked again. All night long, we heard guns firing somewhere outside the building, but it was very sporadic. It didn't sound like a battle. Around midnight, one guy got up enough nerve to step outside and see if the Japanese troops were out there creeping up on us. If so, they didn't shoot him. He came back with a sleeping bag from the barracks. We spread that out on the floor and took turns lying down for fifteen minutes at a time. At two or three in the morning, Lt. Commander Guenther offered to send somebody to the mess hall for sandwiches. I should have been hungry—I hadn't eaten since the night before—but I wasn't. Nobody wanted to eat. All we wanted to do was talk.

Japanese incendiary bombs struck three ships in this dry dock at Pearl Harbor. Foreground, right, is destroyer Cassin *(DD-372), collapsed against destroyer* Downes *(DD-375). Less-damaged ship in background is battleship* Pennsylvania *(BB-38).* COURTESY OF U.S. NAVY, PHOTO #80-G-32511.

I don't think any of us were surprised that Japan had attacked. We just didn't expect them to hit us here, at Pearl Harbor. There was no disagreement about where the enemy planes came from. Everybody knew Japan had no air bases within flying range of Hawaii, so the planes must have been launched from aircraft carriers. At least four of them, we thought, judging by the number of planes. Assuming their carrier planes' fuel range was anywhere near the same as ours, that meant the Japanese carriers were only about two hundred miles from Oahu. We could not understand how such a large task force could have got that close to our base without being spotted by scout planes. We mulled that over for quite a while. Never did come up with an answer.[3]

I also remember discussing why the Japanese planes did not drop any bombs on the submarines or Pacific Fleet headquarters. Our best theory was that it had something to do with the fuel tanks behind our barracks. We guessed they didn't want to blow up all those millions of gallons of diesel because they needed it for their own ships. Which, of course, led us right back to wondering when the enemy soldiers would show up for the ground invasion of Pearl Harbor. We were still waiting for them when the sun came up on Monday morning.[4]

I grabbed a sweet roll from the mess hall at dawn, before Lt. Commander Guenther sent me back to the dry docks. I didn't think I was needed—it looked like all the fires were out—but somebody handed me a fire extinguisher and told me to keep watch. There were clouds of black smoke hanging over the whole base; it looked like most of it was coming from the *Arizona* (BB 39). My friend George's ship was sitting on the bottom of the harbor, but the water wasn't deep enough to cover it all. The upper decks were still burning, and the superstructure was sticking up like a tombstone. It was hard to stand there and wonder if George died in the explosion or in the fires. I was glad when I got the message to return to the submarine base. I probably would have felt differently if I'd known why.

I didn't realize that Lt. Commander Guenther had assigned me to a burial detail until the truck pulled up to the administration building with six other guys in the back. They handed me a rifle and said we were going to a funeral on Red Hill. It was about a forty-five-minute drive. If there were any trenches for mass burials, I never saw them. At the burial I attended, there was one grave and one body bag. It was white—made out of canvas, I think—with a drawstring at the top, and there were two Navy chaplains—one Catholic, one Protestant—standing beside the grave. They both said prayers for the man in the bag. If they said his name or where he was from, I don't recall it. I just remember standing at attention until it was time for the seven of us to fire our rifles into the air, three shots apiece. That's a twenty-one gun salute. There were other funerals going on at the same time, so we had to wait for the bugler to come and play "Taps." As we were walking back to the truck, I heard more shots in the distance and "Taps" again, at least twice more before we drove away. I felt surrounded by the echoes. I think there were a lot of guys buried on Red Hill that day.[5]

It was shortly after noon when the truck dropped me off at the sub base. I had not eaten a regular meal since Saturday dinner, and this was Monday, but I still wasn't hungry. I had to force myself to stop at the mess hall before I reported back to the administration building. Lt. Commander Guenther ordered me back on fire watch in the dry docks again. I was just beginning to figure out why. The Navy didn't really need that many guys standing around with fire extinguishers. I'm pretty sure the object was to give us something to do besides sit around and exchange rumors. Everyone was still speculating on when the enemy planes might strike again and when the ground invasion was going to start. I was too worn out to talk about it anymore.

When I saw the other radiomen heading for the barracks that night, I went, too. We'd left the windows open since Saturday night, so the whole building reeked of smoke. Even the sheets and pillows smelled like diesel, but it felt so good to lie down. The only thing that bothered me was that Japanese pilot. Every time I closed my eyes, I saw him. When I finally dropped off to sleep, he was still there, and he was still trying to kill me. I woke up screaming several times.

The next day was Tuesday, and there was a crane down by the submarine docks lifting the Japanese plane out of the water. I had orders to salvage the radio out of the cockpit. I waited until they removed the pilot's body. When they dragged him out, I saw his face again. It was even more ghastly than in my nightmares, because the little rock crabs had already done their work. His eyes were gone, along with most of his face. I cannot explain why I took out my pocketknife and cut off a piece of his parachute before they put the body in the ambulance and took him away. It's not like I needed a souvenir to remember how close he came to crashing into me on the roof. After that, I crawled inside the wet cockpit. It made me mad when I found the radio: The parts were stamped "Thordarson" and "Mallory." Those were the same companies that supplied radio equipment to the Navy. I wondered how many other American factories had been doing business with Japan over the past few years, and now all those products were coming back to us in the form of weapons.

I didn't hear the President's speech to Congress "live." I just heard the replay of it on the radio, Tuesday afternoon. He asked the House and Senate to declare war on Japan. As far as I was concerned, we'd been at war since that first bomb fell on Pearl Harbor. I guess he wanted them to vote on it anyway, to make it official. I thought the rest of the speech was actually pretty good. I especially remember the part where he said December 7, 1941, was "a day that would live in infamy." I didn't know the meaning of "infamy." At the time, I thought it was just a nicer word for "hell."

I spent the rest of the week on Ford Island, along with dozens of other enlisted men from various sections around the base. They had us posted about ten feet apart, all up and down the runways. I never used the fire extinguisher they gave me. I just stood there all day and stared at all the wrecked ships on Battleship Row.[6] I wasn't close enough to the *Oklahoma* to hear the tapping sounds from the hull myself, but a lot of other guys did. They said it was coming from the crew of that ship, the sailors who were trapped belowdeck when the *Oklahoma* turned upside down. I guess they were pounding on the hull from inside, so the rescuers would know where to cut the holes and get them all out. I never dreamed most of those sailors were going to die a slow death.[7] At the time, I thought the men in the rescue boats had the worst job. They were trolling for bodies in the water. The whole harbor was covered with residue from the oil spills. When the fires burned out, it left a thick layer of nasty-looking black gooey stuff, like tar. Every few minutes, I saw the rescue boats stop and pull another body or part of one out from under that sheet of tar.

Toward the end of the week, the sub base chaplain came by the barracks with a stack of preprinted postcards. There were only two choices: You could check the box for "alive, in the hospital" or you could check the box for "alive, not wounded." I checked that one and signed my name. There was no room to explain about the stitches on my hand. I wrote my parents' address on the front and gave it back to the chaplain. After that, I wrote a letter to Adeline. The weird thing was, I wasn't allowed to seal the envelope. I had to give it to Lt. Commander Guenther. He read it before she did. If I'd written anything that he considered classified or secret, he said his orders were to either cover the words with black ink or cut them out with scissors. The trouble was, practically everything was classified after the attack on Pearl Harbor. I wasn't even sure if it was okay to tell her what I had for dinner.

There were still plenty of rumors going around the submarine base, but they weren't the same as what we heard during the first few days. By this time, everybody knew there were no Japanese paratroopers or ships full of enemy soldiers offshore. We were back to talking about spies and sabotage and terrorist attacks. I never heard anyone say the government should start rounding up Japanese Americans for that reason—I didn't know about that until years later—but, the truth is, if anybody had asked my opinion in December of 1941, I would have gone along with that idea. I'll bet anyone who was at Pearl Harbor would have agreed. We were that scared. If you'd asked me again, six months or a year later, I probably would have said it wasn't necessary. I know I for sure would have objected if I'd known the government was turning the CCC camps into prisons.[8] It still makes me sad to think about it. They should have kept the CCC the way it was: a place for boys like me who needed a job or just to get away from home.

I wanted to go home then—it was the first time I ever really felt homesick—but I also wanted to go to war. I was so angry and anxious to get revenge on the Imperial Japanese Navy, I requested sea duty on a warship. I didn't care what kind. I was positively giddy when I got my orders to board the *Dolphin*. I couldn't tell Adeline why she wasn't going to get any more letters for a while. That was classified. The best I could do was send her a short telegram. The military gave us a special rate—five cents a word, I think it was. I just said "I love you," and "Don't worry" and signed my name. I couldn't tell my parents where I was going either.

Scoop and Spic were the only ones who knew I was assigned to a submarine. On Christmas Eve, they walked me down to the docks. The three of us shook hands and wished each other luck. It never occurred to me that I might never see them again. If I could turn back time, I would have taken more than a couple of minutes to say goodbye to my friends.

See Time Line, page 235, and Historical Notes, page 237.

10

THE SUBMARINE

December 24, 1941–February 3, 1942

I did not know where the *Dolphin* was going until we cleared the channel out of Pearl Harbor. That's when the captain picked up the microphone and spoke to the crew. I didn't need a loudspeaker to hear him, because the command center was less than ten feet from the radio room. There wasn't even a door between us. If the senior officers didn't want the radiomen to know what they were saying around the periscope, I think they would have had to pass notes. But the captain's mission announcement was for everybody. He told us we had orders to spy on the Japanese bases in the Marshall Islands.[1] I didn't know where that was, other than somewhere in the South Pacific. He also said that we would attack any enemy ships we found along the way, especially the ones that might be bringing soldiers to Hawaii. There was still considerable worry that the Japanese might try to invade and capture our base at Pearl Harbor.

The rules of engagement were "unrestricted submarine warfare." I didn't get the significance of that until we started talking among ourselves. The *Dolphin*'s communications officer explained to all of us radiomen that any ship flying a Japanese flag was a target, including their supply ships. They could even be civilian-owned cargo vessels, like our Merchant Marine. The Japanese called them "*maru.*" We all knew these kinds of ships were mostly unarmed, totally defenseless against a submarine, and I remember thinking, *Whoa now. Wait a minute. You mean we're actually going to kill people? Hundreds, maybe thousands of them? On an unarmed ship?* The more we talked about it, the more it bothered me. Finally, somebody said, "Well, yeah. But look what they did to us at Pearl Harbor." And that's how I got past it. From then on, I knew I was going to follow orders. It wasn't my job to press the button that fired the torpedoes, but I'm sure I would have done that, too. We never talked about it again.[2]

I was one of six radiomen on the *Dolphin*. Submerged or on the surface, we spent most of our time trying to locate enemy ships. I didn't have much experience with sonar, but I understood the principle. Sonar was just a variation of a radio transmitter. I never actually saw the device because it was underwater, hanging like a gallon milk jug from the belly of the submarine. When we turned it on, it sent out a constant radio signal for about a hundred miles in all directions. Anything that was big and thick enough to bounce the signal back to us showed up in green lights on a screen in the radio room. It made a pinging sound on the headphones, too. The closer the object, the louder the ping, but you couldn't tell if the ship was friend or enemy without raising the periscope. Sometimes it wasn't a ship at all. It was a whale. It took a lot of practice to hear the difference. Whenever I said, "I have a ping, Sir," one of the officers—sometimes the captain himself—would come over and put on the headphones. The radiomen thought that was hilarious. The senior officers on the *Dolphin* had even less experience with sonar interpretation than we did.[3]

There was almost no sensation of movement when we traveled underwater. It was like living and working in a building with no windows, and we didn't have much to do besides eat and sleep between shifts. We played a lot of board games—mainly acey-deucey—to pass the time. It's similar to backgammon: you just shake the dice and move your pieces up and down the board. We had acey-deucey and chess tournaments pretty much around the clock on the *Dolphin*. The highlight of everybody's day was when we surfaced at night. Anyone could go outside for some fresh air after dark, but never all at once. In case of emergency—if we'd needed to crash-dive for some reason—it would have taken too long to get everybody back inside. The hatch was only big enough for one man at a time. We took turns going outside in small groups of ten or twelve, all night long.

The first few nights were actually quite relaxing. As soon as we were on the surface, the radiomen checked in with headquarters. We could not send or receive any radio messages while we were submerged. After that, the captain let us tune in to a civilian

The radio room of a World War II–era submarine contained both transmitters and receivers. The key used to tap Morse code through transmitter is at right of typewriter; headphones for listening to incoming messages are hooked to right of chairback. COURTESY OF C. E. "TED" AND MARIE T. WIGTON COLLECTION.

radio station. If we picked up one that was playing big band music, we put it on the loudspeakers. Everybody wanted to hear the latest from Benny Goodman—he was the King of Swing—but some guys thought Glenn Miller's band was the best there was.[4] I never got into those debates, because I frankly didn't care what was on the radio when it was my turn to go outside. I usually just stood by myself and looked at the stars. In the warm night air, with no other ships around, you could almost forget that we were at war.

There were about sixty of us on the *Dolphin*. It felt more like six hundred when everyone was inside. If you met somebody coming or going, you had to turn sideways and suck in your stomach to let the other guy get by. I began to understand why I hardly ever saw the sub crews inside the barracks at Pearl Harbor. They were always outdoors, around the pool or on the tennis court, even when it rained. I could also see why the Navy didn't make them live on their subs when they came into port. But I never got why they kept referring to the *Dolphin* and all the other submarines as "boats." The way I learned it in boot camp, a boat was something small enough to carry aboard a ship. Well, the *Dolphin* was nearly as long as a destroyer, and some of the newer submarines were even longer than that. I just chalked it up as one more way of saying sub crews were different from everybody else in the Navy.[5]

I didn't know what to think when we started having so many mechanical problems. First it was leaks, and they weren't just little drips here and there. I'm talking sprays. The boatswains had to run around and patch nearly every pipe and joint just to keep us from sinking while we were submerged. When the fathometer malfunctioned, the captain had to guess how deep we were. The radiomen were guessing, too, because the *Dolphin*'s radio antenna kept shorting out. We were never sure if our nightly reports to headquarters were getting through. It's probably a darned good thing that we didn't locate any enemy ships during that first week out of Pearl Harbor: The captain had too many other problems to deal with.

Every time I turned around, the captain was in conference with the COB, the Chief of the Boat. The COB was the senior enlisted man on the *Dolphin*. Not only was he the oldest chief petty officer, he was also a boatswain, which probably had something to do with his short temper. And, not only that, the COB was what they called a "plankowner." He'd been on the *Dolphin* since it first came into service. If anyone knew what was wrong and how to fix it, it was the COB, and I heard him tell the captain to turn around and go back to Pearl Harbor for repairs. But the captain was also taking advice from the Executive Officer, his second in command. The XO didn't think the mechanical problems were that serious, and even if they were, we should complete our mission or die trying.

I felt sorry for the captain. He was caught in the middle between the COB and his XO, and I could tell that the stress was beginning to get to him. It was his first wartime mission, too. Personally, I agreed with the XO, and so did all the other enlisted men. We didn't have a big meeting or take a vote, and nobody asked our opinion. We just talked it over in small groups. As far as I know, the COB was the only one who thought the captain was making a big mistake when he decided to continue the mission.

Shortly after New Year's Day, the off-duty conversations switched from leaks and mechanical malfunctions to pollywogs. Anyone in the Navy who had never crossed the equator was a pollywog, and there were about ten of us on the *Dolphin*. War or no war, leaks and all, this called for a ceremony. The Navy was real big on tradition. The older men tried to scare us with stories of what happened to them when they crossed the equator. Some said they had to take off all their clothes and walk past a line of guys with paddles. So, yeah, you could say I was a little nervous when the navigator said we were about to "cross the line."

The officers went outside first that night. We had to wait until they called for us, one by one. When it was my turn to climb the ladder, I didn't see any guys with paddles. All I saw were the officers, the COB, the head cook, and a dirty-looking pail with the word "worms" painted on the lid. Somebody said, "Kneel," and they tied on a real thick blindfold, so big it covered my nose, too. It smelled like dirt and dead fish. The captain rattled off a bunch of mumbo jumbo about how crossing the equator is when you meet King Neptune in his mysterious, watery realm. It was pretty funny until he got to the part where he said, "and a polly-wog's gotta eat worms." The cook told me to "open wide and chew 'em up real good." I should have known it was just that old trick from science class, the one where you close your eyes and hold your nose and try to tell which is the apple and which is the onion. I guess I forgot that lesson. I really believed I'd just eaten a big glob of slimy worms. I didn't know the bucket was full of cold, cooked spaghetti until they took off the blindfold. I acted like I was gagging and throwing up over the side of the boat for the benefit of the next guy. It was a short ceremony—forty-five minutes or so—but everybody got a good laugh. It relieved some of the tension.

After we crossed the equator, I was getting six or eight pings a day, and none of them were whales. Everybody was waiting for the captain's order to fire on the Japanese ships. We had twelve torpedoes—six loaded in the tubes and six more in reserve—but he kept saying that the targets were out of range, too far away. Either that, or they were at the wrong angle. I have no doubt that was true. The *Dolphin* wasn't fast enough to catch a maru from behind, let alone a warship, and our torpedoes had no guidance system. They were like firing bullets from an underwater rifle. The captain was probably saving his ammunition for the best possible shot, which would be the broad side of a ship crossing in front of us. It reminded me of hunting deer: You have to hide in the meadow and wait for that big buck to walk right past you. Range and angle was everything.

The XO agreed with the captain's decision to hold his fire—until a big Japanese cruiser came into view. It was well within range of our torpedoes. The only problem was, that cruiser was coming straight toward us. We would have had to aim for the bow, which was a very narrow target. The XO called this a "down-the-throat" shot, and he was desperate to try it.[6] The COB said it was a waste of a torpedo. More than that, he was worried about revealing our position to the cruiser. He was so certain we would miss it, and then they would fire back at us. He advised the captain to let the cruiser go because the *Dolphin* was too slow and too crippled to get away. They had a three-way shouting match around the periscope, until finally the captain couldn't take it any more. The Japanese cruiser was passing out of range when he left the command center. Everyone said he had what they called a nervous breakdown. I never saw the captain again. He stayed in his private quarters for the rest of the mission.

The XO took charge of the *Dolphin,* and all of the other officers accepted him as their unofficial captain. So did the COB, and the rest of the enlisted men followed him. But the XO did not order us to fire on the next Japanese ship that came within range of our torpedoes. At that point, we were too close to the enemy bases in the Marshall Islands. Our orders were to spy on them, and that's exactly what we did. For the next week and a half, we just sneaked around from one island to another and counted the number and type of ships at each base. Sometimes we were less than two hundred yards offshore. I got to look through the periscope myself. I saw two or three cruisers and several destroyers coming and going, but most of the ships in the Marshall Islands were marus. If I'd known how to read Japanese, I could have reported what was in the boxes and crates they were unloading. We were close enough to read the labels. Every time a ship left the dock and came toward us, we lowered the periscope and prayed they didn't see it. The XO quit putting on the headphones when I told him I had a ping. He was ordering crash dives on my say-so.

I don't know how we managed to stay undetected for as long as we did, especially when we started snooping around Kwajalein.[7] That was the biggest and busiest harbor we could find in the Marshall Islands, and that's where I got the loudest pinging I'd ever heard on sonar. It was a Japanese destroyer. We crash-dived and hoped it was on its way out to sea. But the darn thing just sat there on the surface above us. I was probably more scared than anybody because I'd been on a destroyer myself. I used to think it was fun to watch the depth charges explode. Now, they were just the deadliest weapon I could imagine. The XO didn't look scared, but I think he was. He took us deeper than we'd ever been before. I'm sure we were well below two hundred feet that day, because I never saw so many leaks all at once. We had to shut down every system and act dead in the water. If the enemy destroyer's sonar was anywhere near as sensitive as ours, they could have heard our propeller. Nobody talked above a whisper; we didn't dare shake the dice for acey-deucey. We even took off our shoes when we walked from one end of the boat to the other. You could smell the fear. I was almost afraid to breathe. I thought I was going to die that day.

The pinging stayed loud for hours and hours, until it finally faded and stopped. I have never known whether that Japanese destroyer was really looking for us or not. If they dropped any depth charges, I did not feel the concussion. They must have exploded more than thirty yards away. When the XO finally brought us closer to the surface, we had so many serious leaks from one end of the boat to the other, he called off the mission. I guess he finally agreed with the COB, and so did I. We probably could not have survived another crash dive. I wasn't even sure we were going to make it out of the Marshall Islands, let alone all the way back to Pearl Harbor.

We stayed submerged until we were out of enemy territory, and then we started transmitting our reports back to headquarters. That was an adventure, too, because our radio antenna was still shorting out. We didn't know if any of our information was getting through.[8] For incoming messages, we relied on the Fox Schedule. That was a system where each transmission from CinCPac was numbered and broadcast over and over again. If you didn't get it the first time, you might pick it up the next day, or the day after that. You have no idea how relieved I was when I copied the message that said the *Dolphin* had permission to return to base. We were about halfway back to Hawaii when we got that one.

We did not see any enemy ships after we crossed the equator on the way back to Pearl Harbor, but we did see some of our own. One was the carrier *Enterprise*. There were several cruisers and destroyers around it, and the whole task force was headed south. I knew better than to ask where they were going. The movements of the carriers were always highly classified.[9] What I mainly remember about returning from that mission is the crew's low morale. Everyone on the *Dolphin* felt like a failure. We didn't sink a single enemy ship. We didn't even fire any of our torpedoes. All we had to show for over a month at sea was something like thirty-five "deficiencies." I saw the XO's checklist. I also saw that he'd marked over half of those mechanical problems as "serious." I have no idea if the *Dolphin* was ever repaired enough to go out again, and I never heard what happened to the captain. He was still holed up in his quarters when we pulled up to the docks.[10]

I was grateful to come back from that mission alive. I can't remember a time when it felt so good to walk on solid ground. As soon as I got to the barracks, I went looking for Scoop and Spic, but I couldn't find them anywhere. Their bunks were empty, and their seabags were gone. All of the radiomen at headquarters were new. I'd only been gone for a month or so, but nothing at the submarine base was the same. Even Lt. Commander Guenther was gone, and there was a new admiral in charge of the Pacific Fleet.[11] It felt so strange, I requested sea duty again. I thought they'd put me on another submarine, and that was okay with me, as long as it wasn't the *Dolphin*. I couldn't believe it when I saw my orders. I'd never even been close to an aircraft carrier before. I thought I was lucky to get the *Yorktown*.

See Time Line, page 239, and Historical Notes, page 240.

11

THE AIRCRAFT CARRIER

February 3–April 27, 1942

I tried asking around the base, but it was no use. Not one radioman at CinCPac headquarters had ever been to sea on a carrier, and neither had anybody else at the submarine base. Probably because there weren't that many of them. Before the war started, there were only three aircraft carriers in the whole Pacific Fleet. They were never in port for very long. Everybody knew their nicknames—the *Saratoga* was "Sara"; *Enterprise* was "Big E"; *Lexington* was "The Lady"—and that's about all we knew. The *Yorktown* was even less familiar to us at Pearl Harbor because it didn't come over from the Atlantic Fleet until some time after we were attacked. I did hear that the *Yorktown* had a reputation for being real modern, and it was said that the crew lived in luxury. One guy claimed they even had a machine where you could help yourself to a drink of cold milk any time you wanted it, day or night. I didn't quite believe that—sounded like a pet cockroach story to me—but the milk machine was right up there on my list of things to look for on the day I boarded the *Yorktown*.

It was February, exceptionally sunny at Pearl Harbor that morning, like a summer day back home. In Arkansas, this was what you called "bluebird weather." I was feeling a little bit homesick when the motorboat picked me up from the sub base docks, but that went away as soon as we made the turn at Ford Island. I burst out laughing. I mean, yes, I fully expected to see a really big ship, but the *Yorktown* was ridiculous. The darn thing was nearly three football fields long.[1] You could have dropped about six destroyers inside the hull and still have room for a couple of submarines. The guy driving the boat was laughing, too. He promised to stay and fish me out of the water if I fell off the boarding ladder. I wasn't afraid of heights; I just didn't know if I was strong enough to climb that many steep steps with a fifty-pound seabag on my back. I guess you can do a lot of things when you're twenty-one.

I stepped off on the hangar deck level, which looked and smelled like a giant garage, except that it was full of planes instead of cars. I saw dozens of them, all parked in rows with their wings folded. They were so similar to what flew past me on the roof of the administration building in December, I had to ask. The boatswain's mate said they were torpedo planes, all right. "Devastators," he called them. I said I hoped ours were as devastating as the Japanese version.[2] He told me the *Yorktown* carried fighter planes and dive-bombers, too, but I didn't see any of those. According to him, they generally flew off before the ship came into port and stayed on Ford Island until the carrier went back out to sea. He wasn't sure when that would be. Even if he knew, he probably wasn't allowed to say. The Navy was beginning to refer to this as the "loose lips sink ships" doctrine.

As soon as I got my bunk assignment, which was three or four ladders down from the hangar deck, I reported to the radio shack. It was on the flight deck, inside a multilevel tower that sat off to one side. I don't know why this tower was called "the island." It looked more like an office building to me. The radio room was larger than I was used to, even at Fleet headquarters. It took up most of the island's second floor. When I showed my orders to the communications officer, he showed me to my battle station. That was standard procedure. Even before the war, the first thing you had to know was where to run in case of emergency. But on all the other ships—even at CinCPac headquarters—I was always assigned to the radio shack. I couldn't figure out why he was taking me up the ladder, to the bridge level of the island. And I still didn't know why until I opened the door to the emergency radio room. It was about six feet behind the captain's chair.

The emergency radio room on the *Yorktown*'s bridge was not much bigger than a broom closet, or maybe a couple of telephone booths stuck together. Anyone could see that it was designed for only one radioman. I don't know why me. I have always suspected it was because none of the more senior guys in the radio gang wanted the job. Maybe they were claustrophobic. The only good thing about it was the perks: Anyone who was assigned to a battle station on the bridge could go there anytime. I liked that, because of the windows. I also had permission to step out on the bridge catwalk, which was sort of like an outdoor balcony, about thirty feet above the flight deck. There were lots of other catwalks on the *Yorktown*, but the one that wrapped around the bridge was clearly the best. As long as I was careful not to block the captain's view, I could stand out there and watch the planes all day long.

The minute I saw the *Yorktown* had no catapults, I wanted to fly again. About half of the radiomen on that ship did. They were "aviation radiomen," but everyone called them "radio gunners" or just "gunners." The only difference between them and the rest of us was the extra training they got on the planes' machine guns. You didn't have to go to any special school for it; I could have taken the course right there on the ship. In my mind, riding in the gunner's seat behind the pilot was the next best thing to being a pilot myself. But the communications officer said no. There were no openings for aviation radiomen on the *Yorktown* at that time.

The closest I could get to being a gunner was to hang out with them, and that's exactly what I did, starting with Keith Mansfield. I went to lunch with him and several other aviation radiomen that first day. They laughed when I asked if there really was such a thing as a milk machine, but they took me right to it. Oh, yes, and there it was, right outside the mess hall. It looked like a restaurant coffee dispenser, with a stack of paper cups on the table beside it. I grabbed one, pushed the button, took a great big gulp, and gagged. It was cold and it was white, but it wasn't milk. It was "klim." That's "milk" spelled backward—the powdered, reconstituted kind. Nastiest-tasting stuff there is, in my opinion. No wonder the gunners didn't want any. They said there were a few guys on the *Yorktown* who actually did drink klim and liked it. I wasn't one of them. I never touched that dumb machine again.

The Marines were downright creepy. We didn't have them on the smaller ships, but they were all over the *Yorktown*. The gunners said some of the Marines were bodyguards for the captain and the admiral; the rest were the ship's police. As far as I could see, they didn't do anything except stand around like statues and look mean. Their uniforms were so much fancier than ours, we called them "seagoing bellhops." Of course, nobody ever said that to their faces, except maybe the boatswains—ship security was normally their turf—but it was fairly obvious that the whole crew hated them. There had always been bad blood between sailors and Marines. We knew they had more training in hand-to-hand combat than we did, and it was common knowledge that those guys could really fight, with or without a weapon. They were very intimidating. The Marines on the *Yorktown* did carry a sidearm, but I think it was just for show. They didn't need a gun to keep the crew in line.

I spent the rest of my first day on the *Yorktown* inside the radio shack. It was three times bigger than the radio room at CinCPac headquarters, and the equipment was newer. They had more voice channels, too, which I assumed were necessary for communicating with the planes. But there was one piece of equipment I had never seen before. I'd never even heard of radar. The radiomen said they hadn't had it for very long. They were still taking turns at learning how to read the dots on the screen. The way they explained it, radar worked on the same principle as sonar. The signal just beamed out of a big antenna on the top of the island and bounced off objects above the surface of the water instead of below. The signal itself was called "the main bang." The other radiomen warned me to stay out of its path. They thought this radar signal was so powerful it would make a guy sterile. You better believe I took that seriously. From day one on the *Yorktown,* I made it a point to stay out of the main bang.

I went up to the bridge several times while we were still in port, but I did not see the captain until the ship left Pearl Harbor, three or four days after I came aboard. We were just outside the channel when he gave the mission announcement over the ship's loudspeakers. He told us we were going to the Solomon Islands. I don't know how the rest of the crew reacted. In the radio shack, it was "Okay. Where the hell are the Solomons?" Nobody knew. We decided they must be somewhere in the South Pacific, like the Marshall Islands, and all those other little islands and atolls we never heard of before the war. I stepped outside to see how many other ships were going on this mission with us. I counted three or four cruisers and about that many destroyers. I would have loved to see a battleship, too, but there were none. The *Arizona* and the *Oklahoma* were still sitting on the bottom of Pearl Harbor, and all the others were in for repairs. As we began to pick up speed, I realized that it didn't matter how many battleships the Navy did or didn't have in service at that time. They couldn't keep up with a fast carrier task force anyway. The *Yorktown* was doing thirty knots, easy.[3]

A couple of hours out of Pearl Harbor, I heard pilots on the voice channels. The *Yorktown*'s planes were flying out from Ford Island, requesting clearance. I was off duty, so I ran up to the bridge catwalk to watch them land on the flight deck. I saw at least twenty planes circling in the air above the ship. It was even more interesting to watch the LSO, the landing signal officer. He stood out on the flight deck with a big wooden paddle in each hand. When the first fighter plane approached the stern, he crossed the paddles in front of his chest. That must have been the signal for the pilot to cut his engine, because, at that very instant, the plane dropped like a rock. The tailhook dragged along until it caught one of the cables across the flight deck, and that brought the plane to a dead stop, directly below where I was standing on the bridge catwalk. As soon as the plane stopped moving, a whole bunch of guys came running out and hitched it up to a little tractor. They didn't even wait for the pilot to climb out of the cockpit; they just towed the plane forward to the elevator on the bow. Two minutes later, here comes another fighter plane. Same thing. When they had three or four planes around the elevator platform, down it went to the hangar deck. There must have been another big crew on that level, because the elevator came back empty in no time at all. This went on, plane after plane, until all the squadrons were on board.

From then on, the *Yorktown* had planes taking off and landing all day, every day, and it never got old for me. Whenever I was off duty, if I wasn't eating or sleeping, everybody knew where to find me: I was on the bridge, watching the flight deck. That's how I got acquainted with a quartermaster named Siwash Nagombi. He worked in the chartroom, where they kept all the ship's maps and navigation equipment. Since that was also on the *Yorktown*'s bridge level, Siwash had the same catwalk privileges I did. His skin was almost as dark as his hair and his eyes. As we got to know each other better, he told me that his parents came to America from India. He was born after they settled somewhere around Chicago.

Siwash was a couple of years older, more studious, and a lot less talkative than I was. We didn't have much in common to begin with, except that we both loved to stand out on the catwalk and watch the planes in our free time. There were no flight operations after dark—the *Yorktown* didn't have any pilots qualified for night landings at sea—but Siwash and I still took our evening breaks out on the catwalk. The more we got to know each other, the more I enjoyed his company. After dinner, we usually went down to the hangar deck. At the end of the day, it turned into something like a recreation center for the whole crew. The guys who serviced the planes were real nice about sharing their space. We called them "airdales." They pushed open the big hangar deck doors to let the wind blow through, which made it more like a giant covered patio than a garage. As soon as it got dark, they pulled down this huge movie screen and turned on the projector. The *Yorktown* had all the latest movies from Hollywood. It you got there late and all the folding chairs were taken, the airdales let us sit on the wings of the planes.

Sometimes the ship's band came out and played for us on the hangar deck. They were very good musicians, and they took requests. Well, of course, we all wanted swing music, which was great for dancing, but there were no girls on the *Yorktown*. No problem: The sailors just danced with each other. I never learned the jitterbug myself—it was more like acrobatics than dancing—but it was pretty fun to watch. The boxing matches—we called them "smokers"—were even better. On smoker nights, they set up a regular professional-type boxing ring on the flight deck. I'm talking ropes, mats, referees, announcers, and the whole bit. We even had bookies keeping track of the bets. I don't know how they did it. With a total crew of about three thousand, there must have been tens of thousands of dollars riding on every fight. I never bet more than five myself, but some guys wagered a whole month's pay on a single match. The boxers could be anybody, including the cooks and the mess attendants. There were several on the *Yorktown* who boxed professionally before they got drafted or enlisted in the Navy. I always cheered for whichever sailor was in the ring, and sometimes they won. I usually put my money on the Marine.

On Sunday, the hangar deck turned into a church. The ship's chaplain was from one of the Protestant denominations, but, just like in boot camp, he did a Catholic-type service, too. No one was required to attend either kind. He drew a good-sized crowd, though. I saw more officers and enlisted men at divine services on the *Yorktown* than we ever had at the sub base chapel before the war. I think a lot of guys got more religious after the attack on Pearl Harbor. I know I did. I believed I'd already been through hell. I didn't want to go there again when I died.

About a week out of Hawaii, the boatswains set up a stage with a microphone on the flight deck. Everybody who wasn't on duty came up to watch the ceremony when we crossed the equator. We had about twenty-five pollywogs on the *Yorktown* for that mission, and some of them were officers. They got it worse than the enlisted men. The emcee made them put on grass skirts and be hula dancers. After that, he pretended to be a hypnotist, and told them they were ducks and chickens. He had them all running around, quacking and clucking like a bunch of idiots. One officer got a pair of Coke bottles for binoculars. Every few minutes, the emcee made him describe all the enemy ships he was seeing. There was a lot of hooting and clapping for him, but I think we got our biggest laugh from this one enlisted man. He was so young and scared. I doubt if he was even eighteen. The emcee really had fun with him. "Sailor," he said, "I'm ordering you to smile if you were with a strange woman on Hotel Street the night before you boarded the *Yorktown*." That kid's face turned so many shades of red, but he sure did smile, and everybody just howled.

That was the last big entertainment we had on the *Yorktown*. We still hadn't sighted any Japanese ships or planes, but everybody knew we were getting deeper into enemy territory. You could feel the tension all over the ship. I don't think we were more than two or three days south of the equator when I started picking up civilian radio stations from Tokyo. A couple of them were broadcasting American music. It was a little strange to get Glenn Miller from Japan, but we liked it. Sometimes Captain Buckmaster told us to go ahead and play those programs over the loudspeakers. As we got farther west into the Pacific, we passed a lot of little islands. Siwash told me their names. The only one I remember is Pago Pago, probably because the radiomen talked about it, too. It sounded like they had all been there before.[4] It would have been nice to get liberty on Pago Pago—the beaches and palm trees looked like Hawaii to me—but the *Yorktown* did not stop there or anywhere else on our way to the Solomon Islands.

The first ships we saw were our own. That was the *Lexington*'s task force. We joined up with them somewhere between the

Solomons and New Guinea. So now there were two aircraft carri- ers full of planes, all searching for enemy ships, and nobody was finding any. We were pretty excited when one of the *Yorktown* pi- lots finally spotted a whole bunch of Japanese ships. They were on one side of New Guinea, we were on the other, and the enemy didn't seem to know we were there. The *Yorktown* pilot described the Japanese ships as mostly marus—supply ships and troop carriers—but he thought he saw a couple of destroyers and maybe a cruiser, too. They were at anchor or coming and going from two different harbors. I knew the *Yorktown* and the *Lexington* were going to strike both of those New Guinea harbors in the morning.[5]

Siwash was even quieter than usual that night. He was wor- ried about our planes, because they were going to fly across New Guinea, instead of around it, which meant they would be flying over the Owen Stanley Mountains. According to his charts, those mountains were fifteen thousand feet high. He and I both knew that the *Yorktown* fighter planes and dive bombers were capable of that altitude, but the torpedo planes were not. The only way our Devastators could cross those mountains would be to find a certain pass—some kind of a valley—where they could fly lower. But there was no such pass on any of the quartermasters' charts. They were relying on a source that claimed the pass would be vis- ible when the fog lifted over the mountains for two hours in the morning. Siwash did not trust that intelligence. He believed it came from someone's interrogation of a Japanese prisoner of war.

If the *Yorktown*'s torpedo plane gunners were concerned about crashing into the Owen Stanley Mountains in the morning, they didn't show it. My friend Mansfield was snickering when he came back from the mission briefing that night. He said everybody was laughing at this one superstitious pilot. I guess he was a regular fortune-teller who believed he was doomed because the next day was his birthday. In his mind, this was such a bad omen, he was down on the hangar deck, packing his cockpit with all the gear he thought he was going to need if he survived the crash. The gunners said he had a bag full of fishhooks, pocketknives, food, water, and who knows what else. Well, that got all the other *Yorktown* pilots

to teasing the poor guy. They told him there were probably canni-
bals in those jungles on New Guinea. Last we heard, he was in the
galley. The cooks said they caught him stealing their butcher
knives and meat cleavers.

I was on duty when the planes took off the next morning, so
I'm not sure how many there were. If I had to guess, I'd say we
launched about fifty. I suppose the *Lexington* sent the same or
more. I know that both carriers kept a few fighter planes behind,
because they were all flying in circles above us. That was the
CAP—Combat Air Patrol. Their job was to guard against a possible counterattack by enemy planes, which wasn't too likely that
day, and those pilots were not happy about it. I heard them
grumbling back and forth to one another on the radio. It sounded
like they would rather have been with the guys who were flying
over the Owen Stanley Mountains.

It was over an hour before we picked up the frequencies of the
squadrons that were trying to find the pass. Cheers broke out
when they said they did. We put them on the loudspeakers; everybody wanted to know what was happening on the other side of
New Guinea. It sounded like a turkey shoot to me. The *Yorktown*
pilots were jovial. They reported no Japanese fighter planes in the
air and very little antiaircraft fire from the ships in either harbor. I
guess they caught the enemy by surprise. I don't know about the
Lexington, but I can tell you that the *Yorktown* did not lose a single plane over New Guinea that day. They all came back by noon.[6]

We did have one casualty on the *Yorktown.* The pilot was not
physically injured, but he was grounded. He couldn't fly again
until the chaplain cleared him. According to his gunner, it happened when they fired on a Japanese seaplane that was taking off
from one of those New Guinea harbors. The enemy plane exploded in a great big fireball, right in front of them, and that
really bothered the *Yorktown* pilot. All the way back to us, he kept
saying, over and over again, "I just killed my first man today."
His squadron leader referred him to the chaplain, but the gunners
swore that it was actually the other pilots who did the counseling.
We heard they showed him pictures of the *Arizona* and talked to

him about the attack on Pearl Harbor. Whatever it took to cure him, that pilot was back in the air in less than a week.

We parted company with the *Lexington* task force right after the attack on New Guinea. They didn't tell us where they were going. When we saw them heading south, we thought maybe they were going to Australia for liberty. That's what we wanted, but we didn't get it. For the rest of March and most of April, we just cruised up and down the southern shores of the Solomon Islands, looking for more enemy ships. We thought we were invincible. We couldn't wait to attack another harbor full of Japanese ships, but we couldn't find any. Heck, we couldn't even find a maru. The whole crew was joking about it. I think that's when the *Yorktown* got a brand-new nickname. It was one of those things that caught on and spread around the ship: instead of just "Yorkie," we started calling ourselves "the Yorkie Maru."

After several weeks of no action—we were supposed to be at war, but we couldn't find anybody to fight with—it wasn't funny anymore. Everybody was bored, and morale was dropping all over the ship. Even the cooks were cranky, because we were low on supplies. They'd run out of ways to cook beans. The radiomen stayed fairly busy, though. I remember copying a lot of incoming messages from CinCPac at that time. All messages from headquarters were in code, of course, so it looked like gibberish to me. I just typed what I heard and handed the sheets of paper to the communications officer. He put them through the decoding machine and rushed them up to the captain on the bridge.

I was also monitoring the civilian press frequencies. Those came through in plain English, and it was all bad news. The war was not going well. The Japanese were taking territory all over the South Pacific, and our troops in the Philippines were surrendering to them on Bataan. I passed that news, along with everything else I got from the civilian press, up to the bridge. It was up to Captain Buckmaster to decide how much to tell the crew. Most of the time, he didn't give them anything but the baseball scores. The only piece of news I recall him reading over the loudspeakers was when the Army Air Force bombed Tokyo. Everybody on the ship cheered for those guys, even the Marines. I think we would have hollered a lot louder if we'd known the Army had figured out how to launch their bombers from a Navy aircraft carrier.[7]

Toward the end of April, the *Yorktown* stopped at a harbor in the Tonga Islands. Nobody went ashore except for the guys assigned to meet the supply ships, but it was still nice to be at anchor in a friendly harbor. When Siwash and I went out on the catwalk that night, he showed me the Southern Cross and a lot of other constellations I'd never seen before.[8] The whole sky looked different in that part of the world, if you took the time to study it. Siwash did. He was really into astronomy. He was one of the few quartermasters who could steer by the stars, like they used to in the old days. Me, I just stared at the moon and thought about Adeline. The last letter I'd had from her was before I boarded the *Yorktown*. I only read it twice—twice a day, that is. She said she loved me, that she was going to wait for me. I really needed to believe that. I even talked myself into believing that she was out looking up at the moon at the same time I was. Siwash never said a word. When you're that lovesick, you don't want to hear about time zones. He really was a good friend.

The *Yorktown* stayed in that little harbor for several days, until we got a whole flurry of urgent, coded messages from headquarters. The captain must have thought it would be good for morale, because he gave us the gist of it. He said Admiral Nimitz was quite sure that we would find at least two Japanese aircraft carriers in the Coral Sea, and they were headed our way. It never occurred to me to wonder how CinCPac came by this information. All I cared to know was whether these were the same carriers that attacked Pearl Harbor.[9] Everybody on the *Yorktown* wanted revenge for Pearl Harbor. It was just a little more personal for me.

See Time Line, page 241, and Historical Notes, page 243.

12

THE BATTLE OF THE CORAL SEA

April 27–May 27, 1942

The Coral Sea was south of the Solomon Islands and north of Australia. It looked the same as the rest of the Pacific in that part of the world, except for what it did to the *Yorktown*'s radar. The screen was just a mess of purple dots, because the Coral Sea was full of coral. There was no way to tell which dots were coral atolls and which were ships or planes. We just had to stare at the screen and holler for a second opinion if we thought any of the dots were moving. It was even worse for our search pilots, because none of our planes had radar. When they flew over a cluster of coral atolls at about twenty thousand feet, the pilots reported it as a Japanese carrier task force. We got a lot of false alarms that way.[1]

After three or four days of nothing but coral in the Coral Sea, I was beginning to think we were on a wild goose chase. Maybe CinCPac got some bad intelligence. But those messages were still coming in from Admiral Nimitz, and our captain said the *Yorktown* wasn't going anywhere until we found those Japanese aircraft carriers. So, naturally, we were very excited when the Australians told us enemy ships had been spotted in a harbor called Tulagi. That was back in the Solomon Islands, but it was still within fuel range for our planes. Everybody thought these were the enemy carriers we were looking for. Headquarters would surely send us to Australia as a reward for sinking them. I'd heard all kinds of good things about how they treated American sailors on liberty in Australia.

There was a lot of wishful thinking on the *Yorktown* when our planes took off for the attack on Tulagi. But that's all it was. When we listened to the pilots on the loudspeakers, it sounded about the same as when they flew over the mountains on New Guinea. There were no Japanese carriers in that harbor. The enemy ships were mostly marus. I don't know how many they sank. I don't usually remember exact numbers—some of them I never knew to begin with—but I can tell you we lost three planes that day. They were the *Yorktown*'s first combat losses since I joined the crew in February. I wish I could say they were the last.[2]

A day or two after the attack on Tulagi, the *Lexington* joined up with us again. It worked the same as when we combined task forces for the attack on New Guinea the month before. That is, they had their captain and we had ours, but all the ships took orders from the admiral on the *Yorktown*. He had his own bridge—closer to the top of the island—and he never spoke to the crew on the loudspeakers. I hardly even knew he was aboard until we started hunting for the Japanese carriers in the Coral Sea. After that, I saw him every day. Sometimes he came down and talked to the captain and the XO on the bridge, but mostly he was in the chart room talking to Siwash. Every time I poked my head in there to see my friend, I had to back right out again because he was with the admiral. They were usually looking at maps, and the admiral was asking him, "Where are we now?" I'd never seen anyone of such high rank speak directly to an enlisted man before.[3]

I don't recall very many exact dates either, but I know it was the sixth of May when the Fat Lady came. That was what we called the *Neosho,* one of the tanker ships that brought us fuel.

Refueling at sea was not unusual—we'd done it two or three times a week since we left Pearl Harbor—but that was the day I said goodbye to my gunner friend Keith Mansfield. He'd just received orders to attend flight school at Pensacola, and the *Neosho* was his ride for part of the way back to the States. He was so happy, and I was happy for him. I really was. I shook his hand and wished him luck, but, oh, I was so jealous. We both wanted to be carrier pilots, but the Navy picked him instead of me. Mansfield had more flight experience than I did. He was also two years older, and everybody knew the Navy wasn't too gung ho for making pilots out of guys my age. I still thought it should have been me. The last time I saw Mansfield, he was waving at me from the top deck of the *Neosho*. I believe he died at sunrise the next day.[4]

I was on duty in the radio shack when I heard the *Neosho* was under attack. The planes must have come from one of the Japanese carriers we were still looking for in the Coral Sea. After we attacked their ships at Tulagi, I'm sure they were looking for us, too. But it was the *Neosho* they found, and there were very few survivors. My friend Mansfield was not one of them. Oh, gosh, that hurt. I would have given anything to trade places with him when he left, and now I was grateful that it wasn't me that got picked for flight school. And then I felt guilty for thinking that way, and I felt guilty for being alive.

A little later that same morning, a *Yorktown* pilot spotted one Japanese aircraft carrier. Radar could not confirm the sighting, so it must have been at least a hundred miles away. Either that, or it was just another false alarm. None of the radiomen was sure it really was an enemy ship of any kind until we heard more pilots say they saw it, too. Next thing you know, we're listening to all of them while they attacked the thing. It sounded like over a hundred of our planes were converging on that one Japanese carrier.[5] I heard a *Yorktown* pilot say, "Man, it looks like a beehive up here!" I'm sure it did. Five or ten minutes later, it was all over. I heard one of the *Lexington* pilots say, "Scratch one flattop!" That was about as close as any of our pilots came to cheering. There was no celebrating in the radio shack either. We just wondered if this was the same enemy carrier that attacked the *Neosho* and killed our buddy Mansfield. I chose to believe that it was.[6]

All of the *Yorktown* planes were low on fuel when they came back from sinking the Japanese carrier. I heard them arguing on the voice channels about who should land first. That was really the LSO's decision, but those pilots were so polite to each other, they even argued with him. One guy kept insisting that his wingman should come in ahead of him, because "He's got less in his tank than I do." And they weren't kidding. A couple of the *Yorktown*'s planes actually did run out of gas before they made it to the flight deck. They had to splash down in the water around us instead. The planes sank pretty fast, but the pilots and their gunners were okay. They just climbed out and sat in their rubber rafts until one of the destroyers came over and got them. We did have a few injuries, though. I was out on the catwalk when one pilot climbed out of the cockpit. It looked like he was bleeding pretty bad, but he would not let anyone touch him until they brought the stretcher for his gunner. I saw him walking beside the stretcher, and I can tell you that he never let go of his gunner's hand all the way to the elevator. I didn't follow them down to sick bay, but I believed it when I heard that pilot was still holding his gunner's hand when he died.

I did not go down to the hangar deck at all that afternoon. It was best to stay away when the airdales were refueling and rearming the planes. Those guys must have worked like the devil, because they had most of the bombers back on the flight deck and ready to launch again in a couple of hours. I'll bet they cussed like the devil, too, when the word came down from the bridge: The admiral said wait until morning. It probably was a little too late in the day. The planes might not get back by sundown. Even if the pilots could find us after dark, there was still so little experience with night landings on the *Yorktown*. So I left the catwalk and went back down to the radio shack, and that's where I was when I heard the ship's antiaircraft guns firing. That was strange. We were used to hearing the guns when they had target practice in the morning, but this was well after sundown. I had no idea what happened until word spread around the ship that the gun crews were not practicing. They were firing at a whole bunch of Japanese planes. The funny thing was, the enemy pilots were not attacking. They were just trying to land on our flight deck. In the dark, I guess the *Yorktown* looked like one of theirs.[7]

I don't recall anybody laughing about the Japanese pilots' confusion that night. We didn't sleep much either. In my section, everybody just sat there and stared at Mansfield's empty bunk. We knew there was at least one more enemy carrier out there, and we knew it had to be close. How else could those pilots have mistaken our flight deck for theirs? Everyone believed something big was going to happen in the morning. Nobody wanted to admit to being scared. It was better to think our planes would find and sink the Japanese carriers before their planes found us. Well, actually it was better not to think about it at all, so we talked about girls and whether or not the cooks had anything besides powdered eggs for breakfast. I saw a few guys writing letters. Some pulled out the acey-deucey boards and started shaking the dice. One radioman showed us how strong he was: He was popping the caps off our Coke bottles with his thumbs.

I think it was close to dawn when the klaxon went off. That was the most horrible clanging alarm, like a cross between a buzzer and a bell. I'd heard it before, but only in practice drills. The officers timed us to see how long it took the crew to get to battle stations. I usually just walked a little faster when I heard the klaxon. But not this time. It's different when you know it's for real. I jumped out of bed and ran like hell. Captain Buckmaster was already on the bridge when I got there. He looked tired—maybe he was up all night, too—but he was so calm. He just stood there, looking out the window through his binoculars. The XO and about half a dozen other senior officers were there, too, all lined up beside the captain. I didn't stop to salute any of them. I just ran to my little room behind the captain's chair and turned on the radios.

The first frequency I picked up was from the *Lexington*'s search planes. They were giving the location of two Japanese carriers, and the *Yorktown*'s planes were launching. I didn't think to count how many. I just listened to the pilots after they were in the air, and some squadrons came in more clearly than others. I'm sure the *Yorktown* launched at least thirty. The *Lexington* probably had that many or more.[8] I was switching back and forth between different frequencies in the emergency radio room—the pilots said they were about an hour away from the Japanese carriers—when I heard the scariest message of all. It came from the *Yorktown*'s radio shack. Somebody down there was tracking a whole cluster of purple dots on the radar screen, and they were definitely moving. The communications officer advised the captain to expect enemy planes over our heads within the hour.

If there was ever a time for panic on the bridge of the *Yorktown,* I'd say that was it, but Captain Buckmaster stayed calm. He just picked up the mike and spoke to the CAP fighter pilots. I heard him tell them we had bandits, incoming. After that, he switched over to the loudspeakers and warned the entire crew. I was startled when he turned around and asked me if I was okay. I didn't think he even knew I was there, but I guess he did.

The next thing I remember is planes falling out of the sky. It was hard to tell ours from theirs, because they were all exploding or on fire. There were some I couldn't see at all, because the captain was standing right in front of me. The first Japanese planes I actually recognized were the torpedo bombers. I remembered those from Pearl Harbor. I was scared when I saw the torpedo wakes. That reminded me of Pearl Harbor, too, except that the *Yorktown* was not at anchor. We were at sea, full speed, which made it more like a bullfight, where the matador just steps aside and lets the bull go by. Every time the XO called out the direction of a torpedo wake, the captain ordered the helmsman to change course. I got slammed against the wall every time we made another sharp turn, but that was okay with me. I believe he avoided at least six or seven torpedoes that way.

Next came the Japanese dive-bombers. That's when the captain picked up the mike and told the *Yorktown*'s CAP fighter pilots to clear the area, because he was going to order the ship's antiaircraft gunners to open fire. Those guys were good. They shot down several enemy planes.[9] Some of them exploded in the air so close to the island, I thought the shrapnel was going to smash through the bridge windows and hurt the captain. He didn't even duck. The only time he stepped back was when he turned around and closed my door. After that, I couldn't see anything except the dials on the radios, but I could feel the ship shaking from all the near misses. At least one bomb must have exploded close to the stern, because it felt like the whole back end of the ship lifted up out of the water. I lost my balance when it dropped back down. There was another big explosion shortly after that, and I knew the ship was on fire. I could smell the smoke.[10]

It seemed like forever at the time, but I doubt if that whole attack on the *Yorktown* lasted more than ten minutes. There was no sound of planes in the air when I picked myself off the deck and pushed open the door. The captain was still standing in front of the bridge window. He was on the ship's phone, taking damage reports from all over the ship. As soon as I saw he wasn't injured, I started listening to the radios again. I picked up a squadron of *Yorktown* pilots on their way back from their attacks on the Japanese carriers. They said they left one on fire—they thought it was sinking—but they couldn't find the second carrier, and they were too low on fuel to keep looking for it.[11]

I don't think anyone ever told our pilots that we had a big bomb hole in our flight deck. The ship's carpenters were already out there, and I heard the XO say they would have that hole patched before our planes needed to land. I also heard him say there was no damage to any of the cruisers or destroyers around the *Yorktown* or the *Lexington*. I guess the Japanese pilots had orders to focus on the two carriers.

Well, they didn't sink the *Yorktown*, and it sounded like the *Lexington* was okay, too. I did hear that the Lady took a couple of torpedo hits, but no one thought the damage was that serious until the *Lexington* pilots started requesting clearance to land on the *Yorktown*'s flight deck. That was most unusual. It was even stranger when Captain Buckmaster invited those pilots up to the bridge catwalk. I stood with them for a while. They said the Lady had some explosions below deck and the fires were out of control. I guess the enemy torpedoes did a lot more damage than anyone realized at the time. It was around midafternoon that day when the radiomen on the *Lexington* told us they were about to abandon ship. We watched the destroyers come over and pick up the crew, and I heard the admiral order one of those destroyers to sink her. They put her out of her misery, like a horse with a broken leg. Two torpedoes, I think, was what it took to send her down.[12]

The *Lexington* pilots were lined up on the catwalk, and I saw them come to attention and salute their ship when it disappeared into the ocean. Every one of those guys had tears in his eyes. A little later that night, Captain Buckmaster summoned them to his ward room, which was like a conference room on the hangar-deck level. He also ordered the surviving *Yorktown* pilots and gunners to that meeting. Nobody in the radio shack knew what all that was about until the gunners came back and told us. They said the captain set a couple of bottles of whiskey on the table, and everybody drank straight shots until it was gone. We were shocked. Alcohol was not allowed aboard any Navy ship, ever. If the captain actually had some, we couldn't understand why he hadn't already drunk it all himself.

It was very late, probably close to midnight, when Captain Buckmaster finally spoke to the whole crew on the loudspeakers. He said he was proud of us, that it was his honor to serve on the *Yorktown* in the Battle of the Coral Sea, and then he read off the names of the dead. Most of them I didn't know. They were mainly "black gang"—mechanics and engineers who worked around the machinery on deck four. That was where the bomb we took through the flight deck actually exploded. A lot of firefighters died down there, too. The corpsmen were still bringing the body bags up to the hangar deck. There was nowhere else to store them, and no way could we keep them on board until we got home. The captain had no choice, really. All those men had to be buried at sea.[13]

The ceremonies were on the hangar deck, and the place was just packed. By the time I got there, it was past two in the morning, and there were still about fourteen body bags to go. They were all lined up along one of the hangar-deck catwalks. There was a long board sticking out over the side of the ship, with the American flag draped over it like a tent. They picked up one of the body bags and placed it under the flag. The chaplain said the guy's name, where he was from, and a prayer for him. Everybody stood up and saluted when they tipped the board. We stayed at attention until the body slid off into the water, and then we were at ease again, until the next one was ready to go. This went on until the wee hours of the morning. When all the bodies were gone, the chaplain read off the names of the men who went down with their planes. Those were the guys I knew, the pilots and the gunners. Their bodies were never recovered, but we saluted and said a prayer for every one of them, too.[14]

We always wondered whatever happened to the second Japanese carrier that our planes saw that day. The search pilots said it was there, and then it just disappeared. If the admiral had asked for a show of hands on the *Yorktown*, I'm sure the crew would have voted to chase it. But the Navy was never a democracy. We were back in the harbor at Tongatabu in the Tonga Islands the next night. There was no big victory party or anything like that, but the captain did tell the radio shack to find some good ol' American music and put it on the loudspeakers for the crew. Everybody liked the Japanese girl with the sexy voice, so we tuned in to her program. In between the songs, she gave the news in English. We laughed ourselves silly when she said the Imperial Japanese Navy had just won a great victory. According to her—we called her Tokyo Rose—they sank two American aircraft carriers in the Coral Sea. She even gave the names: *Saratoga* and *Yorktown*. I think that was the first time I laughed since we crossed the equator.[15]

No one went ashore at Tongatabu, but the supply ships

brought us ice cream and a fresh batch of movies. Even the captain came down to the hangar deck that night. He just about lost it when we all stood up and cheered for him. I was amazed to see him so emotional. He was a completely different person when the *Yorktown* was under attack the day before. I can't quote his speech exactly: It was mainly compliments to the crew. He never said a word about any great historical significance to the battle we'd just been through in the Coral Sea. I frankly doubt if he knew or cared about that. The only thing that mattered to him, or any of us, really, was winning the war.[16]

The *Yorktown* needed serious repairs—anyone could see the trail of oil leaking from the stern—but Tongatabu had no facilities for that. It was just a place to rest for a couple of days. We lounged around on the flight deck; I got myself a pretty good sunburn. There was lots of talk about where the *Yorktown* was going next. The ship's mechanics said we needed at least three months in dry dock, probably at the Puget Sound Navy Yards in Bremerton. Well, that was in the state of Washington, less than a day's bus ride from Spokane, and, oh, boy, did I ever run with that idea. When we left that harbor in the Tonga Islands, I thought I was on my way to see Adeline. I was long overdue for a thirty-day leave. I thought I might even work up the nerve to propose to her. If she said yes, why, maybe we could get married and still have time for a honeymoon before my leave was up.

That little fantasy lasted for a week or two. We were halfway across the Pacific when the captain broke the news. The *Yorktown* wasn't going to Bremerton or anywhere else in the state of Washington for three months. We were on our way to Pearl Harbor, for three *days*. Captain Buckmaster said it was because CinCPac had another urgent mission for us.[17] And when he asked if he could count on me to stay on board for the next mission, I said yes. For all I know, he put that same question to every guy in the crew. At the time, I was just so flattered that he knew my name. I would have gone to sea in a rowboat with that man.

When the *Yorktown* came within our planes' fuel range of Pearl Harbor, all that were still flyable took off for Ford Island. I expected that. I was surprised when the captain ordered us to change out of our dungarees, put on our dress whites, and report to the flight deck. The older men in the crew didn't know why either. They said this had never been done before, at least not on this ship, but there we were, all lined up by section when the *Yorktown* came through the entrance channel. As we passed by the *Arizona* and the *Oklahoma,* the officers called us to attention, and the entire crew saluted those sunken battleships and the men who died on them.[18] I needed that. I needed to remember why we were at war.

See Time Line, page 244, and Historical Notes, page 245.

13

THE BATTLE OF MIDWAY

May 27-Noon, June 4, 1942

Everybody on the *Yorktown* was look-
ing forward to liberty in Honolulu. After nearly four months at
sea, even three days ashore sounded pretty good. I was still out
on the flight deck with the rest of the crew when Captain Buckmaster came over the loudspeaker and told us he was sorry. No liberty cards for anybody. All hands were needed to get our ship
repaired and resupplied and ready to sail in time. In time for what,
he couldn't tell us yet, but he said it was important. Of course the
captain was sorry. Everybody was sorry. And, yes, there was plenty
of grousing. I did my share of that, too. But I never once heard anyone blame the captain. We just cursed the war.

There was a regular mob of workers waiting for us. Hundreds of guys with toolboxes came swarming aboard the minute
we pulled into dry dock. They hammered and sawed around the
clock for the next three days and nights, and so did the crew. My
job was hauling supplies. I bet I carried a hundred crates full of
pineapples and oranges down to the galley. The cardboard boxes
were heavier yet. Canned goods, I suppose. The Navy bought a

lot of pork and beans. It was during one of those trips between
the supply trucks and the ship when I noticed the other two carriers. They were on the far side of Ford Island, so I never got a
close look at them. Somebody said *Enterprise* was one; the other
was *Hornet*. This was the first time I'd ever heard of the *Hornet*.
It was also the first time I could remember seeing three carriers
inside Pearl Harbor at once. That hardly ever happened before
the war. They were both gone the next time I checked. I hope
their crews got more rest between missions than we did.[1]

The thirtieth of May was our deadline to get back out to sea,
and we met it. I still didn't know where we were going or why
we were in such a hurry to get there. And I couldn't imagine why
Admiral Nimitz himself came aboard to see us off. He was the
top dog at Pearl Harbor, Commander in Chief of the whole Pacific Fleet. In the radio shack, we referred to him as CinCPac.
For him to take such a personal interest in our next mission, it
had to be important. Somewhere in the South Pacific, probably.
All the radiomen thought so, until the *Yorktown* cleared the
channel. The cruisers and destroyers were just getting into formation around us when the whole task force turned north. That
was our first clue. The captain hadn't said anything yet, but it
seemed obvious to us. We guessed we were going to Midway.[2]

I was still waiting for the mission announcement when I felt
the ship's speed increasing, and we were turning into the wind.
That meant the air group was flying out from Ford Island. The
pilots needed a headwind to help slow the planes when they
touched down. I hustled up to the bridge catwalk to watch. Siwash wanted to come with me, but he couldn't leave the chart
room just then. The admiral was on his way down. This was the
same admiral that was with us in the Coral Sea, so I'm sure my
friend was used to him. I still couldn't get over it myself. I mean,
Siwash was senior to most of the other quartermasters—probably
the smartest, too—but he was not an officer. He was an enlisted
man—petty officer, second class—the same as me.

I saw nothing unusual when the first fighter plane came in. The
airdales towed it forward; the pilot was still in the cockpit when

the next plane approached the stern. Landing accidents were not unusual either. About once a week, a plane would veer off the runway and bump into the island. They were never going very fast by the time they got that far. The pilots were just embarrassed. Until that day, the worst accident I ever saw on the *Yorktown* was during a storm in the Solomon Islands: A wave lifted the stern just as a plane was touching down, and it caught a piece of the landing gear. The plane flipped over backward and landed upside down in the water behind the ship. That was nothing. The pilot got wet— he was still cussing when we fished him out—but they just gave him another plane, and he was back in the air the very next day.

So I wasn't all that worried this day when the second fighter plane came in "hot"—too fast. I could tell by the sound of the engines. The LSO tried to wave him off. He was jumping up and down like a crazy man. I laughed when he dropped his paddles and scrambled out of the way. I don't know why that pilot didn't pull up and try again. Maybe he didn't see the LSO's signal to abort; maybe he thought it was too late. Either way, I knew he was going to get grounded for a day or two. That was the worst thing that could happen to any pilot, or so I thought, until that plane touched down. It came in so fast, the tailhook bounced over every cable across the stern, didn't catch a single one. After that, it plowed through the last barrier, which was a rope net below the island. I braced myself for the impact, but there was none. This plane crashed into the one that had landed a minute before, with the pilot still in the cockpit. I saw the propeller blades cut through the canopy of that parked plane, and I watched them chop that pilot's body into little pieces. There was blood spattered all over both planes, all across the flight deck, and all over me.[3]

That was the last time I ever watched a plane land on the *Yorktown*. It wasn't entertaining any more. I did not know the pilot who died in that accident or the one who was in the plane that killed him. They were both new to the *Yorktown*, as were all the other pilots and gunners that landed afterward. I heard that in the radio shack, right before the captain told us where we were going.

Midway was one of few islands in the Pacific I'd ever heard of before the war. I copied a lot of messages from there while I was in the radio shack at the submarine base. As far as I knew, Midway was just a Naval Air Station, and that's all that was there, except for the Marines that guarded the place. I pictured it as being just like Ford Island, except that it was way out there in the middle of the ocean, all by itself. If the captain knew how many Japanese Navy ships were expected to attack Midway, he didn't say. It's just as well he didn't. After what I saw in the Coral Sea, even one Japanese aircraft carrier sounded pretty scary to me.[4]

I didn't know what to make of it when the captain said this could be the *Yorktown*'s most important battle of the war. It wasn't like him to exaggerate, so that sure got my attention, along with the note he read over the loudspeakers. He said it was a personal message to all of us from Admiral Nimitz. I wish I'd thought to write it down. I just remember that it went something like this: "I'm sorry you didn't get the liberty you deserved after your victory in the Coral Sea. When the *Yorktown* returns from Midway, I promise all of you a long vacation on the West Coast. And, furthermore, the Navy's going to throw a party for the whole crew, and it won't be peanuts." I was still tired; my arms were sore from carrying all those crates and boxes. But, all of a sudden, I felt better. Thanks to Admiral Nimitz, I had something to look forward to again.

The *Yorktown* was more than halfway to Midway on the first of June. I didn't tell anyone it was my birthday—I was twenty-two—but it was still a good day because I spent all my free time with Mike Brazier. He was one of the new aviation radiomen that hung out with us in the radio shack. I'm not sure how we got to be such good buddies in such a short time. Maybe that's just the way it is when you're stuck together on a ship, especially in wartime, but I think Brazier and I would have been friends anywhere. If we'd been ashore, we'd have gone for beer at the Tin Roof and played some pool. At sea, it was just coffee, black, and acey-deucey.

Brazier was even more like me than Siwash, because he had a girlfriend back home. He showed me her picture. I lied and said

En route to Midway, Yorktown *sailors play acey-deucey on the platform of a 5-inch (shell-size) antiaircraft gun.* COURTESY OF U.S. NAVY, PHOTO #80-G-312011.

she was as pretty as Adeline. But he was in love with her, and they were going to get married the next time he got leave. Assuming he survived this mission, which we both knew was not a given for any of us on the *Yorktown.* I was more afraid for him than I was for myself, because Brazier was the gunner for the pilot of a torpedo plane. By this time, everybody knew those Devastators weren't really devastating at all. They were too slow. When they had a thousand-pound torpedo under their bellies, they could barely make 100 miles an hour. If a Japanese fighter plane—a Zero—got on his tail, the gunner was even less likely to survive than his pilot, because he was in the rear seat. Brazier never said he was afraid on the way to Midway. We never even talked about it. But I know that he wasn't concentrating very well when we played acey-deucey that day. I beat him two games out of three.

On the second of June, Siwash told me we were getting close to Midway. I never saw the island, but I saw a lot of ships in the distance. It didn't take long for word to get around that we were about to join task forces with the *Hornet* and the *Enterprise*. Counting all the cruisers and destroyers around the three carriers, there must have been at least twenty warships altogether.[5] I would have liked to talk to the other radio gangs, but that was not allowed. Under radio silence, the only way we could communicate was through the signalmen, the guys that ran up the flags or flashed the lanterns. We couldn't even talk to our own pilots on the radio for fear of giving away our location to the enemy.

Everyone had an opinion on how CinCPac knew that a Japanese carrier task force was on the way. Some said Admiral Nimitz had a spy inside their government. Personally, I thought it had to be somebody really high up in the Imperial Japanese Navy.[6] I was more interested in discussing the enemy's strategy. In the radio shack, we thought Japan wanted Midway as a base for their next attack on Pearl Harbor. If they could get Pearl Harbor, too—well, that was the ball game. There would be nothing left to keep the enemy carriers away from the West Coast. I could just see the bombs falling on San Diego and Los Angeles.[7]

I remember the night of June third, too. That was when I heard we were looking for at least four Japanese carriers. Maybe five.[8] They were expected to attack Midway in the morning, but we still didn't know where they were. It was the same kind of tension as in the Coral Sea, only ten times worse, because I had a better idea of what was going to happen. I couldn't eat or sleep, and I sure as heck couldn't pretend I wasn't scared. So I went down to the hangar deck by myself and just walked around. It looked like they'd added more antiaircraft guns than we had before. There were all different sizes of guns, every ten or twelve feet around the hangar deck. I wasn't sure it was enough. Those Japanese carrier pilots were so skillful, and all it took was one to plant another bomb on our flight deck. I didn't want to see any more burials at sea. That was the worst outcome I could imagine at the time.

The klaxon went off on the morning of June fourth. When I got to my battle station on the bridge, I heard the officers say that Midway was under attack. That was actually a relief to me. It meant that the enemy carriers had no idea we were there. They never would have sent their planes to bomb Midway if they'd known three American carriers were near enough to strike back. I heard the captain say *Hornet* and *Enterprise* had already launched their torpedo planes. The *Yorktown*'s took off a while later. When Brazier's squadron was in the air, I tried tuning in to their frequency. All I got was static. It was over an hour before any of the *Yorktown* pilots broke radio silence. The first pilot's voice I heard was from a dive-bomber squadron. He said they had just sighted a Japanese carrier, and, oh, boy, was that guy mad. He'd accidentally lost his bomb somewhere over the ocean, shortly after takeoff. I guess there was something wrong with the release lever. But he was going to dive on the enemy carrier anyway, unarmed. That was just crazy. I think there was an awful lot of that kind of courage at Midway, on both sides.

I put the dive-bomber frequency on the loudspeaker; all the officers on the bridge of the *Yorktown* were listening. I heard the lead pilot say, "That carrier is getting ready to launch!" and "Let's go get it!" and "Okay, then, follow me!" The next five or ten minutes were awful. We didn't know what was happening until the dive-bombers spoke again. I could hardly believe it when they said nobody was shot down. They also said that the enemy carrier was in flames.[9] They didn't have enough fuel to stay and watch it sink, but they all agreed it was done for. The pilots also told us they saw two other Japanese carriers, and they were burning, too. We didn't know who was responsible for that.[10] I hoped it was Brazier's torpedo squadron. I still had nothing but static from them.

The communications officer had an urgent message for the captain: The *Yorktown*'s radar had just picked up a group of planes. They were less than forty miles away, and everybody knew they weren't ours.[11] Apparently, the enemy had caught on to the idea of flying low when they approached the ship. They came in under the radar. Captain Buckmaster grabbed the mike and told the CAP fighter pilots to intercept the Japanese planes. I also heard him reminding all the senior officers on the bridge to be careful when they spoke on the radio. They were not allowed to refer to us as the *Yorktown*. They were supposed to use our code name, which was "Scarlet." That made no sense to me. I thought they should have just told the Japanese pilots who we were. If they listened to Tokyo Rose as much as we did, maybe they would believe they were bombing a ghost ship.[12] If that wasn't enough to make them nervous, maybe they would at least wonder what else their leaders got wrong. Anything to mess up their aim.

The *Yorktown*'s fighter planes were about twenty miles out when they engaged the approaching enemy planes. I heard one of our pilots say, "Where's my wingman?" and another was shouting, "Get that Zero off my tail!" The first plane I saw shot down was a Japanese dive-bomber. There was a trail of fire and smoke behind it and a huge splash when it hit the water. I heard the antiaircraft guns on the cruisers and destroyers booming in the distance. They shot down several more. But I know at least a few enemy planes got through all that, because there was one coming right at us on the bridge. For a second or two, that was all I could see. I thought it was going to crash into the island and kill us all, until that plane disintegrated into a million pieces. Somebody shot it down before it hit us, but the plane had already released its bomb. So then I watched the bomb, and the bomb filled the window, and it was like in slow motion, the way the thing tumbled end over end. I couldn't take my eyes off it until it exploded, and then I hit the deck.

When I looked up, I saw a huge cloud of black smoke and shrapnel outside the bridge, and the captain was not standing in front of the window anymore. He was inside the radio room with me. I wanted him to stay there, but he didn't. He stepped out again, because the helmsman couldn't hear his turning orders, and another plane was coming toward the bridge, and there was another big explosion, and I fell down again. The dials on the radios were flickering, and I didn't believe this was how I was going to die because I'd just turned twenty-two. I heard men shouting—no, screaming—somewhere outside the bridge, but there was no sound at all from the ship's engines. The *Yorktown* was dead.[13]

See Time Line, page 247, and Historical Notes, page 248.

14

ABANDON SHIP

12:20 P.M.–mid-afternoon, June 4, 1942

I'm not sure how long I was out. I came to dizzy and disoriented. My ears were still ringing from the explosions. It hurt to breathe because of all the smoke on the bridge. Worst of all, I was alone in the dark. I have no memory of when the captain closed the door to the emergency radio room. I wasn't even sure the enemy planes were gone until I heard his voice. He was not shouting anymore; he was talking to someone on the ship's phone. At least that still worked. It sounded like he was taking damage reports from the engine room. He was so cool and steady, you'd have thought he was inquiring about his dry cleaning or the price of fish.

The *Yorktown* was not moving when I opened the door. I honestly believed the captain was about to give the "abandon ship" order. Which was a scary thought, because I didn't know how. The Navy didn't teach us that in basic training. Then again, maybe they did. I missed a lot of stuff while I was in the pool. You don't know how glad I was when I heard the captain say the engines were going to restart. I even heard him tell the XO that we could start launching and recovering planes as soon as the flight deck was repaired. I thought that was a pretty big if. There was only one hole in the flight deck, but it was huge—ten or twelve feet wide—and it was less than thirty feet from the island. If that bomb was intended to kill the captain and all the senior officers on the bridge, I would call it a near miss. I knew I was lucky to be alive.

There was no reason for me to stay inside my battle station at that time, so I volunteered to help repair the hole in the flight deck. Not being a carpenter, there wasn't much I could do there either, but I figured they could use another hand for the grunt work. I don't know if I would have done that if I'd known that the hole was really the least of the bomb damage. I didn't see the bodies until I climbed down from the bridge. I don't know how many—twenty, thirty, maybe more. They were hard to look at and hard to count, because most of those men were just blown to pieces. The guys in the ship's band—I remember the harp insignias on their sleeves—were helping the corpsmen lay out all the body bags. I was having flashbacks from the smell. There is nothing close to the odor of cooked human flesh. I smelled it at Pearl Harbor, I smelled it in the Coral Sea, and somebody must have burned to death on the flight deck at Midway, because I smelled it there, too.[1]

The ship's carpenters were calling for more lumber and sheet metal to repair the hole. I turned and ran with the guys who were going down to the hangar deck to get it for them. There were a lot of casualties on that level, too. I saw the assistant chaplain on his knees next to a row of about fifteen body bags. I thought he was praying for those men, which he probably was, but then I saw his hands groping around inside the bags. He was searching for their dog tags, and he would not allow the corpsmen to pull the drawstring until he found them. There really was no other way to identify those poor guys. Their faces were just gone.

The chaplain himself was already doing burials at sea, or I should say, he was trying to. He had five or six sailors to help him set up the board with the flag draped over it, but they weren't doing very well. I saw one guy slip and fall down in the blood, another was passed out, and two of them were hanging over the rails vomiting. They were just teenagers, probably fresh out of boot camp when they joined us at Pearl Harbor. I felt sorry for them. They hadn't even been to sea for a week, and now they're in combat, picking up parts of bodies and putting them in bags and hosing the blood off the deck and tipping the board.

There was no time for a proper funeral for anyone at Midway. Everyone knew there were at least one or two more Japanese aircraft carriers out there, and it was still early in the day. Their search planes had plenty of daylight to find the *Yorktown* and hit us again if they wanted to. I assumed they would. And I'm not going to lie and say I was any less afraid of the next attack than those guys that were fainting and puking on the hangar deck. But I guess I'd finally got to the point where I could let go of the

Radioman (RM2c) Ray Daves stands atop the lumber he carried from hangar deck to flight deck of Yorktown *(CV-5), Midway, June 4, 1942. (Dungarees and chambray shirt are typical of those worn by U.S. sailors aboard ship during World War II.)* COURTESY OF RAY DAVES COLLECTION.

fear and do my job. I don't know why I never got sick to my stomach. It never affected me that way. It just made me more angry, made me want to fight harder. I dropped my load of lumber on the flight deck and went back for more. The ship's carpenters worked up more of a sweat than I did. They had that hole patched in less than an hour.

I was inside the radio shack when I heard the engines come back on line. A few minutes later, I felt the ship begin to move. The radio gang was cheering. We cheered some more when the radios stopped shorting out, but I still couldn't get anything but static from Brazier's torpedo squadron. The other radiomen were worried, too. We were all friends with the gunners, and they were long overdue. I didn't want to discuss what could have happened to the torpedo planes.[2] I just wanted to keep listening to that frequency, and that's what I was doing when we got the next radar warning: Another large group of planes was approaching the *Yorktown*. We couldn't tell how many or what kind; we just knew they were Japanese. I didn't think it was a social call. I was halfway up the ladder to my battle station when the klaxon went off for the second time that day.

The ship was still not up to full speed, but it must have been something close to twenty knots because I saw fighter planes taking off from the flight deck. Captain Buckmaster was already talking to the pilots in the air when I got to the bridge. He always told them, "Protect the fleet," but this time he also said, "Don't start chasing tails." I'm sure they knew what he meant. Everybody knew the Japanese fighter planes were faster than ours. It was useless to try to get behind a Zero. As my friend Brazier explained it to me, our pilots were just beginning to learn some new maneuver where they flew in pairs. The object was to let the Zero get behind you, and then lead him in front of your wingman's guns.[3] It was just funny to hear the captain put it that way. "Chasing tails" was something we did on liberty. It's what sailors called it when we were trying to get the attention of the girls ahead of us on sidewalks and beaches in Honolulu. In any other situation I would have laughed. But not at Midway. Those fighter pilots were the *Yorktown*'s first line of defense, and they were willing to die to protect her.

I don't know how many enemy planes our fighters shot down. I'm sure they did their best, and so did the cruisers and destroyers around the *Yorktown*.[4] I could hear their antiaircraft guns going off in the distance. But I still didn't know what kind of planes were attacking us until the XO hollered, "Torpedoes!" I did not see the wakes—the captain was blocking my view—but I knew what was coming. I braced myself. I did not fall down when the ship swerved out of the way. Captain Buckmaster was so good at that, I'm sure he would have avoided them all if the engines had been at full speed. But then I saw the plane approaching low from the port side. It was only seven or eight hundred yards away when it dropped the torpedo. I heard the captain call out another turning order, but the *Yorktown* wasn't fast enough. There was nothing anybody could do but stare at the wake of that torpedo and wait for the hit.

I wanted the captain to take shelter inside the radio room with me, but he did not. He was just holding on to the door when the torpedo exploded. It felt like some giant hand reached down and grabbed the *Yorktown* like it was a toy, lifted us out of the water and shook us for a few seconds before it let go. There was another big jolt after that, and then the lights went out, and the engines stopped again. It was worse than before, because this time the ship was listing—turning over on its side—and if it didn't stop, we were going to be upside down in the water. For a couple of minutes, I thought I knew what it must have been like for all those sailors on the *Oklahoma* at Pearl Harbor.

The *Yorktown* was sitting at about a twenty-degree angle when the captain gave the order to abandon ship. I still didn't know the procedure, but, one way or the other, I knew I had to get off. Right now. I already had my life jacket on. I wore it like a vest all the time—never took it off except when I was in bed. I just had to make sure the fasteners were good and tight, which gave me all the time I needed to remember the stories that went around after the *Lexington* sank in the Coral Sea. As far as I know, most of those guys got off okay, but there were all kinds of what-ifs. Like, what if the enemy pilots had come back and strafed them while they were bobbing in the water close to the ship. And sharks. But the one that really got to me was the meaning of the term "displacement." As I understood it, anything that floats displaces a certain amount of water, which is like saying it makes a hole in the ocean. Whenever a ship sinks, the ocean comes rushing in to fill that hole, and it creates a whirlpool—the same as water going down the drain in a bathtub. The bigger the ship, the bigger the hole, the bigger the whirlpool. Well, they didn't come much bigger than the *Yorktown*. I was trying to calculate the physics in my head. I didn't know if I could swim fast enough to escape getting sucked into the whirlpool when the ship went down.

I followed the quartermasters down the ladder from the bridge. Siwash was not with them. I ran back up to see if he was still in the chart room. He was not. I didn't see him on the flight deck either. That's where everybody was gathering, waiting in lines for a turn to climb down the ropes they had thrown over the side. There was some confusion, but no great pandemonium. I even heard a few guys joking about what a nice day it was to go for a swim, but it was that false, nervous kind of laughter, so I know I wasn't the only one that was scared. I saw several sailors refuse to wait their turn. They stepped out of the rope lines and ran up to the edge of the flight deck and jumped. Well, the ship was tilting closer to the water on the port side, but it was still a good thirty-foot drop. I wasn't about to do that. But there were at least two hundred guys ahead of me in every line. I didn't know if we had that much time. I was trying to think of a faster way to get off the ship myself when I saw a couple of radiomen going down the ladder to the hangar deck. They called out to me; I ran and joined them.

There were ropes thrown over the side of the hangar-deck level, too, and hundreds of guys in the lines for those. We ran past them, and we didn't stop until we got to the fantail. I don't know why nobody else had thought of jumping off the ship from there. It was only about twelve feet above the water at that time.

Maybe they thought the screws—the ships's propellers—were still turning. I knew they weren't. It was perfectly safe to jump off the fantail as long as the ship was dead in the water, which it most definitely was, but I didn't want to leave without Siwash. I was about to go back and look for him in the rope lines when somebody said he was probably with the admiral. That made sense to me. The admiral left us right after the first attack, and I hadn't seen my friend since I volunteered for the work party on the flight deck. I wouldn't be surprised if the admiral did take Siwash with him when he got off the *Yorktown*. I was just sorry I never got to say goodbye.[5]

So I stayed where I was, along with about fifty other sailors. There was an officer on the fantail, dividing us into groups of about fifteen. When the first group stepped up to the edge, I heard him shout: "Stay together! Swim as far away from the ship as you can!" I don't know what time that was. It must have been midafternoon, because when it was my group's turn, I looked down at the ocean and saw rainbows. The sun was shining on the water, making rainbows on the oil leaking from the stern. The men on either side of me were jumping, and the officer was yelling at me, "Go! Go *now!*" I could feel the next group of guys crowding behind me, pressing against my back. It was too late to change my mind. I took a deep breath and jumped into the rainbows.

See Time Line, page 249, and Historical Notes, page 250.

15

RESCUED AT SEA

Mid-afternoon, June 4–June 9, 1942

I swam until I was out of breath, and then I turned over on my back and paddled some more that way. The chief boatswain in charge of the pool in basic training would have been surprised at how far and how fast I could swim if I really had to. I even surprised myself. When I took my first look back at the *Yorktown,* I was nearly a hundred yards away. I thought the ship was lower in the water than before, and I was sure it would sink in the next few minutes. I was not at all sure that I was far enough away to escape the whirlpool, but I was too tired to swim another stroke. There were dozens of men floating in the water around me. I don't think any of us believed we were going to live another day until we saw the destroyers approaching.

The destroyers' lifeboats were not rubber rafts with oars or paddles, like on the planes. These were regular metal boats with motors, more like the liberty boats at Pearl Harbor, only not as big. It looked like they were picking up maybe fifteen men at a time. Well, there were more than a thousand of us in the water by then, so I knew it might be hours before they got around to me. I heard a few guys holler "Taxi!" at the lifeboats; some whistled and waved. I was saving my breath in case I had to make another mad dash. I just floated on my back and watched the sky for enemy planes and tried not to think about sharks. The water wasn't all that cold; the wind just made it seem so. In about thirty minutes, I was numb all over. I couldn't even talk when the lifeboat finally came.[1]

There were twelve or thirteen of us in that lifeboat when it pulled alongside one of the destroyers. We had to climb a Jacob's ladder to get aboard. I'd never done that before either. It was like crawling up the side of a big ship on a spiderweb made out of ropes. I was not very graceful at it. The destroyer crew was lined up on the main deck, cheering for me, telling me where to put my feet so I wouldn't fall off. I was still a couple of ropes away from the top railing when somebody reached down, grabbed me by the armpits, and yanked me the rest of the way. I landed in a wet heap; somebody threw a blanket around me. After that, it was all hot coffee and "Welcome to the *Hughes*." I believe every man on that ship came by to shake my hand or pat me on the back. In less than an hour, they had me warmed up and showered and walking around in somebody else's clothes. I don't know what they did with mine. Probably threw them away. They were covered with oil.

The other ships must have rescued hundreds from the *York-town* that day, but there were only about twenty-five of us on the *Hughes*. Maybe that's why we got so much special attention from the crew. The cooks gave us extra-big helpings of meat and potatoes and gravy; we had all the ice cream we could stand. Even the officers stepped aside for us on the ladders, like we were some kind of heroes. I didn't think that was right. I knew I was not a hero. I was just a survivor. All the heroes I ever knew died in combat, and I was afraid my friend Mike Brazier was one of them. The only special privilege I wanted was for the *Hughes*'s radiomen to tell me what happened to his squadron. At that time, which was close to sunset on the fourth of June, they didn't know anything except that a few *Yorktown* planes had landed on the *Enterprise* (CV 6). I was told that they refueled and took off again when somebody sighted the fourth Japanese carrier. Everybody was praying that our planes would find and sink that one, too.[2] I was mainly praying for Brazier—and all my other gunner friends—to come back alive.

The *Hughes* did not have any spare bunks for us *Yorktown* survivors, but they had lots of blankets. They told us to bed down wherever we wanted to on their ship. I stayed outside and watched the *Yorktown*. When it got too dark to see it any more, I spread my blankets under an antiaircraft gun and curled up out of the wind. Several of my shipmates did the same, but nobody slept. We stayed up all night talking. There were no other ships around the *Hughes,* so it seemed pretty obvious to us that we were on the destroyer that drew the death watch. If by some fluke the *Yorktown* was still afloat in the morning, we expected the captain of the *Hughes* had orders to sink her.[3] That's what happened to the *Lexington* in the Coral Sea. I didn't want to watch that, and neither did the other survivors, but we promised each other that we would. I didn't know any of those guys before—we were from all different sections, and I was the only radioman—but we had a lot in common. It went far beyond the fact that we'd left everything we owned on the *Yorktown*. Every one of us had at least one buddy who was either killed or missing in action on the fourth of June.

I did not expect to see the *Yorktown* at dawn, but, by golly, there she was, about six hundred yards away. No lower in the water than the night before, no fires, no explosions, no nothing. Just deserted. The *Hughes* had a whole rack full of torpedoes, all loaded in the tubes and ready to fire. I thought I was hallucinating when I heard the machine gun. It sounded like the shots were coming from the *Yorktown,* which was impossible, because there was no one left aboard. But then I heard it again, and others heard it, too. Some said the *Yorktown* was haunted—they thought it was the ghosts of our antiaircraft gunners. An awful lot of those guys were killed while we were under attack the day before. Well, I didn't believe in ghosts, and, apparently, the captain of the *Hughes* didn't either. He sent a lifeboat and crew over to see who or what was firing that machine gun.

The lifeboat came back with two seriously wounded men. They told us they woke up in sick bay, probably left for dead when we abandoned ship. One guy had a really bad head wound; the other was soaked in blood from the waist down. I can't imagine how he dragged himself up all those ladders in the dark, much less how he managed to fire the machine gun that got our attention. He died shortly after we got him aboard the *Hughes*. A little later that same day, we let down the Jacob's ladder again, only this time it was for one of the *Yorktown*'s fighter pilots. He came paddling up to us in his rubber raft, and said his plane was shot down by a Zero during the torpedo bomber attack. I do not recall any blood on his flight suit. I think he was just bruised and tired and thirsty after rowing all night. Like me, he went straight to the radio shack and asked for news about his buddies. The radiomen on the *Hughes* went to a lot of trouble to find out for both of us. They contacted all the other destroyers in the area. There were several of them picking up downed pilots and gunners from all the carriers at Midway.

I found out that Brazier's pilot was rescued. According to the radiomen on the destroyer that picked him up, his was one of the few torpedo planes that was not shot down over the Japanese carriers. He gave my friend a lot of the credit for that. He said Mike was shot several times in the back and bleeding badly, but somehow he kept on firing at the Zeroes on their tail. He also said Brazier was near death when he made the adjustment to the plane's radio so they could receive the *Yorktown*'s homing beacon. I don't know how he did that, but his pilot said he did, and I believed it. They couldn't have found their way back to us without it. I heard they were only a few miles away from our task force when they splashed for lack of fuel. The pilot swore that Brazier was still alive when he dragged him out of the plane, but he died shortly thereafter. The radiomen on the destroyer that rescued the pilot said he was found crying and praying over his gunner's body in the raft.[4]

I wanted to cry, too, but I did not. I just thanked the *Hughes* radiomen and went back to staring across the water with my shipmates. I was so angry when the war started at Pearl Harbor—the first six months was all about anger and revenge—but I think I lost most of that at Midway, too. I just wanted it to end.

It would have been better if they'd given me some work to do on the *Hughes,* but they never did. The crew was still treating us like celebrities. We perked up a little when the tugboat arrived. We heard they were actually going to tow the *Yorktown* back to Pearl Harbor. Well, they tried. That little tugboat just wasn't strong enough for the job. We watched the towline break several times that afternoon. I doubt if they pulled her more than ten miles before dark.

The next morning, when I crawled out from under the antiaircraft gun, I saw five or six destroyers. One was tied right up to the *Yorktown* on the starboard side. That was the *Hammann.* I also saw dozens of men walking around the flight deck. I was too far away to make out their faces, but I heard that Captain Buckmaster was one of them. He and the rest of the salvage party must have arrived sometime during the night. Well, naturally, I volunteered to go over and help him, as did all the other survivors on the *Hughes.* But the captain did not choose me. He wanted yeomen. I could understand why: The yeomen were the ship's office workers. They knew where to find the personnel files, not to mention all the keys and combinations to the safes where they kept the *Yorktown*'s code books and cash. I'm sure that was a lot higher priority than anything I might have been able to salvage from the radio shack. It was just so frustrating to have to stand there and watch.

I don't know how the enemy submarine got past the *Hughes* and all the other destroyers that were guarding the Yorktown that day. It might have been because the ocean was too rough, or maybe the radiomen on sonar duty were confused by all the pings they were getting from the debris around the ship. Either of those conditions could have explained why no one detected the submerged submarine before it fired at the *Yorktown.* I never saw that Japanese submarine. All I saw were the wakes of the torpedoes—four of them—and I was still shouting "No! No!" when they hit. The explosions were a little muffled, like distant thunder because they were underwater, but it was still very loud, and I could see where they made contact. There were two huge columns of spray on the *Yorktown*'s starboard side. At least one of the torpedoes must have hit the destroyer that was tied up next to the *Yorktown*. That's when I finally understood why destroyers were called tin cans. The *Hammann* just exploded and broke in half.

I saw dozens of men in the water, all trying to swim away from the destroyer before it sank. We were still letting down our lifeboats to rescue them when I heard another explosion, and all those heads in the water around the *Hammann* just disappeared. I don't think the Japanese submarine fired another torpedo. I'm sure I would have seen the wake. I believe it was one of the *Hammann*'s own depth charges or torpedoes that went off when the ship went down, and that's what killed all those men in the water.[5]

The *Hughes* took off on a mad hunt for the Japanese submarine. We looked for it all afternoon and into the night, along with two or three other destroyers. I never saw so many depth charges exploding all at once, but there was no sign of debris from a sunken sub. I think it got away.[6] When we finally gave up searching for the enemy sub, we came back to the *Yorktown*. I was amazed that she was still afloat. To me, that ship was beginning to feel like a person in intensive care in the hospitals like she was fighting to stay alive. I really thought she was going to win that battle, until I saw her for the last time.

When I crawled out from under my blankets on the deck of the *Hughes* at dawn the next day, I knew it was over. The *Yorktown*'s flight deck had sunk so low, it was touching the water on the port side. For about fifteen minutes, my shipmates and I just stood there and watched our ship roll the rest of the way over and sink upside down.[7] We came to attention and saluted when she disappeared. The *Hughes* captain was kind enough to show his respect for the death of the *Yorktown*. He ordered his crew to lower their flag. I felt tears rolling down my face. I was kind of embarrassed until I looked down the line of sailors beside me. They were all crying, too. One guy put his head down on the railing and just sobbed. For some reason, that made it okay. For the very first time since this damned war started, I broke down and had myself a really good cry.

The ride back to Hawaii was so strange. The *Hughes* crew was still very cordial, but all of the *Yorktown* survivors noticed that nobody wanted to talk to us anymore. They seemed to go out of their way to avoid any contact with us at all. I never understood why. Maybe they thought we wanted to be left alone; maybe they believed we were bad luck. Whatever it was, I felt like an untouchable for the next three days.

When we came through the channel at Pearl Harbor, my shipmates and I went out on the main deck and stood at attention. The destroyer crew had no idea what we were doing. I guess it was not their custom to enter the harbor that way, but, bless their hearts, they all dropped what they were doing and saluted the *Arizona* and the *Oklahoma,* right along with us. They were really good guys, but they sure didn't waste any time getting us off their ship at Pearl Harbor.

See Time Line, page 250, and Historical Notes, page 252.

16

THE SUMMER OF '42

June 10–September 1942

We had no orders, and there was no one waiting to meet us at the dock. I could have caught a ride to Honolulu and just melted into the city until the war was over. The thought did cross my mind. I don't know where the other survivors went: Everybody took off in different directions. I walked over to the submarine base alone. I had no reason to believe that I belonged there, but that was the last place I'd been before I boarded the *Yorktown*. I couldn't think of anywhere else to go.

The administration building looked about the same—I noticed they had a few more machine guns on the roof—but there was not one familiar face inside. The radio gang at CinCPac headquarters must have had another complete turnover since February. Even the communications officer was new again, and I had no papers to prove I was me. I just told him what happened, and I guess he believed me, because he let me stay. He took me in like a stray pup.

The sub base barracks were a lot more crowded than I remembered.[1] I got the last empty bunk on the second floor. I wandered around, looking for Scoop and Spic. Nobody had ever heard of either of them. It was like my best friends in the Navy never existed. I had a real hard time with that. Everybody probably thought I was a little crazy because I kept asking, "Are you sure?" But I think I was even lonelier for my shipmates from the *Yorktown*. When you've been at sea for as along as I was, the ship is your home and the guys you work with are your family. I had one required counseling session with the sub base chaplain, right after my postcombat physical, also required. I wouldn't be surprised if a lot of *Yorktown* survivors had to have major psychiatric treatment. In my case, the chaplain said I just needed time. He cleared me for duty at CinCPac headquarters in less than a week.

I was still lonely and a little depressed, but I did go to the party that Admiral Nimitz had promised. Boy, did he ever follow through. Toward the end of June, the Navy sent buses to pick up all the *Yorktown* survivors at Pearl Harbor. They took us to the Royal Hawaiian Hotel in Honolulu and wined and dined us all night. We even had an open bar, with all the fancy tropical drinks and cocktails you could imagine—anything you wanted, with or without alcohol—and it was all free. Two or three different bands took turns playing for us, and then here came the girls in the grass skirts, and we took turns with them, dancing in the sand. I was kind of looking forward to the fights. What else would you expect from a few hundred sailors, and all that free booze, and maybe one girl for every ten guys? But would you believe it, nobody threw a single punch. Not that night. It seemed like everybody just had this real mellow attitude toward the whole human race. We knew we'd beaten the Imperial Japanese Navy at Midway, and we thought that was the end of the war in the Pacific.[2] I never saw so many guys hugging each other. I actually saw sailors hugging Marines. I thought that was going a little too far, myself.

I stayed out pretty late that night—okay, I partied 'til dawn—but I swear it wasn't for the free mai tais, or the hula girls. I didn't want to leave because I knew this was probably the last time I would ever see most of those guys. Oh, there was lots of scuttlebutt to the contrary. Everyone was talking about the Navy's new aircraft carrier. We heard they were going to name it after our *Yorktown,* and wouldn't it be great if we could be her first crew.[3] I would have liked that. I just didn't think it was very realistic. Some of the radiomen and gunners I talked to that night already had orders to other ships in the fleet, and I was sure Japan would surrender long before the new carrier was ready to go to sea. If not, it wouldn't matter to me, because I only signed up for four years in the Navy. My biggest concern at that time was, how much more education can I possibly get out of the Navy before I'm out on the street in a few months, looking for a job in the civilian world.

The radio gang at the submarine base advised me to try for Radio Materiel School in Washington, D.C. That was the most advanced training a Navy radioman could get. You didn't just learn how to repair radio equipment, they taught you how to build a whole radio station from the ground up. All I had to do was get past the entrance exam, which was pretty funny, because you had to know a whole lot of geometry and trig, and I didn't. Basic algebra, yes. I took that before I dropped out of high school after tenth grade. But there was this one chief radioman at the sub base: He'd just come out Radio Materiel School himself. He had all the books. He even promised to help me study for the exam. I had a thirty-day leave coming—that was Admiral Nimitz's other promise to everybody on the *Yorktown*—but I was afraid to take it. As fast as the Navy moved guys around, I knew that chief radioman might not be there when I got back. And I wasn't all that sure where I stood with my girlfriend at that time.

I didn't get a single letter from Adeline while I was on the *Yorktown,* and there were none waiting for me when I got back to Pearl Harbor after Midway. I didn't know she'd been writing to me all along. The letters just piled up at the Fleet Post Office in San Diego for months and months. When the Navy finally got around to telling the FPO where I was, I got about twenty letters all in one day. She wrote numbers on the envelopes, so I knew in what order I was supposed to read them. That was scary. Every time I opened the next letter in the sequence, I thought, okay, this must be the one that says she's tired of waiting for me. But she never said that. From first to last, every letter said she still loved me. I wanted to write back and explain why she hadn't heard from me for such a long time, but I knew better. The censors would have cut out anything about what happened on the *Yorktown*. Shoot, I couldn't even say what happened to my wallet. I just told her it got wet, and could she please send more pictures.

There was another big stack of letters from my mother. She didn't number hers, so it was a little harder to follow all the news from home. My two older brothers were joining the Army, which was no surprise. Mom said practically all the guys in my hometown were either drafted or volunteered for some branch of the military right after the attack on Pearl Harbor.[4] What shocked me was the women, especially my mother. She had always been a prayer warrior. That's what we called the folks that prayed for everybody in the military, right on up to the Commander in Chief of the whole country, which was President Roosevelt. Now she tells me it's also her patriotic duty to get on the bus to Little Rock every day, along with all the other ladies in the church. Most of those women had never worked outside their homes in their entire lives, and now they'd all got jobs in a factory. I couldn't believe it when my mother told me she was making airplane parts for the military.[5]

I was still going through my mail when a *Yorktown* survivor dropped by the barracks. He was a yeoman, one of the guys that helped salvage the ship's files before it went down at Midway. He brought me my liberty card from the *Yorktown,* and we both had a good laugh about that. I never had a liberty while I was on the carrier, so this was the first time I'd ever seen the thing. If I had, I would have told them to fix the mistakes. The most obvious was my rating: I was not an RM3c on that ship; I was an RM2c. I'd been wearing two stripes and drawing the higher pay of a second class radioman and petty officer for almost a year before I boarded the *Yorktown.* The second error was my date of birth. I guess the Navy hadn't got around to correcting the lie I told on my application. They still had me a year older than I really was. But I knew my mother would like the picture, so I signed the card and put it in the mail. I told her to keep it as a souvenir from her son in the U.S. Navy. That's about all a canceled liberty card is good for.

I could have been assigned to another submarine crew. I didn't ask for that, and, quite frankly, I hoped I wouldn't get those orders. I think there were at least two submarines that never came back that summer.[6] The sub crews that did survive their missions were generally disgusted and discouraged. According to them, about every other torpedo they fired was a dud. Some said it was because the explosive chemicals were old; others claimed there was something wrong with the firing mechanism.[7] The worst story I heard was from a guy who'd been on a mission with the *Perch*. He said they fired twelve torpedoes and never got a single kill.[8] I don't know if all the submarines had such bad luck. I didn't get to talk to those guys as much as I did before the war, because they weren't around the pool much anymore. The Navy was putting them up at the Royal Hawaiian Hotel instead. I thought that was great. As far as I was concerned, submariners deserved every bit of pampering they got between missions. I just wish the Navy had done that a little sooner. I would have loved to spend a week or so at the Royal Hawaiian after that hellish mission on the *Dolphin*.[9]

I did see a lot of Admiral Nimitz that summer. He had to walk past the radio shack to get to his office in the administration building. Sometimes he poked his head in and spoke to our communications officer. The civilian press reporters were always asking for interviews. He didn't grant very many while I was there. He didn't much care for the photographers either. When Admiral Nimitz did consent to a picture, more often than not he wanted it taken with a few enlisted men. I think all of us who worked at CinCPac headquarters got called for that kind of duty at least once. But the main thing I remember about him is the two times he spoke to me, and both times he called me "son."

My first conversation with Admiral Nimitz was in his office. I'm not sure why he was moving his desk and generally sprucing up the place. It may have had something to do with the rumors. We heard President Roosevelt was planning a visit to Pearl Harbor, maybe even that summer.[10] Whatever the reason, Admiral Nimitz wanted his desk in the center of his office, and the cord on his telephone was too short to reach it. It was a very simple job. The only reason it took me more than a few minutes was that I wanted to wrap the extra cord around the leg of the desk. I was afraid he or the President might trip over it if I didn't. I was still on my knees behind the desk when the admiral returned with his coffee. He watched me finish up, and then he said, "Son, that's a mighty fine piece of work." He thanked me several times while I gathered up my tools, and he was still thanking me when I left. I was so embarrassed. All I did was install a longer cord on his telephone. The way he carried on, you'd have thought I won the war.

The second time Admiral Nimitz spoke to me, I thought he was going to throw me in the brig for assaulting an officer. I didn't mean to scare him, and I wasn't trying to knock him on his keister. It was an accident. I was just running errands around the submarine base, and for some stupid reason, I decided to take a short cut by jumping off the torpedo loading dock. It was about a six-foot drop. I really should have looked to see if there was anyone on the sidewalk below. I landed on my haunches, right in the middle of three admirals. Two of them came up cursing. I didn't know who they were. The only one I recognized was Admiral Nimitz. I thought I was dead meat, and I probably would have been if not for him. He just chuckled and said, "That's all right, son. Were you in a hurry to get to the mess hall before they close for lunch?" I said, "Yes, Sir. I'm sorry, Sir."

Everyone at CinCPac headquarters thought Admiral Nimitz was a genius. I don't know anyone at Pearl Harbor who didn't admire the way he was running the war in the Pacific.[11] But, in my experience, he was also the kindest man in the world, and he had the bluest eyes you ever saw. I will never forget how they sparkled in the sun that day. He winked at me and told me to keep running.

Everyone at the submarine base was good to me that summer. I could have made a lot of close friends there, but I didn't want to. It seemed like every guy I ever really cared about in the Navy either disappeared or got killed during the first six months of the war. I didn't want to go through that kind of grief again. The radiomen at headquarters did invite me to the beach with them once or twice. All I remember is the rolls and rolls of barbed wire all along the shore. I guess the Army and the Navy in Hawaii was still thinking Japanese troops might try to land on Waikiki.

The nights in Honolulu were pretty strange, too. The whole city was blacked out. The military and civilian police could write tickets and fine anybody who showed a light from their houses

The USO center in Honolulu served up to 250 gallons of ice cream per day to American military personnel. This and 75 other USO centers and mobile units in the Hawaiian Islands provided entertainment and services to 2.25 million troops in one month during World War II. COURTESY OF THE USO.

or businesses after dark, so a lot of the stores locked their doors at sunset. Of course, the bars and the taverns never closed. They just boarded up the windows and lit candles. That didn't bother the sailors any. Some thought it actually enhanced the nightlife. Candlelight is more romantic, I guess. The USO clubs were always open, too. That was really the best and cheapest entertainment there was for guys in the military.[12] Whenever I went to the USO in Honolulu, I tipped my cap back like everybody else. Two fingers above the eyebrows was regulation; beyond that it was a signal that you were single and available. But I hardly ever asked the USO girls to dance. Where I came from, most churches considered dancing a sin, so I never learned how. I just listened to the bands. There weren't enough girls to go around anyway.

I took the entrance exam for Radio Materiel School in August. Glory be, and thanks to the chief radioman's tutoring, I passed it. All I had to do was get the communications officer to put through my application, which turned out to be an even bigger challenge. Every other day, I asked him if he'd done the paperwork yet. He was a patient man, but he finally blew his stack: "Sailor, don't you know we're in the middle of a war here?" Well, no, I didn't know that. I thought we were at the end. I mean, good grief, we sank four Japanese aircraft carriers in one day at Midway. I didn't think they had anything left to fight us with. I was not aware that Japan also had a powerful Army.[13] I didn't know there were Japanese troops on islands all over the Pacific, and I most certainly did not understand how hard they intended to fight to keep them. None of that was really clear to me until I saw the lists of casualties from Guadalcanal and other islands in the Solomons.[14] The Marines were obviously in heavy combat on the ground, and I was so sorry for all the times I called them seagoing bellhops on the *Yorktown*. It was only after I saw the reports from Guadalcanal that I understood what the Marines really were. Those guys were warriors. Incredibly *brave* warriors.

I don't recall what was going on with the war in Europe that summer. We didn't get much news from there at Pearl Harbor. All I remember is the long lists of Merchant Marine ships that were reported sunk by German submarines in the Atlantic. The lists were shorter in August than they were in June.[15] According to the scuttlebutt at CinCPac headquarters, this was due to all the new destroyers the Navy was getting. I heard a lot of them went right to convoy duty. They were protecting the troop and supply ships that were going to England.

Toward the end of the summer, it was beginning to dawn on me that the war might last another year or two, and, yes, I did feel a little bit guilty for wanting more education instead of another tour of duty on a warship. But not that guilty. The minute I found out I was accepted into Radio Materiel School in Washington, D.C., I put in my request for a thirty-day leave and shot off a letter to Adeline. I told her I was on my way back to the States.

See Time Line, page 253, and Historical Notes, page 254.

17

FIRST LEAVE

September–October 1942

The troopship out of Pearl Harbor was just packed—three, four hundred rowdy sailors—and we were all headed home on leave. I don't remember the name of that ship, but it was huge. The main deck was so big they even had room for six or seven cars parked at one end. I didn't know whose cars they were. If they belonged to any of the enlisted men on board, it must have cost them a month's pay to take up that much space on a Navy ship. If I'd bought a car in Hawaii, I might have done the same. It was worth it, because you couldn't just go out and buy yourself a new one when you got home, not for any amount of money. The car companies weren't selling cars any more. They weren't making anything but weapons and vehicles for the military. If you were lucky enough to own a car before the war, you would do just about anything to keep it.[1]

We were still admiring those cars when the ship began to move. Just outside the channel, the captain turned on the loudspeaker and told us we weren't going to San Diego. We were on our way to San Francisco instead, to some Navy base called

Treasure Island.[2] I'd never been there before. Everybody groaned when the captain said it would take us six or seven days to get to San Francisco. A destroyer could have made that trip in half the time. The smokers complained about the rules: They weren't allowed to light up outside after dark. That was fairly standard policy for all ships during the war, to keep from being spotted by the enemy at night. I didn't think there were very many Japanese submarines on the prowl between Hawaii and California. The greatest danger I could see was right there on the ship, when they broke out the dice and the cards. The stakes were way higher than normal.

The poker games were especially rich. Guys were betting ten- and twenty-dollar bills like they were nickels and dimes. I had over three hundred dollars myself, but I wanted no part of that action. It took me all summer to save up for this leave. I was going to keep my wallet in my pocket and watch everybody else's money change hands. The poker game that drew the biggest crowd had six players; the rest of us were standing about three-deep behind them when this guy named Scott ran out of cash and bet his car. So then we all ran across the deck to see which car. It was the dark red Zephyr, and, oh my, that was a beautiful car.[3] He could have sold that thing for five hundred dollars to just about anybody on the ship, but now it was in the pot. And he lost it. All he had was three of a kind. What an idiot. I never would have bet that much on a hand of poker unless I had a royal flush. I lost all my money in the latrine.

The sanitary facilities on that ship were, shall we say, a little primitive. For the enlisted men, it was basically a horse trough with boards on each side if you needed to sit down. There was a constant stream of saltwater piped in from one end, and the whole contraption was tilted so everything emptied into the ocean through a big drain hole at the other end. So that's where I was, along with about ten other guys, when this joker sneaks in with a great big wad of toilet paper and lights it on fire just before he drops it in the trough. It went sailing like a torch underneath our bare behinds. We all stood up cussing and laughing and pulling our pants up so we could go chase the guy, and then I saw my wallet go down the drain. It was probably sticking out of my back pocket to begin with, and must have fallen the rest of the way when I jumped up and grabbed my pants.

I hardly noticed the Golden Gate Bridge when the ship pulled into Treasure Island. I was too busy looking for the nearest pay phone. I felt bad about calling Adeline collect. I hadn't heard her voice in over five years. When I told her how I lost my wallet this time, she couldn't stop laughing. I didn't think it was very funny at all: I was flat broke until next payday. Thank goodness, I still had my travel voucher from CinCPac. It was good for a seat on a civilian airline from Oakland to Spokane. The only catch was, I had to make my own reservation. I didn't think that was any big deal until I started calling the airlines. Every single plane out of Oakland and San Francisco was full for the next three days. I couldn't even get sympathy from the guys that came in on the same troopship as me. Some of them had to wait longer than I did. I guess the trains and buses were full, too.[4]

Everybody had to stay on Treasure Island for at least a day or two. I ended up bunking with about twenty other sailors in a special section of the barracks curtained and roped off from the rest of the building. We didn't know why. We didn't even know each other. As far as I could tell we had just one thing in common: We were all *Yorktown* survivors. It got weirder when we went to dinner. They had a separate table set up for us in the mess hall, away from all the others, and there was an announcement over the loudspeakers as soon as we sat down. It went something like, "The men at table number such and such are from the *Yorktown*. Do not approach them and do not ask them any questions." We couldn't understand why the Navy didn't want anybody talking to us. I still wonder about that.[5]

There were no other restrictions on us at Treasure Island, at least not that I remember. I know most of the *Yorktown* survivors went out on the town in San Francisco that night. I saw them slapping on the aftershave, and they were all joking about who was going to be writing his name in that book in sick bay in the morning. No question about it, those guys were hunting quail. That's what sailors called the women they met for one-night stands in the port cities. If she was less than eighteen, she was "San Quentin Quail." San Quentin was the name of a prison in California, where you might end up if you got caught messing with the younger girls. I was invited to go along—they even offered to chip in a few bucks apiece so I could—but I said no. I wasn't interested in meeting any girl but Adeline. I just went to the library on Treasure Island and checked out all the books they had from Radio Materiel School. Took a couple of cold showers, too.

I was really looking forward to my very first ride on a regular civilian airline. The plane was a DC-3, similar to the military's C-47 cargo plane, only bigger. When I boarded that plane in Oakland, I thought I'd be with Adeline in three or four hours. It was only a few hundred miles from there to Spokane. Well, that flight took all afternoon and most of the night, because we touched down in about a dozen cities in between. Sacramento, Portland, Boise. I think we even stopped in Walla Walla—twice, it seemed like—and every time we landed, the flight attendants ordered all the passengers who weren't getting off to stay seated and pull down the window shades. I assume that was for security. As if I was going to look out and count all the military planes on the runways and tell it to an enemy spy. Whatever. Anyway, because of all those stops, it was two or three in the morning when I finally landed in Spokane. Thanks to Adeline and Western Union, I had enough money for a taxi and a room at the YMCA.

I never even turned back the covers on the bed. All I did was change clothes. I would rather have stayed in my whites. My two black petty officer stripes showed up better on the whites, but the dress blues were warmer, and it was pretty chilly in Spokane. I know, because I spent the rest of the night walking around downtown. I called Adeline at six thirty in the morning; she promised to meet me in an hour. So I'm pacing back and forth on the sidewalk in front of the YMCA, waiting for my big breakfast date. Every five minutes I checked my watch. Seven thirty. No Adeline. Seven fifty-five. She didn't come. Five more minutes. I decided to give her five more minutes. If she wasn't there by eight, it meant she changed her mind, and I was going to be on the very next plane out of town, and I didn't care where it was going. And then I saw this '38 Plymouth come screeching around the corner and stop in the loading zone.

The engine was still running when Adeline jumped out. She didn't even close the door on the driver's side. She just ran to me on the sidewalk. And she was crying. Something about trains—too many trains—waiting for trains to go by. I didn't care about trains. I just wanted her to stop crying. I'm sure we made quite a spectacle of ourselves. I remember cars going by, honking at us, and there were lots of people on the sidewalk. I could feel them brushing against my back as they walked around me. I didn't care about them either. Nothing mattered except the way she was kissing me back.

I could hardly put three words together over breakfast. I don't remember saying anything intelligent at all, except that I liked her new hairstyle. It was longer, below her shoulders, turned under at the ends. She said it was the latest thing, something called a pageboy. I liked it. I did not like the parking ticket that was on her windshield. The fine for leaving your car in a loading zone was very high, something like five or ten dollars, as I recall. I thought it might help if I talked to the judge, so we drove straight to the courthouse. I told him it was partly my fault, and could he maybe give a poor sailor a break and reduce the fine, just this once? "Well, no," he said. "Can't do that." And then he tore up the ticket and thanked me for my service to the country.

Adeline's mother would not hear of me staying another night at the YMCA. Nothing would do but for me to move into their guest room for a week. Better yet, Adeline took time off from her job—she was still working for the newspaper then—so I got to spend seven whole days with her. I couldn't get over how much more beautiful she was than when we first met. None of the pictures I'd lost did her justice. She was so pretty, guys would turn and whistle at her when we walked down the street. I didn't mind a bit. It just showed I had good taste. I loved everything about her, including the clothes she wore. Adeline was really into the latest fashion, and the skirts were getting shorter—several inches above the knee. They were a lot longer than that the last time I was on the mainland, before the war. The more leg, the better, as far as I was concerned.[6]

The nights with Adeline were wonderful, too. We went out to dinner a couple of times, and I think we saw two or three movies. I can't tell you which ones.[7] We always sat in the back row, and I wasn't exactly paying attention to what was happening on the screen. I do remember the night we got home late—very late— and we decided to just sit there, parked in her parents' driveway for a while longer. We were sort of looking at the stars, but then the car windows got all steamed up and we fell asleep. Next thing you know, the sun was up and so was Adeline's mother. She was out there in her bathrobe, tapping on the windshield with a wooden spoon. And she was laughing. "Breakfast is ready, you two!" Well, her dad was in the kitchen, reading the newspaper, drinking his morning coffee. He was not laughing. I was in the middle of a big long apology for keeping his daughter out all night when he slammed his cup on the table and said, "You sailors think you can get away with anything!" It was all I could do to keep a straight face. Adeline had two older brothers in the Navy.

I hadn't seen my own family in over three years. As much as I would have liked to spend the rest of my leave in Spokane with Adeline, I knew it wasn't right. I had to go home to Arkansas. When I got off the plane in Little Rock, there was my brother Velton, fresh out of basic training in his brand-new Army Air Force uniform. Some people called it the Army Air Corps; Velton said that was the old name.[8] He wanted to know about the Navy. It felt so strange for my older brother to be asking me, "What's it like to be in the war?" I told him as much as I could, which wasn't very much. It was only a half-hour drive from the airport to Vilonia.

When we pulled up to the farmhouse, my parents were standing out on the porch. Mom was crying. My little sister Jo said she did that a lot since the war started. I think that was when I made a conscious decision not to talk about the war while I was home. I couldn't keep my mother from knowing about the attack on Pearl Harbor. She read the newspapers, and I guess it was all over the radio, too. If she'd known what happened after that, especially on the *Yorktown,* it would have just scared her more. It was better for her and easier for me to avoid telling her anything at all.

I spent most of my leave at home on the farm, but I did drive into Vilonia a few times. Most of the guys my age were in the military. I think I was the first to come home after the attack on Pearl Harbor. I hope all of the other soldiers and sailors from my hometown got the same reception I did. Wherever I went, people wanted to shake my hand, and my money was no good. I don't believe I bought a single hamburger or a Coke or even a bag of popcorn at the movies the whole time I was in town. It was all "on the house" or paid for by the folks in line behind me. Some of them I didn't even know. I guess that was their way of showing their support for the war and how much they appreciated everybody in the military. That was fine. I just didn't like it when they called me a hero. I knew very well that I was not, and I told them so. It was embarrassing.

If I heard it once, I heard it a dozen times—how the whole town thought I was dead for several weeks after the war started. They said the post office closed down on the day that card I filled out at Pearl Harbor finally arrived. The postmaster pulled down the shades and locked the door and delivered it himself. Nobody had ever seen him drive that fast. My sister said she saw this big cloud of dust come up the lane, and he jumped out hollering and waving that postcard, "He's all right! He's all right!" I made a special trip to the post office to thank Mr. Moore for that. I also paid a visit to my high school principal, Mr. Bollen. Of all my teachers, he was the one who took the most interest in me, and I wanted to thank him, too. I'm glad I did. He told me there was some new test for guys like me. If you passed it, you could get your high school diploma. He made me promise that I would take that GED test and let him know how I did.[9]

I never meant to lie to my parents while I was home on leave, but I had no choice. When my mother asked me why I didn't ask that girl in Spokane to marry me, I said it was because I wasn't sure. The truth is, I was very sure, and I had every reason to believe she would say yes. I just didn't think it was right to ask her until I was sure I was going to survive the war. If it wasn't over by the time I got out of Radio Materiel School, I assumed the Navy would send me right back to a warship in a hot combat zone. I couldn't think of a truthful way to explain that to my mother. She had three sons in the military, and she knew there was a lot of war left to fight. The last thing she needed was another reason to cry.

See Time Line, page 256, and Historical Notes, page 257.

18

THE NAVAL RESEARCH
LABORATORY

October 1942–July 1943

My parents drove me to the train station in Little Rock. It was a regular civilian passenger train, but most of the seats were filled with guys in uniform. Some reserved space in the sleeping car, but that cost extra. I rode for free in the section with the reclining seats. It was a three-day trip to Washington, D.C., but it wasn't that bad. I just read a lot and took naps between stops until the train pulled into Arlington. I caught a bus from there, and it was loaded with soldiers and sailors, too. I don't know where they were going. I was the only one that got off at the Naval Research Laboratory.

I couldn't get past the main gate without showing my orders to the Marines. That was normal for any kind of military facility during the war, at least in my experience. What surprised me was the way it looked once I got inside. The Naval Research Laboratory was exactly what I had always imagined a college campus would be: dozens of two- and three-story buildings, all red brick, with ivy growing up the sides. There were big green lawns and shade trees, statues, fountains, and park benches. Guys walking around with books under their arms. Good gosh, I thought I took a wrong turn and ended up at Harvard or Yale. I could hardly wait to go to my first class in the morning.[1]

Turns out, my orders were mistaken. The next session of Radio Materiel School was not starting until the first of November, so I had almost a month to kill in Washington, D.C. I spent most of that time with my sister. Verna was the oldest of seven children in my family. She was nearly thirty, but she was still single. She used to be a schoolteacher, which she said she loved, but "men's jobs" paid better. She didn't especially like her job at the Bureau of Engraving. I don't know what she did, other than that it had something do with printing money. All she ever said about it was that most of her coworkers were women. Verna thought this was because the federal government was in the same boat as the civilian employers. They had no choice. They had to hire women to replace all the men who quit their jobs and joined the military after the attack on Pearl Harbor.

I thought Verna had it made. She had her own apartment in Washington, D.C., and a car. She couldn't drive it all that much because of the gas rationing, but still.[2] She could also afford to take me out to all the best restaurants in the city, and we hit quite a few of them. I was shocked when she finally broke down and told me that she was going to give it all up and join the Army herself. She wanted to be a nurse. It was not my place to argue with her, and she sure didn't need my permission. I just felt sorry for our poor mother. I could almost hear the wailing back home whenever Verna got around to telling her. I wasn't that worried about my sister being in the Army, mainly because I still believed the war would be over by the time she finished her training in a year or so. I might have thought otherwise if I'd been paying more attention to the news from overseas.[3]

It's not that I didn't care how the war was going against the Nazis in Europe or the Japanese in the Pacific. I just couldn't spare the time to listen to the radio or read the newspaper after I started my classes. I truly thought the instructors were joking on the first day. One said he was compressing about two years' worth of advanced math into this eight-month course. Another told us not to look down if we dropped a pencil, because we might miss something that would be on the final exam. They were serious. I had to hit the books every night and all day on the weekends, and so did everybody else in Radio Materiel School that term. There were about thirty of us, all enlisted men, mostly first or second class petty officers and experienced radiomen. Several of my classmates had a year or two of college before they joined the Navy, and even they thought it was hard. The math was way beyond anything I'd ever learned in algebra and geometry, or even trig. "Operator j" was especially difficult for me. I thought I was just dense until the instructor told us this was actually a concept from calculus.

The one thing I never did understand was why the Navy called the whole place a laboratory. I didn't see any scientists in white lab coats, and there were no test tubes or microscopes. All I ever saw were regular classrooms, with desks and blackboards and charts on the walls. If there really were scientists working in laboratories, they must have been in the other buildings, the ones I was not authorized to enter. I never questioned why. Everybody knew the Navy was obsessed with secrecy after the war started, and I think I just got used to it. We had all kinds of buildings at Pearl Harbor where you had to be an admiral or on the staff to get past the Marines at the front door. So, if there was something going on with nuclear weapons at the Naval Research Laboratory while I was there, I'm not surprised that my classmates and I were not aware of it. I never even heard the words "Manhattan Project" until the war was over.[4]

I was not restricted to campus while I was at Radio Materiel School, but I hardly ever stepped outside the gates after Verna left for the Army in December. I had no reason to. I only took the bus downtown one time, and that was to go shopping. I wanted to buy something really special for Adeline's twenty-third birthday in January. I spent a fortune on a bathrobe—it was purple velvet with a satin lining—and then I had to pay the store to wrap it up and mail it to her. Altogether, I think it came to over twenty-five dollars. I was happy when she wrote back and thanked me. I was less than pleased when she told me about her new job. She was still a civilian, but she was now a secretary to one of the Army doctors at Fort George Wright in Spokane. She said she sat behind a curtain and took notes in shorthand while he examined and talked with the pilots.

Those flyboys were dangerous. I was afraid one of them would make a pass at Adeline, and she might like it. I especially hated it when she told me about the "Pretty Legs Contest." She said all the men on the staff at Fort George Wright got to vote on which secretaries had the best-looking legs. Oh, yes, and guess who made it into the top five. I didn't want to be the jealous boyfriend, so I wrote back and said, "Congratulations." I never really believed she would ever go for some hotshot pilot over a handsome sailor like me. But you never know what goes on in a girl's mind when her boyfriend is three thousand miles away.

My four years in the Navy were up in April. When they called me to the administration building on campus, it was decision time. I knew they weren't going to let me go. By then, everybody who was in the military knew we were in "for the duration." The only choice I had was whether I wanted to commit to another four years or take my discharge as soon as the war was over. The personnel officer really pressured me to reenlist. He even offered me a signing bonus—a coupon for a chicken dinner. I said no. So then he threw in another bonus. That was another coupon, for a ham-and-egg breakfast. We're talking real ham, not Spam, and real eggs, not powdered. Okay, now that was tempting. You'd be surprised how many guys in my class actually went for it. If the Navy had offered cash instead of a couple of decent meals in the mess hall, I probably would have reenlisted. As it was, I decided it was worth more to have the choice of being a civilian at the end of the war. I guess you could say I took a gamble that the war would be over in less than four years.

I did not go out for beer on my twenty-third birthday. The first of June fell in the middle of the week, and, besides, I had nobody to celebrate with. We were all studying for our final exams.

I believe everyone in my class passed. Even me. I figured I was on a roll, so I asked to take the Navy's promotional exam for radiomen. Compared to the finals in Radio Materiel School, it was easy. That gave me the next higher rating in my specialty. I was now a radioman first class, with three stripes on my sleeve to show that I was also a petty office first class. I got an extra ten or twelve bucks in my pay envelope, too. By the end of June, I was making somewhere close to $85 a month. Pretty decent money for a high school dropout in 1943.

We didn't know what the Navy was going to do with us until the day we graduated. There was no ceremony. An officer just brought a big stack of orders into the classroom and called our names out, one by one. As soon as he left, we ran around and looked at each other's orders. Not one of my classmates was assigned to a warship. I thought that was unusual, considering all the action in the South Pacific at that time. Some said it was because the Navy didn't want to get us killed right away, not after they'd invested so much time and money in our training. I doubted that was why, because several guys had orders to what they called "lighter-than-air craft." That was as hazardous as a warship, in my opinion, if not more so, and I did not envy them. I mean, I still wanted to fly and all, but I preferred a vehicle with wings.[5]

About twenty of us were assigned to naval air stations. There were so many new ones going up around the world, I'd never heard of most of them. My orders were to the naval air station at Cold Bay in the Aleutian Islands. I had no idea where that was. I went over every inch of the map from Hawaii to the Marshalls to the Solomons. Couldn't find the Aleutians. So then I checked all the little island chains around New Guinea and Australia. Not there either. Finally, one of my classmates said, "Try Father Hubbard territory." Well, everybody knew Father Hubbard. I saw one of his films in grade school. It was all about dogsleds and Eskimos and wildlife in Alaska.[6] Sure enough, there was Cold Bay: right at the tip of this long peninsula that stuck out from Alaska. And all those little islands lined up west of that peninsula—those were the Aleutians. I could not imagine why the Navy needed an air base for carrier planes all the way up there. As far as I knew, the North Pacific was not a combat zone. I even wrote and told my parents to stop worrying. I couldn't say where I was going, of course. The censors would have crossed that out. I just told them I was in no danger from anything, except maybe a case of frostbite.[7]

My travel orders to Alaska started with a train ride, from Washington, D.C., to the Sand Point Naval Air Station in Seattle, with a short layover in Spokane. I thought this might be my last chance to propose to Adeline before one of those darn flyboys beat me to it, so I sent her a telegram. I hardly looked out the window for the next five days. All the way across the country, I was rehearsing how I was going to ask her to marry me. When the train finally stopped in Spokane, I took a taxi to her house— paid the guy extra to drive fast and avoid the railroad crossings— and then I asked her to step outside and walk with me. Halfway around the block, I forgot my speech. I just blurted it out: "Adeline, I think we should get married." She didn't answer. I panicked. Asked her if she wanted time to think about it. But then she kissed me and said, "No, I don't need any more time. I'll marry you." I was the happiest guy on earth, for about five minutes. That's how long it took us to walk back and tell her parents that we were engaged. To which her mother said, "Don't be too sure, Ray. She'll probably back out, like she did with all the others." I hoped she was kidding. Adeline's mother had a great sense of humor. If I'd had more time, maybe I could have figured it out, but my taxi was waiting. I had a train to catch.

Sand Point Naval Air Station was on the outskirts of Seattle, close to Lake Washington. They gave me a bunk in the barracks, but I didn't bother to unpack my seabag. I was supposed to be on a plane to Cold Bay in the morning. Well, that flight was canceled. There were no planes flying in or out of the Aleutian Islands because the weather was bad. That should have been my first clue, especially when the radiomen said this happened a lot, even in the summer.[8] At the time, I was just mad because I could have stayed another day with Adeline in Spokane.

I didn't know anyone in Seattle, and I had nothing to do but wait for that stupid plane to Alaska. Somebody said I should check the bulletin board in the barracks. This was where the Navy posted names and phone numbers of civilians who liked to entertain sailors. Most of the offers I saw were for lunch or dinner in their homes. There were also a few invitations to parties and special events at the yacht club. I picked the one for a seafood dinner and a concert. When I called that phone number, it turned out to be the office of a surgeon named Dr. Burden. The first thing she said to me was, "You can call me Minnie."

Minnie Burden was real old. I'm sure she was at least forty-five, but the guys in the barracks at Sand Point told me she was well known for showing sailors a good time in Seattle. Well, I guess so. She took me to a fancy restaurant—first time I'd ever tasted Dungeness crab and Pacific salmon—and then she paid for a taxi to the concert hall. She had season tickets, best seats in the house. I'd never heard classical music performed live. The soloist was Yehudi Menuhin. I didn't know who he was, but Dr. Burden said he was pretty famous. Maybe that's why it was standing room only that night. I couldn't understand how a solo violinist could draw such a big crowd, until he began to play. It was the most beautiful music I'd ever heard in my life. For two whole hours, I actually forgot about the war. I doubt if I ever would have discovered how much I liked classical music if it hadn't been for Dr. Burden and the Yehudi Menuhin concert in Seattle.[9]

There was no plane to the Aleutians the next day or the day after that, so I just hung out with the radiomen in the Sand Point control tower. They directed all the Navy pilots who were landing and taking off on the runway. I thought I would be doing the same thing at the naval air station at Cold Bay, if the Navy ever figured out a way to get me there. I would have been happy to go by sea—there were several destroyers and a cruiser in the harbor—but they weren't headed to Alaska. The only ship that was, was this big ugly civilian cargo vessel, full of lumber. I was afraid that would be my ride, and, sure enough, it was. The guys in the barracks laughed when I showed them my boarding orders. They handed me a heavy wool peacoat and a pair of thick gloves. I thought this was their idea of a joke. Of course I knew it might be a little cooler in Alaska, but this was July, for crying out loud.

I still had a few hours to kill before the lumber ship was due to leave. Somebody told me I should go to the USO, because they were letting guys make free long-distance phone calls.[10] That much was true. The catch was, you could only talk for three minutes, and they wouldn't let you dial it yourself. You had to write the phone number on a piece of paper, hand it to a volunteer, and then go stand in line until it was your turn. Well, there were at least twenty sailors ahead of me, so it took over an hour to get to the front of the line. The guy ahead of me had just hung up the phone. As he was leaving, he says to me, "Is your girl named Adeline?" I said, "Yes, how did you know?" And he said, " 'Cuz I just talked to her." I didn't have time to go back and try again.

The lumber ship turned straight north from Seattle, and we stayed in sight of the coastline on both sides for the next three or four days. The crew said this was called the Inside Passage to Alaska. We stopped for one night in the harbor at Ketchikan. That's where I put on the coat. The day after that, I broke out the gloves. I think we were somewhere in the middle of the Icy Straits when I got a little ticked off at those guys back in the barracks at Sand Point. They should have given me a set of long underwear, too.

See Time Line, page 258, and Historical Notes, page 261.

19

COLD BAY

July Through December 1943

I saw snow on the mountains in the distance, but the sun was shining as we approached the Aleutian Peninsula. Temperature was about sixty degrees. I didn't think that was bad at all, until the ship's crew informed me that this was what you called a scorcher at Cold Bay in July. We had to wait outside the harbor entrance for the Coast Guard cutters to lift the sub net.[1] It worked sort of like an automatic garage door, except that it was underwater. Pearl Harbor had a sub net, too, for keeping enemy submarines out and away from the warships, but there were no warships inside the harbor at Cold Bay. There wasn't even a base. All I saw was a few small fishing boats and a tiny little village.

The name of the village was King Cove, and the fishermen were obviously civilians. I was warned not to call them Eskimos. The lumber ship crew referred to them as "Aleuts." I don't know what they called themselves.[2] What really got my attention was their dock. I'd never seen such a dock—military or civilian— anywhere in the world. It was over eight hundred feet long and wide enough for trucks, but there was only one jeep on it that day, and the driver was waving and calling to me. I had a lot of questions for that guy.

We drove inland for about fifteen miles, which seemed a little odd for a naval air station. They were usually closer to the water. I thought I would see forests along the way, but there was not a single tree in sight. Not even a bush. It was just grass and moss, as far as the eye could see, all the way to the mountains, and the ground looked kind of wavy, like there was water sloshing below the surface. The jeep driver called it "tundra." He said it felt kind of squishy when you walked on it. The only animals he'd ever seen on his trips between the harbor and the base were seabirds and caribou.[3]

There were tanks on the hill above the base. As we got closer to the runway, I saw planes with Army Air Force markings. The jeep driver said they came from Fort Randall, the Army base a few miles farther down the road. He didn't know why the Army was parking tanks and bombers at a naval air station, but he was able to explain all the strange-looking buildings. "Quonset huts," he called them.[4] They came in all different sizes; the smaller ones were buried in the ground, almost up to the roof. I thought this was probably for extra insulation from the cold, but the driver said, "No, it's to keep the darn things from blowing over in the wind." And then he stopped at the hut with a sign over the door. The sign said PARADISE LOST.

Paradise Lost was one of the dozens of Quonset huts that were used for barracks at Cold Bay. It had an oil-burning stove and bunks for about fifteen enlisted men. Half of my bunkmates were radiomen; the rest were torpedomen. I had a lot of questions for them, too. By the time I unpacked my seabag, I thought I knew the score. They told me about the thousands of Japanese troops on the islands west of us. About a month ago, they said, there was a terrible battle with them on the island of Attu. It sounded like a bloodbath. I heard our guys ended up killing every last enemy soldier on that island, because the Japanese Army didn't believe in the concept of surrender. They didn't care if they were outnumbered or outgunned. They would rather die in combat than be taken as prisoners of war.[5]

According to the radiomen who bunked at Paradise Lost, there was going to be another big battle with the Japanese troops on the island of Kiska. They thought it would be even worse than Attu, because there were even more enemy soldiers on that island. They also believed that Japan would invade us at Cold Bay eventually. Well, that sure explained why the Army had tanks on the hills around us. The torpedomen said that the Navy had all kinds of warships to defend us, too. Whenever they needed more ammunition or supplies, the torpedomen had to haul it across the tundra to that huge dock in the harbor. They hated that job, but I guess that was the Navy's deal with the Aleuts. The villagers were kind enough to put up with the dock, the sub net, and all the warships that came and went in their fishing waters. They just drew the line at the Navy's request for an air base next to their homes on shore. I could understand that.

The Aleuts at Cold Bay were clearly on our side. Maybe they were as afraid of the Japanese Army and Navy as we were.[6] But I think the main reason we got so much cooperation from the local civilians was our base commander. He was an Aleut. The way I heard it, he used to be a fishing boat captain, until the Navy gave him the rank of commander and put him in charge of this base on the Aleutian peninsula.

For me, being at Cold Bay in the summer of 1943 felt like I was right back at Pearl Harbor in those first few days after the attack in December 1941. There weren't any palm trees or tourist hotels on the beaches, but the paranoia—the fear of invasion by Japanese soldiers on the ground—was exactly the same. And the radiomen were laughing at me. All I said was "Where's the radio shack?" They were still laughing when they took me outside and pointed to a big, fresh-dug hole in the ground. The joke was, the Navy did not have a radio station on the base at Cold Bay. We had to build it ourselves, from scratch, in a hurry.

Setting up the Quonset hut was easy: The pieces snapped together like a tinker toy. We had that thing in the hole with the roof on in a couple of hours. The wiring was something else. It takes a lot of electricity to power a full-blown military radio station. For about a week, we worked day and night. Well, actually, there was no night at Cold Bay. When you're that close to the Arctic Circle, it doesn't get dark in the summer. I couldn't sleep at all for the first couple of days. I finally got so tired, I didn't care if the sun was up, down, or sideways. There were some advantages to working under the "midnight sun": You could read a technical manual outside at midnight. We didn't even need flashlights when we sneaked around the base and stole tools and equipment from the Army at two in the morning.[7] The Navy had a special term for this. It wasn't stealing. It was a "midnight requisition from small stores."

The only really big thing we filched from the Army was a generator. It took four of us to haul that monster down into the hole. We almost had it through the door when it slipped off the dolly and pinned me against the wall. I woke up in sick bay; the corpsman was standing over me with a bedpan. He said I had three crushed vertebrae, and it might be awhile before I could walk again. When the radiomen came by to see how I was doing, they said I probably did it on purpose, to get out of all the wiring we still had to do. Yeah, right. My back was in traction, I'm sipping dinner through a straw, and all the doctors and nurses had beards. There were no women anywhere on the base at Cold Bay.

The one good thing about being laid up was that it gave me time to study for the GED test. I promised to write and tell my high school principal when I passed it, which I did. A month or so later, here comes this little package in the mail from Vilonia High School. It was my class ring. The note from Mr. Bollen said it was a gift from the class of '38. I knew better. I'm sure he bought and paid for that ring himself. The stone was a red ruby. I don't know how much it cost—probably thirty or forty dollars. That was a lot of money for anybody in 1943.

By the time I got out of the base hospital, the new radio shack was up and running, and we were swamped. Some of the messages came from CinCPac at Pearl Harbor, but it was mostly requests

Radioman (RM1c) Ray Daves, 23, at door to stairs leading to below-ground radio shack ("Navy Radio Communications Duty Office"), Naval Auxiliary Air Field (NAAF) Cold Bay, 1943. COURTESY OF RAY DAVES COLLECTION.

for more torpedoes and supplies from our warehouses. I think every Navy warship in the Aleutians stopped at Cold Bay at least once that summer. We were also functioning as air traffic controllers for all the Army Air Force pilots who were flying in and out of Fort Randall that summer. Whenever their runways were overcrowded or fogged in, they requested clearance to land on the Navy's runways at Cold Bay.[8] On top of that, we were getting all kinds of enemy sightings from the Aleuts. Their fishing boats had radios; some even had sonar. Whenever the Aleut fishermen spotted a Japanese ship or submarine, they called in the location to us. We relayed that information to any Army plane or Navy ship that was close enough to go out and chase it down. The Aleuts were really valuable allies in those waters, but we had to be extra careful whenever we communicated with them on the

Radioman Ray Daves at work inside the radio shack, NAAF Cold Bay,
1943. Courtesy of Ray Daves Collection.

radio. Very few of the local fishermen were as fluent in English as
our base commander.

Toward the end of July, I thought the Aleuts were imagining
all the Japanese submarine sightings they were calling in. There
were so many, I wondered if they were seeing whales. I'd made
that mistake on sonar myself, lots of times. But then I started
picking up Japanese transmissions on my own headphones, sometimes two or three times a day. It happened so often, I got so I
could recognize their fists. The Japanese radiomen's key taps
were every bit as distinctive and individual as ours. One particular Japanese radioman broke into our frequencies so often, I was
pretty sure he was doing it on purpose, to disrupt our transmissions. That was only a nuisance: It made me stop and start over
from the beginning. It was just scary to think how close he must
have been to break in to our military frequencies. And unless
Japan's radio technology was a whole lot better than ours, it
meant those submarines were on the surface, too.

There were never enough planes or ships in the area to chase
down all the submarine sightings we were getting at Cold Bay
that summer, so the base commander ordered us to start flying

Radioman Ray Daves in flight gear, including Mae West life vest and leather helmet, prepares for aerial search and destroy mission. NAAF Cold Bay, 1943. COURTESY OF RAY DAVES COLLECTION.

search-and-destroy missions ourselves. None of the radiomen had taken the course for aviation gunners, but there was no time for training. We just put on our Mae Wests, climbed in the backseat behind the pilot, and hoped for the best.

The only Navy planes we had on the base at that time were OS2U Kingfishers. It wasn't much of a sub killer. The Kingfisher was nothing more than a scout plane—the same kind they catapulted off the cruisers, the kind I swore I would never fly in again. But that was before the war. I was pretty relieved when I saw our Kingfishers had wheels instead of pontoons. They could take off and land on a normal runway, like a normal plane. They also had bomb racks—one underneath each wing—but the bombs were only a hundred pounds each. I don't know what made us think we could do any damage to an enemy ship or submarine with such a small bomb load. The only other armament on that plane was the radioman's thirty-caliber machine gun, unless you count the two Colt .45 pistols. I carried one in a holster on my right hip; the pilot had the other. I'm sure the Japanese sub crews were real scared of those, too.[9]

We flew in pairs, but we didn't always stay together for the whole mission. Whenever I looked over and saw my wingman, I got a real warm-fuzzy feeling. It was actually kind of fun to fly search-and-destroy missions out of Cold Bay, but the truth is, it's a wonder any of us ever lived to tell about it. I think we were just lucky. The Japanese submarines were always submerged by the time we got to the Aleuts' coordinates. We never found any enemy ships on the surface either. They must have been out of our fuel range or hidden in the fog. If we'd ever tried to bomb a Japanese ship or sub on the surface, their antiaircraft guns would have shot us down like a dead duck. Other than that, I suppose the greatest danger was the weather, unless it was your turn to fly with Fish.

Of all the Navy pilots at Cold Bay, Fish was the daredevil. We called him Fish because he flew so low over the ocean that the propeller splashed icy cold water all over the radioman in the backseat. The only reason anybody put up with being his gunner was that he was a darn good pilot, most of the time. Fish liked to fly low over the ground, too. When we saw caribou on the way back to base—and if he had enough fuel to fool around with—he would tell me to take target practice. You don't have to be a very good shot to bring down a caribou with a thirty-caliber machine gun. I could usually pick off three or four in a single pass over the herd. And then I would get on the radio and tell the cooks where to find them. The meat was a little tough and stringy, but we were glad to get it. Anything was better than Spam.

Fish had this one real nasty habit when the fog rolled in. If we couldn't see the runway in the fog, he would order me to give him a fix on the homing beacon. He would just dive—nose down, full speed, and blind—and he would not pull up until the very last second before we hit the ground. And then he'd turn around and ask you if you'd wet your pants. Twice he did that to me. I decided he was crazy. I flat refused to fly with him again. It wasn't very long before all the other radiomen did the same. I have no idea whatever happened to Fish. The base commander had him transferred out of Cold Bay. They could have used him on an aircraft carrier. He would have made a great dive-bomber.

I especially remember coming back from one of those search-

and-destroy missions in the month of August. I was still in the hangar, putting away my flight gear, when I heard another plane approaching our runway. I knew by the sound of the engine that this was no Kingfisher, so I went out to see what it was. I didn't always recognize the Army Air Force plane types, but I knew this was a P-38 Lightning as soon as I saw the two tails. The pilot made a perfect landing. I thought I was dreaming when he climbed out of the cockpit and hollered my name. It was Gale Stevens. There were only thirteen in my class at Vilonia High School, and he was one of them. We'd known each other since first grade. I heard he'd joined the Army right after graduation. Cold Bay was the last place in the world I ever expected to see him again.

Gale and I didn't have a lot of time to visit: There was a jeep coming for him from Fort Randall. I know he sure thought a lot of his P-38. He told me he flew it in combat against the Japanese on Attu. He said that was where he learned to fly low and strafe the enemy soldiers on the ground. I did not ask him how many he thought he killed that way or how many Zeroes he shot down over Attu. I assumed he hated those kinds of questions as much as I did, and we were both pretty sick of the war in general. We just talked about old times, and wouldn't it be great if we could both go back to Arkansas and be kids again. I wished him luck at Kiska. Everybody knew there was going to be a real showdown with the Japanese troops on Kiska Island any day.[10] I'm sure the enemy knew it, too, because I saw the leaflets our bombers were dropping on them. One pilot left a whole bundle of those leaflets in the radio shack at Cold Bay. We didn't know what it said: All the words were in Japanese. I took one for a souvenir.[11]

Gale never landed his P-38 on our runway again, but a lot of other guys from his squadron did. They told me my friend's plane was not shot down over Kiska. Nobody was. According to them, the island was totally deserted when our troops landed on the beaches. We didn't know how the Japanese managed to get that many thousands of soldiers off that island without detection, but I guess they did. Maybe those leaflets did the trick.[12]

It was a little later in August when another pilot stopped by the

"Kiri leaflet" dropped on Japanese-occupied Attu and Kiska translates as follows: "This sign tells you the military of Japan is powerless now and only gives you tragedy and misfortune." Translated by Michiko Takaoka, Director of Japanese Cultural Center, Mukogawa Fort Wright Institute. COURTESY OF RAY DAVES COLLECTION.

radio shack and showed me a Japanese officer's diary. He said he found it beside the man's body after the battle on Attu. It was in Japanese handwriting, of course, but somebody had already translated the whole thing into English, and I typed a copy of that. He must have been a doctor, because I remember the part where he said he used grenades to kill all of his patients. I assumed he did it to prevent them from being captured alive. I don't know if he committed suicide afterward or if he was killed in combat the next day. All he said was that it was an honor and a privilege to die in service to the Emperor. The pilot who found his diary told me he was sending the translated copy to the War Department in Washington, D.C. The original, he said he was going to keep until the war was over. He swore he was going to take that diary back to Japan and turn it over to the man's family. I don't know if he ever found them. I'd bet a month's pay that he tried.

Reverse side of "kiri leaflet" reads: "In next spring, the pouring American bombs will give you tragedy and unhappiness like falling down paulownia leaves." Translated by Michiko Takaoka. COURTESY OF RAY DAVES COLLECTION.

The Aleuts' sightings tapered off quite a bit in September. There was very little we could do about them anyway: The fog got thicker and lasted longer in the fall. I doubt if even Fish would have been crazy enough to take off in a williwaw. That was the local word for this peculiar kind of windstorm. It was even worse than the blizzards in the mountains of northern Idaho when I was in the CCC. The williwaws in the Aleutians came swirling in from all directions at once, sometimes with rain, sometimes with snow, always with fog.[13] You couldn't see more than a few feet ahead of you, in the air or on the ground. The thermometer was irrelevant. We didn't measure windchill. It felt like fifty below when the Navy started issuing these real heavy parkas with no buttons or zippers down the front. You just pulled it over your head like an oversized sweatshirt. On me, it was more like a dress.

From about October on, nobody wanted to go outside. I never missed a meal myself, but there were some who did. They said they would rather starve than walk the hundred yards to the mess hall in a williwaw. The snow got even deeper in December, and, of course, that whole midnight sun thing reversed itself in the winter. It was dark all the time. We couldn't fly, and there were hardly any ships coming into the harbor. Nobody had anything to do, and it began to feel like the whole object of being at Cold Bay was to keep warm and stay sane. Some didn't. I remember one yeoman who developed a weird fixation on his hair. He couldn't seem to quit combing it. For hours on end, he would part it this way and that way and then back again. He finally got so bad he just stood there and stared at himself in the mirror all day. The base commander had him transferred to a psychiatric hospital on the mainland.

The base recreation officer did the best he could. He got the Navy to bring us some treadmills and weight-room equipment. We even had a hot tub of sorts—it was more like a whirlpool bath— and the corpsmen gave great massages. At night, we had movies in the mess hall. We had to show the same ones over and over until the fog cleared enough for the cargo planes to bring in a fresh batch. I ran the projector—the cooks brought me an extra piece of cake or pie for that—and every movie came with a newsreel. They were usually a week or two out of date by the time we got them, so it was hard to keep up with the war. I was glad when I heard the Italians switched sides and joined the Allies. The bad news was how many of our bombers—they called them Flying Fortresses— were lost over Europe. I could hardly believe the Germans shot down sixty in a single day.[14] The newsreels from the Pacific were even worse. The Marines were taking heavy casualties again, only this time it was on Tarawa, in the Gilbert Islands. I never saw the casualty lists from that battle. Based on the newsreel footage, I assumed the numbers were as bad or worse than Guadalcanal.[15]

There wasn't quite as much concern about Japanese troops coming ashore at Cold Bay after winter set in, but no one knew if they had really given up on the idea of invading Alaska altogether. Every few days, when the air raid sirens went off, we had to grab our rifles and run to battle stations until we got the all

Recreation officer Ensign Bell, left, and radioman Ray Daves, outside the Navy's post office at NAAF Cold Bay, 1943. COURTESY OF RAY DAVES COLLECTION.

clear. It was always a false alarm. But I never heard much "woe is me." I think everybody just accepted where we were, and we all knew it could have been worse. The weather was miserable, but we weren't dodging any bombs or bullets on the beaches.[16]

I don't know how the other barracks passed the time between shifts. I suppose they played cards, the same as we did in Paradise Lost. When I got tired of that, I read books and magazines from the base library. Everyone looked forward to the days when the fog lifted enough for the planes to land with all those sacks of mail from home. It was a special treat to get a letter from your girlfriend with a "kiss" inside. Girls blotted their lipstick on a tissue and put that in the envelope with the letter. I got lots of those from Adeline. Whenever she sent me a picture, I pasted it on the wall next to my bunk. I taped black paper over half of the lightbulb so the other half shone on her, like a spotlight. And I remember how my arms ached—it was a real, physical aching

Radiomen and torpedomen re-
turn with rifles to Paradise Lost
barracks after an air raid alarm.
NAAF Cold Bay, 1943. COUR-
TESY OF RAY DAVES COLLEC-
TION.

sensation—when I stared at those pictures. I wanted to hold her
again.

Studying helped. I knew it was probably a waste of time to
take the next promotional exam, because I was a first class petty
officer. After that, you're a chief petty officer. Everybody knew it
didn't matter how high you scored on the chief petty officer exam.
You couldn't "make chief" unless there was an opening in your
specialty. Besides that, I was only twenty-three, and all the chief
petty officers I'd ever known were guys in their forties and fifties.
They were like a bridge between the officers and the enlisted men
in the Navy. Whenever the officers wanted to know what the enlisted men in any section were thinking or worried about, they depended on the chiefs to give it to them straight. Which is why I
had no business taking the chief petty officer exam in December at
Cold Bay, but—hey—what else was there to do.

The other radiomen were as bored as I was, so we put together
a civilian-type radio show and started broadcasting our own programs. This was totally illegal. You were supposed to get FCC ap-

proval for a new radio frequency in U.S. territory. We never even applied for it. The base commander's permission was good enough for us. I think that's one of the reasons everyone at Cold Bay liked him so much. He wasn't afraid to break the rules. He even signed our supply requests for all the newest records from the big bands. When the Navy sent those, we started taking song requests like disc jockeys. If it had been up to me, we would have played more classical music—I was really getting into it after that concert in Seattle—but most of the guys in the barracks wanted top forty. The only request I dreaded was "Red Sails in the Sunset." That was Adeline's favorite; she called it "our song." I always got depressed when somebody asked for that one.

The torpedomen had absolutely nothing to do. There were so few ships coming in for ammunition or supplies that winter. The only torpedoman who didn't seem to mind having all that time on his hands was Hector Lebree. Hector was perfectly satisfied as

Radioman Ray Daves, 23, relaxes on his bunk, NAAF Cold Bay, winter 1943. (Photos on wall are Adeline Bentz, also 23.) COURTESY OF RAY DAVES COLLECTION.

long as he had his sketchbook and pencil. I thought he was a great artist; everything he drew was signed "by Hec." His dream was to be a cartoonist for the Disney studios, if he survived the war. All the other torpedomen were making trips to the warehouse. They claimed it was part of their job to check on the torpedoes. Everybody knew they were just drinking the fuel. We called it "torpedo juice." I have no idea what it tasted like—I never touched the stuff—but I know it had a very high alcohol content. The torpedomen were getting snockered on it. We told them it was dangerous. The Navy was sending all kinds of warnings about torpedo fuel. The memos said it could cause blindness, if it didn't kill you first. Well, the torpedomen in Paradise Lost drank it anyway. One guy got so drunk, he grabbed his rifle and ran outside in his underwear. I guess he got it in his head that we should have an armed guard at the door. He just kept saying, "I are at *war!*" We wrapped some pants around him before we took his picture. Then his buddies dragged him back inside and tucked him into bed.

The only normal, legal alcohol you could get at Cold Bay was at the Officers Club. Enlisted men could go there, too, if they were guests of an officer. I usually went with Ensign Bell. He was the base recreation officer, and we were friends. The first time he took me to the O Club, I realized officers weren't that much different from the rest of us. They sat around, played cards, shot pool, and told jokes. I think they also drank a lot, because I remember what happened when I asked the bartender for a 7-Up. He looked at me kind of funny and said, "How do you mix that?" I never was much of a drinker. I just enjoyed the view from where I stood at the bar. The first time I saw that painting of the girl on the beach, I knew it was "by Hec." I never asked how much the officers paid him for that mural. Knowing Hector, he probably did it for a ham sandwich and a couple of beers.

The Navy did not send any Christmas trees to Cold Bay, but we did get a planeload of Red Cross parcels, enough for everybody on the base. Counting the officers, there were about five or six hundred of us. The boxes were all the same size—about a foot and a half across—but the contents were all different. It was kind of fun to see what everybody got, and then we swapped with each other. Mine was full of socks and cigarettes. I also got a package from my mother: a fruitcake with no fruit. The card said she was afraid real fruit would spoil by the time it got to me, so she baked it with gumdrop candies instead. Another radioman got a quart-sized jar of his mother's home-canned cherries. The way he hopped around Paradise Lost that day, you'd have thought it was a fifth of whiskey. He told us he was going to get drunk on Christmas Eve, and, by golly, he did. We thought he'd lost his brains and got into the torpedo juice, but it was his mom's home-canned cherries. They were preserved, all right—in bourbon. My mother never would have thought of that. The only time she allowed booze in the house was when the doctor prescribed it for my dad: "Two or three straight swallows at night, to improve the appetite."

A couple of days before New Year's, the base commander's yeoman came running into the radio shack. He hollered at me, "Daves! Daves! Guess what! You made chief!" I thought it was a prank until I saw the papers. Everybody said the only reason I got that promotion was because the war was creating so many new openings. They called me a "Tojo Chief."[17] I suppose that was an insult, but—guess what?—I didn't care. It nearly doubled my pay.

It would have been a lot nicer if I'd had some place to spend all that extra money at Cold Bay, but there were no stores or taverns or anything like that. Heck, I couldn't even spend my uniform allowance. The Navy gave me a voucher for three hundred dollars, which was enough for several sets of chief petty officer uniforms in all the different colors. The one I really wanted was aviation green. You weren't entitled to wear that color unless you flew—all those search-and-destroy missions with Fish were good for something—but there were no uniform shops either.

There were only five or six other chief petty officers at Cold Bay at that time. When they heard I made chief, they gathered up all the different pieces of the uniform I needed. It didn't bother me to wear hand-me-downs, but those guys were so much taller and heavier than I was. The jacket, the pants, the shirt—everything was two or three sizes too big for me. The only part that fit was the hat. I knew I looked ridiculous; I felt like a little kid playing dress-up. Maybe that's why I didn't get the usual initiation for a new chief petty officer. I guess they thought I'd been humiliated enough.

Shortly after I made chief, the base commander called me to his office. This was the first time he'd ever spoken to me, one-on-one. I thought I was in trouble. When he said, "Congratulations," I thought it was for making chief. That wasn't it either. He just wanted to tell me that I was leaving Cold Bay. He didn't know why, but, for some reason, I had orders to report to the naval air station on Kodiak. Immediately. Well, that was funny. Kodiak was an island in the Gulf of Alaska, less than five hundred miles east of us on the Aleutian Peninsula. But there was no way for me to get to Kodiak. Not in January. None of our planes were flying in the fog, and there were no Navy ships in the area at that time. Lucky for me, that base commander at Cold Bay really did have a lot of connections with the civilian boat captains in the Aleutians. He radioed the captain of the *Algonquin* and called in a favor. I boarded that ship to Kodiak the very next day.[18]

See Time Line, page 262, and Historical Notes, page 264.

20

KODIAK

January Through December 1944

The *Algonquin* was about half the size and speed of a destroyer, but we still should have made it to Kodiak in two days. I'm sure we would have if we hadn't run into a storm in the Gulf of Alaska. I wouldn't call it a typhoon. It wasn't even as bad as a williwaw, but it was a pretty good storm. The winds really slowed us down, and on a ship that small, you could really feel the waves. I don't know why I didn't get seasick. At least ten guys did, and that was over half the crew. The rest of us went belowdeck and played poker with the captain for the next four days and nights.

I've never had such good luck at cards in my life. In one hand of five-card draw, I was dealt ace, king, queen, and jack, all in spades. Lo and behold, I drew the joker. That gave me a royal flush, the highest hand you can get in poker. Luckier still, nobody folded. Everybody at the table must have thought he had the winning hand, so the bet came around to me several times. I just kept raising and tried to look worried until they called. There was over eight hundred dollars in the pot. I even got to keep most of it. We were only a couple of hours out of Kodiak at the time.

The harbor at Kodiak was full of destroyers. I didn't need to wait for a jeep at that dock, because the base was right on the water. I saw lots of snow on the ground, but none of that awful wind or fog. Compared to Cold Bay, this was the tropics. The base was about ten times bigger, too, with all kinds of shops and stores.[1] First thing I did was find the one that sold uniforms. I bought my first chief's uniform that actually fit. And then I hit the coffee shop. I was surprised at the prices on the menu: A cheeseburger cost thirty-five cents. Everything was about twice as much as you'd expect to pay in a restaurant on the mainland, but even that was okay. I hadn't had a burger and fries for so long, I would have paid a quarter just for the smell.

The radio shack on Kodiak was next to the runways. All the planes I saw taking off and landing were Navy, but they weren't carrier bombers or fighters. They were PBYs. I did see a few other planes with Army Air Force markings, all parked in plain sight outside the hangars. The radiomen said they were too damaged or obsolete to fly in combat. They were just decoys, for drawing the first fire from a Japanese carrier attack. No one thought this was very likely, and they didn't seem too worried about an enemy invasion on the ground either. According to the radio gang at Kodiak, the only major threat to us in Alaska at that time were the Japanese submarines.[2] I was kind of looking forward to flying submarine search-and-destroy missions out of Kodiak on a PBY—they were a lot bigger and faster than the Kingfishers at Cold Bay—and I was really disappointed when the communications officer told me I couldn't. He didn't need any more gunners. What he needed was an assistant communications officer, and I was it. My official job title was NCOIC, for "noncommissioned officer in charge."

Lieutenant Commander Meeker was the commissioned officer in charge. Everybody liked him, but we called him "Beeker." That's how it sounded when he said his name. He had a chronic sinus condition, from allergies or something. Meeker's worst problem was that he didn't know squat about the latest technology in communications equipment. He'd been in the reserves for years before he got called up to active duty because of the war. I'm guessing the Navy assigned me to assist him because I was less than a year out of Radio Materiel School. I was okay with that. In fact, I liked being Meeker's right arm. He gave me a lot of authority over the lower-ranking enlisted men, and he seldom interfered with my decisions. We got along just fine.

The one thing Meeker could not give me was a thirty-day leave. Wanting to go home and get married was not an emergency, and those were the only kind of leaves the base commander at Kodiak was approving at that time. I did get the job of escorting a prisoner to Seattle. I don't know what that poor sailor did, but he was handcuffed to my wrist when we boarded the plane, and the key stayed in my pocket the whole trip. I couldn't even let him go to the bathroom by himself. We made small talk during the flight; he seemed like a really nice guy. Probably got drunk and hurt somebody in a fight. I didn't ask. I just turned him over to the Shore Patrol at Sand Point and called Adeline.

Her boss at Fort Wright was even nicer than mine. He gave her three days off, and she caught the next flight to Seattle from Spokane. I was out pacing on the runway when that DC-3 came in with one engine on fire. I will never, ever forget that sight. I truly thought her plane was going to explode before it touched down, and there was absolutely nothing I could do to stop it. I just watched and prayed and praised God when it did not. Adeline asked why I was shaking when she hugged me. I told her I was just nervous. I was afraid she would never fly again if she knew the truth.

We spent the next three days together in Seattle. I would have preferred to spend the nights with her, too, but she said, "No, Ray. We're not married yet." So then I offered to buy a marriage license and find a justice of the peace, but she wouldn't go for that either. Adeline wanted a regular church wedding in her hometown. There was no sense arguing with that girl, especially when I knew she was right. We stayed in separate hotel rooms.

I got another special assignment as soon as I returned to duty in Kodiak. Meeker wanted me to start meeting the planes that brought in the USO entertainers. About once a month, they came and put on a show for us. I never saw any big movie stars like Bob Hope—I heard he was there before I got to Kodiak—but I sure did see a lot of other comedians and pretty girls.[3] I helped them get their luggage off the plane, showed them to their quarters, and gave them tours of the base. Sometimes I stayed backstage in case they needed anything during the shows. The way those sailors hooted and whistled, you'd have thought the girls were strippers. They most definitely were not. They were just a bunch of really nice girls who could sing and dance. Not one of them ever acted like she was offended, though. I guess they were used to it. I'm sure the USO girls realized that there were probably a lot of guys in the audience who hadn't seen their wives or girlfriends since the war started.

Thirty-day leaves were fairly rare during the war, no matter where you were stationed. If you weren't sick or injured—or lucky enough to survive when your ship went down—you might get a day or two on liberty now and then, and that's all. So I really don't know how Meeker managed to get one for me in late February, but he sure did. I grabbed my seabag and caught the next plane out of Kodiak before the base commander could change his mind. I landed in Seattle on a Wednesday night, called Adeline, and asked her if she still wanted to get married. She picked me up from the airport in Spokane on Thursday morning. She said she already had her dress, and she'd already spent most of my poker winnings from the *Algonquin* on silverware for her hope chest. There wasn't much left for me to buy her a wedding ring, but she thought it was pretty. If you held it up to the light just right, you could almost see the diamond.

There was considerable discussion about the wedding cake. What with the wartime sugar rationing, Adeline's mother had to call several bakeries before she found one with enough sugar on hand to make the frosting. I couldn't understand why she was so riled up. She had all day Friday to phone all the friends and relatives she wanted to come to the wedding on Saturday. I don't re-member much about the ceremony, but I know that we spent our first night together at a hotel in Spokane and boarded a train in the morning. I did pay extra for a berth in the sleeping car that time, and, oh yes, we had a beautiful trip, all the way to Arkansas. I'm sure the scenery was nice, too.

My parents picked us up at the train station in Little Rock. I thought it might be a little awkward when they met Adeline for the first time, but it really wasn't. She just melted right into my family. The only thing that made me nervous was when she started talking politics with my dad. I should have warned her about that. Dad was a real strong Democrat, and so was every-body he knew. One of the biggest newspapers in the state was called the *Arkansas Democrat,* so that tells you something. Well, Adeline thought the Republicans were better. I held my breath when she asked him, "So, A.V., just what would a person do if they weren't a Democrat in this part of the country?" I was shocked when he said, "You'd keep your damn mouth shut, that's what!" But then he winked at her, and they both burst out laughing. As far as Mom and I knew, this was the first time any-body had ever disagreed with A. V. Daves on politics and made him laugh at the same time.

We spent the rest of my leave going to one family reunion af-ter another. All of the relatives in Vilonia and Conway and Little Rock wanted to meet Adeline and wish us well. The most special day for my mother was when she had all seven of her kids home at once. Five of us were in uniform. A lot of families had that many or more in the military during the war, so there was noth-ing unusual about that. It was just rare to see all five of us to-gether in the same place on the same day. Verna was on liberty from the Army hospital in Hot Springs; Lloyd and Velton were in the Army, too. They were both expecting to ship out for Eu-rope in a week or so. Our younger brother Max followed me into the Navy. He was fresh out of boot camp. We all swore not to talk about the war while Mom was around, and we didn't. But she still cried some that day.

An American family in uniform during World War II. From left, Ray Daves, 23, Navy; Velton Daves, 26, Army Air Force; Verna Daves, 30, Army Nurse Corps; Lloyd Daves, 28, Army; Max Daves, 17, Navy. Vilonia, Arkansas, March 1944. COURTESY OF RAY DAVES COLLECTION.

Adeline was crying when I left her with her parents on my way back to Kodiak. I thought it would be easier to be away from her after we were married, but it was worse. Much worse. I don't believe I ever cursed the war as much as I did then. The only thing that kept me from going crazy was the work that piled up on my desk while I was gone. Some of the reports I had to write required the signature of a commissioned officer, so Meeker got the base commander to make me an ensign. He called it a field commission. There was no ceremony, and my job didn't change. I just got paid more for it. And then I had to go out and buy another set of uniforms. Commissioned officers' jackets had six buttons instead of eight.[4] If you define a mustang as an enlisted man who gets promoted to commissioned officer, then I guess I was a mustang. I never thought so, because I didn't take officer's training and I didn't go to Annapolis. And, besides that, it was only temporary. Meeker made it real clear to me that I'd get busted right back to chief petty officer if I ever left Alaska. He knew darn good and well that I had already put in a request for transfer to a base on the West Coast.

About a month after I made ensign, Meeker called me into his office and told me to shut the door. That was pretty unusual, so I knew something was up. He said we were getting a new radioman on our staff at Kodiak, and he was colored. "Colored" or "Negro" was how the Navy referred to African Americans at the time. Meeker wanted to know if I had a problem with that. I was shocked. I didn't know what to say. I couldn't think what I had ever said or done that would cause my commanding officer to ask me such a question. But then I realized he didn't really mean to insult me. He just made the mistake of assuming I was prejudiced because I was from the South.

Well, I have to admit, there was such a thing as Jim Crow laws in the southern states.[5] We even had one in my hometown. Believe it or not, it was against the law in Vilonia, Arkansas, for "colored" folks to be out on the streets after dark. My dad told me that. But he also said that this law had never been enforced, so far as he knew. If anybody had ever tried to, I think Dad would have organized the protest. My parents didn't believe in any of that racist nonsense, and they wouldn't tolerate it from any of us kids. I guess it all depends on how you're raised.

As far as I know, the newest member of the radio gang at Kodiak was the first and only African American on the whole base, and I was the first to meet with him on the day he reported for duty in the spring of 1944. He was a third class petty officer, just graduated from radio school. He seemed a little nervous about that, too. I told him not to worry. All I cared about was whether he could carry his share of the weight as a Navy radioman. He thought he could. He said he used to be a chef at some fancy restaurant in New York City until he got drafted. We had a pretty good laugh about that. He knew as well as I did that the Navy was just getting used to training African Americans for something besides cooking.[6] So what does the Navy do when they get a really high-class civilian chef? Why, send him off to radio school, of course. We couldn't either of us figure that out, unless maybe it was because the Navy needed radiomen more than they needed gourmet cooking at the time. Whatever. I gave him a shift, told him to do his job, and let me know if anybody gave him any grief.

I never got to be friends with that man—the Navy frowned on socializing between the commissioned and noncommissioned officers at Kodiak—so I can't say what it was like for him outside of the radio shack. I do know that he bunked with all the other enlisted radiomen, and I saw him eating and talking with them in the mess hall.[7] I heard he wasn't much of a poker player, but he really was a talented chef. On his days off, he would walk down to the docks and fish for salmon. Whenever he caught one, he cooked it up and shared it with us. The regular cooks let him have the run of the mess hall kitchen any time he felt like it. I suppose they thought it was a privilege to watch how he seasoned all the different dishes. He was a darned good radioman, too.

I was still at the base on Kodiak when we heard about the D-Day in France. To us, this was no more or less important than all the other D-days we'd had with the Japanese all over the Pacific since the attack on Pearl Harbor. The first day of any military offensive was called D-day. I didn't begin to pay extra attention to this one until I saw the numbers.[8] And I just knew my brothers were there. All summer long, I was looking at the casualty reports from Europe, and I was scared to open my mother's letters. I was afraid that she would tell me Lloyd or Velton had been killed in action. She didn't know if they were dead or alive for months after D-Day. There was no news from either of them until she finally started getting letters again in the fall. They couldn't tell her where they were, of course. The family just assumed they were on the move with the Army, somewhere in France or Belgium.[9]

I wasn't allowed to tell anyone what I was doing in Kodiak that summer either. Our business with the Russians was still a pretty big secret at the time. I never quite got used to seeing their planes touch down on our runway. There were usually about a dozen Russian pilots on board, and Meeker assigned me to meet them, too. After I showed them to their quarters, we usually had dinner together in the officers' mess. It was my responsibility to make sure none of those Russian officers walked around the base without an escort. It was an odd situation for them and for us. We knew we were allies against the Germans, but I don't think either of us knew if we were really "good" allies. I'm guessing their orders were exactly the same as mine: "Be cordial; be careful; make small talk."

As soon as the Russian pilots were trained to fly our bombers and fighters, somebody painted over the American markings, slapped on the Soviet Union's red star, and off they went. I have no idea how many planes we handed over to them while I was at Kodiak. Hundreds, at least. Maybe thousands.[10]

The only Russian officer I got to know fairly well was "Lieutenant B.B." He wasn't supposed to give me his full name. B.B. was one of the few who spoke English fluently, and also one of the few who came to Kodiak more than once. It was kind of a strange friendship, I guess. When he and I had dinner together, we talked about our wives and families back home, and how much we wished the war was over so we could see them. I was surprised when he slipped and told me that the Russians knew about our new radar equipment. The Kodiak radar was really state of the art in 1944. We could pick up a formation of planes halfway between Hawaii and Alaska. When my Russian friend asked permission to see it, I had to say sorry. I couldn't even show him which building it was in. I think I made it up to him, though: I took him backstage after a USO show. He got such a kick out of that, he let me take his picture with the girls. After that, he even told me to go ahead and take one of him with all the other pilots as they were leaving. I have never known if Lieutenant B.B survived the war; I have always hoped that he did.[11]

I wish I could have gotten a picture of President Roosevelt. My dad would have loved that, but I didn't even know the President was on Kodiak until after he was gone. He must have come by ship—I'm sure I would have seen him if he'd landed on our runway. Nobody I knew caught so much as a glimpse of him, coming or going, so it must have been a pretty low-key event.[12] I never idolized FDR as much as my parents did, but I did think he was a great Commander in Chief during the war. I would have voted for him if I'd had a chance. I don't believe anyone in the radio gang at Kodiak was a registered voter in the fall of 1944. If it was possible for us to vote in that election, the word never got around.[13]

I did do a little bit of sightseeing on Kodiak, thanks to the hunting guides on that island. I got acquainted with several of them while they were out on the runway, waiting for the com-

An American bomber, recently painted with the USSR's red star, was one of thousands transferred to the Soviet Air Force during World War II. All photos of these transactions were forbidden by both countries until July 1944. (In this group of Russian officers and pilots at Naval Air Station Kodiak, Alaska, "Lt. B.B." is second from right May 1944.) COURTESY OF RAY DAVES COLLECTION.

mercial planes to bring in another batch of tourists. One guide invited me to spend a liberty at his hunting lodge. I wasn't interested in going out with the tourists that came to hunt the Kodiak bears—never saw the point of killing any animal that I didn't plan to eat—but I did take advantage of the free room and board, and it was fun to walk around the town. Kodiak Town was very small. It reminded me of my hometown in Arkansas, and so did the school. The children were outside for recess, and they all wanted to come and talk to me. Their teacher was close by. She said it was good for them to practice their English on somebody from the mainland. The kids were very curious. I don't think they were used to seeing sailors in the residential part of town. When I told them it hardly ever snows in Arkansas, they thought I was joking.

My request for transfer to the West Coast came through in

A hunting guide displays hide of a Kodiak bear at his hunting lodge, Kodiak, Alaska, 1944. COURTESY OF RAY DAVES COLLECTION.

December.[14] The Navy had an opening for an instructor at the radio school in San Diego, and I took it. I knew it meant a cut in rank and pay—from ensign back to chief petty officer—but I didn't care. If they wanted to bust me down to apprentice seaman, with leggings, I probably would have said okay. It's not that I didn't like my job on Kodiak. I really did, and the weather was pretty mild, too, for Alaska. I just wanted to be somewhere closer to my bride. I was in San Diego when I called her on New Year's Eve.

See Time Line, page 266, and Historical Notes, page 270.

21

VICTORY DAYS

January 1 Through August 28, 1945

I did not ask Adeline to quit her job at Fort Wright and move to California. That was her call. Had I known how hard it was to find off-base housing in San Diego, I would have tried to talk her out of it. If I'd been a high-ranking commissioned officer, the Navy would have provided living quarters for both of us, but enlisted men and their wives were on their own, and, I swear, every single apartment building in that city was full. People were renting out their spare bedrooms and garages for twenty-five dollars a month.[1] I actually thought Adeline and I were going to have to set up housekeeping in somebody's garage until I called Mr. and Mrs. Driver. I knew them from boot camp—they used to treat us sailors to Sunday barbecues in their backyard—and I knew they had a guest room in their house. When I asked if we could rent it, Mr. Driver said no way. He insisted that we move in and live with his family for free.

Difficult as it was to find housing in San Diego during the war, civilian jobs were just the opposite. There were so many openings for secretaries, Adeline could take her pick.[2] She chose the Navy. They put her on the staff of some admiral on North Island and paid her nearly three hundred dollars a month for typing his memoirs. That was about twice what I was making as a chief petty officer. I should have known it was too good to last. As soon as I finished the three-month training course for radio school instructors, I got travel orders to Mississippi. I didn't even know the Navy had a base on the Gulf of Mexico.[3]

I had two weeks to report for duty as an instructor at the Naval Training Center in Gulfport, Mississippi. I didn't expect Adeline to go with me, but that's what she wanted, and she wanted us to take her car. Well, a road trip from California to Mississippi did sound like fun, but it wasn't possible because of the gas rationing. You couldn't buy a gallon of gas without a token from the government. It would have taken us months to save up enough tokens to drive halfway across the country. Everybody hoarded their tokens during the war. If you had more than you needed, you traded them with your neighbors for extra coffee or sugar coupons. All that stuff was rationed, too. Adeline didn't see this as a problem. She just called her mother in Spokane and told her to start wheeling and dealing. I guess she did. When we left San Diego, Adeline had a whole purse full of tokens from her mother. And she was so mad when it turned out that we didn't really need them after all. Most of the gas stations wouldn't take our tokens because I was in uniform. Some of the owners were so patriotic they wouldn't even take our money. Well, that turned it into a game. Whenever we gassed up, right before we drove away, Adeline would sneak in and leave a little pile of tokens next to the cash register.

We listened to the war news on the car radio. The Allied armies were crossing the border into Germany, but there was no mention of the Nazi concentration camps they were finding along the way. I don't think that was reported until some time in April or May. I'm sure I did not hear the word "Holocaust" to describe what the Nazis did to all those millions of people until after the war was over.[4]

There were no official reports of kamikazes at that time either, but there were plenty of rumors going around. Before I even left Kodiak, I'd heard talk of Japanese suicide pilots in the Philippines. By the time I got to San Diego, everybody was talking about the kamikazes. It was said there were hundreds of them crashing into our warships all over the Pacific.[5] I hoped that was an exaggeration. I suspected it was not, especially when I saw the casualty lists from the Marines on Iwo Jima. They took that island, too, of course, but it looked like they must have had to kill the entire enemy army in the process. I gathered that it was still the Japanese soldiers' custom to commit suicide rather than surrender.[6]

You could turn off the radio, but you couldn't forget about the war. Every time Adeline and I stopped somewhere to eat, half the items on the menu were crossed out because of the food shortages. The better cuts of meat were hardly ever available in the civilian restaurants. I couldn't believe it when I saw steak on the menu at this small town in Texas. I thought it was a mistake, but the waiter insisted that it wasn't. They really did have top sirloin. I didn't mean for him to hear me tell Adeline it was probably horsemeat. The waiter threw a fit. He said, "Sir, this is a very respectable restaurant, and we don't serve horsemeat!" I apologized and ordered the steak. Raved to the waiter about how great it tasted. I could eat anything if I had enough ketchup. I'm pretty sure it was horsemeat.

The base at Gulfport was almost as big as the town, so the housing shortage was actually worse than in San Diego. Even the garages were taken. The closest we could get to the Naval Training Center was in the town of Pass Christian. We got lucky there. We found an apartment for rent in a two-story house, right on the beach. Our landlady lived on the main floor; we had the whole upstairs to ourselves. And not only did we have a beautiful view of the Gulf of Mexico, Mrs. Kristovich treated us like family. She let us use her kitchen any time we wanted. Adeline and I often wondered whatever happened to her husband and whether or not she had any children, but she never talked about them. I'm not sure if Mrs. Kristovich was Jewish. Her accent sounded a lot like Russian to me. All she told us was that she came to America from Poland.

President Roosevelt died shortly after I started teaching at the Navy's radio school in Gulfport. That was a terrible shock for all of us—FDR had been in office for so long, he was more like a king than a politician—but my first concern was for my dad. Roosevelt was such a hero to him, I knew his death would hit him hard. As for me and most of the guys I worked with, we were mainly wondering what, if any, changes the new president might order for the Navy. Well, there were none, so far as I could tell. The base lowered all the flags to half-staff for several days. I don't recall any other special observance. We knew we had a new Commander in Chief, and his name was Harry Truman. But the war went on, same as before. I was beginning to think it would last forever.

In May, I was on my way home from work when I got caught in a traffic jam in downtown Gulfport. All the cars had stopped, right in the middle of the intersection, and everybody was honking their horns. I assumed it was a traffic accident, until I saw all the drivers get out and hug each other. And then I saw what appeared to be an impromptu parade: Hundreds of people walking arm in arm down the middle of the street, toward the town square. That's when I turned on the car radio. I really had to crank up the volume to get the news: The Germans had surrendered. The war in Europe was over. I hurried home to tell Adeline, but I guess she already knew. I found her and our landlady together in the kitchen. They were giggling and pouring this reddish-brown, syrupy liquid into tiny little glasses. The bottle had a fancy-looking label and a real long neck. I knew it was some kind of booze. Mrs. Kristovich called it a "liqueur." She said she was saving it for a real special occasion, and this was it. So we clinked our glasses and toasted V-E Day with Mrs. Kristovich. That was the eighth of May.

The next day was not a national holiday. Adeline and I both went to work as usual. It was good to be down to one war instead of two, but the Japanese were fighting harder than ever in

the Pacific. I saw the casualty estimates from both sides on Okinawa, and they were even higher than Iwo Jima.[7] Word was just
beginning to leak out that we were going to invade Japan itself in
the fall. According to the scuttlebutt I heard around the base, the
Navy was planning to deliver something like a quarter of a million troops to one of Japan's home islands on the first of November. If that was true, it would be an even bigger operation than
the D-Day invasion of France the year before. I couldn't imagine
such numbers, and I couldn't imagine how many ships it would
take. I just knew I would be on one of them.[8]

I expected to be rotated back into the combat zone in the Pacific eventually, but for the time being I was with Adeline, and
we were comfortable in our little apartment on the beach. It was
completely furnished. The only thing we did not have was an
alarm clock. I don't know why that bothered her so much. I just
got one of the other radio school instructors to call me every
morning and wake me up in time to go to work. If we didn't
hear the phone ringing downstairs, Mrs. Kristovich came up and
banged on our bedroom door. She never complained about that,
but Adeline thought we should have our own alarm clock. I was
amazed when she came back empty-handed. Not one store in
Gulfport or Pass Christian had any brand of alarm clock for sale.

What really put a bee in Adeline's bonnet for an alarm clock
was when she started her new job as a secretary for the Merchant
Marine in Pass Christian.[9] She did not like depending on wake-
up calls from her coworkers. She was always afraid she would be
late to work. So Adeline sat down and wrote this long letter to
the Westclox company. She told them why we needed an alarm
clock to get to our jobs in the military, and couldn't we just buy
one straight from the factory. Well, that got results. The manager
wrote back and said he was sorry. He couldn't sell us a new
clock, because Westclox didn't make them any more. They were
too busy making timers for the fuses on the bombs. The best he
could do was send us a used Baby Ben.[10]

For the rest of that summer, Adeline and I prayed that the
war in the Pacific would end before I got orders to ship out. We

started going to church every Sunday, and we prayed together every night before we went to bed. I thought our prayers were answered when I heard about the bomb. I didn't know we had such a powerful weapon, but, according to the newspaper, one atomic bomb had just destroyed an entire Japanese city.[11] I was thrilled. For the first time since Midway, I actually believed that the war was over. Surely the Japanese would surrender now. The newspaper did not say how many people died in the city of Hiroshima.[12] At that time, I didn't really care. What mattered to me was all the American soldiers and Marines and sailors, including me, who would not die during the invasion of Japan in November. I did not want to see another burial at sea for as long as I lived.

I was so certain that President Truman would announce the end of the war that day, I let my students at the radio school monitor all the civilian frequencies. I wanted to hear it "live." Well, there was no presidential announcement on the radio. Not that day, or the next, or even the day after that. We were still at war. I was the opposite of thrilled when the newspaper said a second atom bomb had just destroyed another Japanese city. It was just depressing and sad to think of all that death and destruction. I went back to believing that the war would go on forever. We were picking up rumors from the ships in the Pacific Fleet, but I was afraid to get my hopes up again. I didn't believe any of the happy talk until I heard it from the President himself. He went on the radio and told the whole country that Japan had surrendered.

I could have gone to a dozen parties on the base that day. There were V-J celebrations breaking out all over Gulfport. Adeline said it was pretty wild in Pass Christian, too. I didn't feel like partying. I just wanted to go home. When I drove up to the house, Adeline and Mrs. Kristovich were out on the front porch with a pitcher of lemonade. They made sandwiches; we sat up late and watched the fireworks over the water. Every car that went by had its horn honking, and the people were hanging out the windows, waving the flag, whooping and hollering. We could also hear the music from the bandstand in the park down the road. It was all patriotic songs at first, like "The Star Spangled Banner" and "America the Beautiful," but then it turned into dance music. There must have been several bands; they were still going strong when we called it a night. That was the fourteenth of August.

I don't think it hit me that the war was truly over until about two weeks later, when the communications officer at Gulfport told me I was free to leave the Navy. He explained the point system: Everybody who was in the military during the war got a certain number of points for however long you were on active duty. You got extra points for going overseas; they tacked on a few more for the number of days you were in combat. I don't remember how many points I had altogether. According to the communications officer, it was more than anyone else on that base, so he had no choice but to offer me the first discharge from Gulfport. And then he tried to talk me into staying in the Navy.

The base commander at Gulfport promised to reinstate my status as a commissioned officer. At the very least, he said that the Navy would make me an ensign again. They might even bump me up a notch, to lieutenant, junior grade. All I had to do was agree to one year of duty overseas. I actually considered that until he told me where. It was in the Marshall Islands, at a base called Eniwetok. Well, I'd already heard the rumors about that place. According to the scuttlebutt, this was where the military was planning to test more of those atomic bombs.[13] I wanted nothing to do with that. It wasn't because I was afraid of radiation poisoning. I didn't know there was such a thing then. I was just sick of being around bombs in general. I said, "No, thanks. I'll take my discharge now."[14]

I had to sign a lot of papers that day. One said I'd been in the Navy for six years, four months, and eighteen days. That was wrong. According to my watch, it was six years, four months, seventeen days, sixteen hours, and forty-two seconds. I signed it anyway. And then I called Adeline. I felt kind of bad about asking her to quit her job and move again, but she sounded happy.

I guess she was ready to go home, too. By the time I got to our house in Pass Christian that day, she had all of our suitcases and boxes stacked out on the front porch. Of course, we didn't have that much to begin with. Adeline probably spent more time saying goodbye to Mrs. Kristovich than she did packing. It was close to sunset when we left Mississippi. The Gulf of Mexico was even more beautiful in my rearview mirror.

We spent our first night as civilians at a hotel in downtown Little Rock. Adeline was never in the military, but she was a war veteran, too. I doubt if I would have made it through the war years without her. So when she asked me to dance with her in the hotel ballroom that night, I danced. I still wasn't much of a dancer, and it felt really strange to be out of uniform in public, but I was not sorry for my decision. I wouldn't even say that I was sorry for joining the Navy in the first place. I was looking for an education, and that's exactly what I got. There was a lot I wish I'd never learned—an awful lot I wish I could forget—but no one will ever hear me say that I hated the Navy. I just hated the war.

See Time Line, page 272, and Historical Notes, page 275.

EPILOGUE

I probably would have stayed in Little Rock if I hadn't married a girl from the Northwest. We both wanted to be close to our families, but I'd been away from home for almost ten years. I was used to it. Adeline was not. So that was our first big decision after the war—to settle in Spokane—and I was in a terrific hurry to get there and find a job in the fall of 1945. Everybody knew there were millions of guys on their way home from overseas at that time. You didn't have to be a genius to figure out what that would do to the competition for jobs in the civilian world.

My oldest brother, Lloyd, beat me home by several months. He was with one of the tank battalions in France until the Army gave him a medical discharge. The Army doctors didn't know what was wrong with him, and it was years later before we found out that he had leukemia. Lloyd died in 1952. My brother Max got a medical discharge from the Navy. They sent him home with a broken eardrum, from standing around those big guns on the warships a little too long, I suppose. Velton had to

U. S. Air Force — Aerospace Power For Peace . . .

FAIRCHILD Times

The FAIRCHILD TIMES is an unofficial newspaper published weekly in the interests of personnel at Fairchild Air Force Base of the Strategic Air Command. It is published by the TIMES PUBLISHING COMPANY, Morgan at 9th, Davenport, Washington 99122, RA 5-3141, a private firm in no way connected with the Department of the Air Force. Opinions expressed by the publishers and writers are their own and are not to be considered an official expression by the Department of the Air Force. The appearance of advertisements in this publication including supplements and inserts, does not constitute an endorsement by the Department of the Air Force of the products or services advertised.

Vol. 22—No. 28   Spokane, Washington,   Friday, October 31, 1969

Civilian air traffic controller Ray Daves, 49, displays a Halloween sense of humor in the control tower at Spokane International Airport, October 31, 1969. COURTESY OF RAY DAVES COLLECTION.

"HEY FELLAS, LOOK AT THIS," cries air traffic controller crew chief Ray Daves as he sights an "unidentified" flying object on the radar screen. Witches are expected to be circling Fairchild and joining young "trick-or-treaters" as they canvass the neighborhoods in search of goodies. (U.S. Air Force Photo

stay in the Army Air Force for another year or so after the war. He was in Tokyo, serving with the occupation forces.[1]

Thanks to Adeline's connections with the Army in Spokane, I got my first civilian job at Fort George Wright. They hired me to check the pay records for guys who thought the Army owed them more than what they got with their discharge papers. I did the research to prove if they were right or wrong. In the majority of cases I handled, the Army was right. It was not a fun job. I wanted something better, and I found it in the spring of 1946. That's when I started as an air traffic controller for the CAA.[2] No question about it, being a radioman on an aircraft carrier was perfect training for the control tower. I was not at all surprised that so many other civilian air traffic controllers were Navy radiomen during the war. Some of us had more experience with tracking planes on radar than others, but

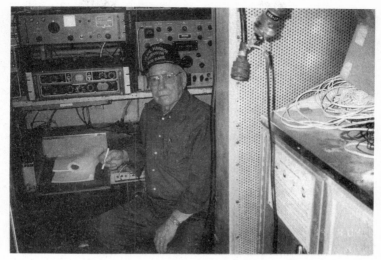

Former Navy radioman Ray Daves, 84, visits the radio room of the restored World War II submarine Cavalla *(SS-244), Galveston, Texas, April 2004. ("It's very similar to the* Dolphin's," *says Daves.)* COURTESY OF RAY DAVES COLLECTION.

we all knew how to carry on a conversation with several pilots at once.

Adeline went back to her old job as a secretary for the Army at Fort Wright. They were glad to have her, but she didn't stay long. It was her choice to quit working outside the home when we had our first child. Rayma was born in 1946.[3] Three years later, we had Janet. She was barely forty when she died of cancer. That was an awful blow to the whole family, especially her husband and children, but the Bible says I'll see her again in heaven, and I do believe that. In 2007, Adeline and I celebrated our sixty-third wedding anniversary. To me, she is as beautiful as the day we met at the CCC camp in Idaho when I was sixteen. She still has the music box, the compact, the purple velvet bathrobe, and most of the letters I wrote during the war years. We have five grandchildren and five great-grandchildren, so far.

The veterans hospital in Spokane has treated me well. I had

The American Defense Service Medal. All U.S. Navy, Coast Guard, and Marine personnel on active duty for any length of time from September 8, 1939, through December 7, 1941, were eligible for this medal. (U.S. Army and Army Air Force personnel who were on active duty for at least 12 months during that period of time were also eligible.) COURTESY OF CAROL EDGEMON HIPPERSON COLLECTION (PHOTO BY TINA McGOVERN).

back surgery to fix more of the damage from the accident with the generator at Cold Bay. I've also had surgery to remove some precancerous spots on my face and neck. The doctors said I got them from spending too much time in the sun, probably from all those months I was out on the catwalk watching planes take off and land on the *Yorktown* (CV 5) in the South Pacific. The Navy didn't issue sunscreen to anybody in the Coral Sea. Other than that, I'm in pretty good health. I'm sure this has a lot to do with the fact that I never smoked while I was at sea. I quit smoking altogether a few years after I got out of the Navy. I haven't had a cigarette in fifty years.

I bought my first life insurance policy in boot camp. The Navy gave me the option to drop it or convert it to something called twenty-pay life when I took my discharge. All I had to do was keep paying the premium, and after twenty years it would start paying me. Best investment I ever made. Every September for the past forty years or so, I've got a check in the mail for $170. I love it. I'll be eighty-seven in June 2007. I've collected thousands of dollars more from that Navy life insurance policy than I ever paid into it.

I retired from the FAA in 1974, but I still copy Morse code.

The American Campaign Medal. Eligible recipients included all U.S. military personnel who served for an aggregate period of at least one year—December 7, 1941, through March 2, 1946—within the continental United States. COURTESY OF CAROL EDGEMON HIPPERSON COLLECTION (PHOTO BY TINA McGOVERN).

I have a ten-channel receiver sitting next to the typewriter in my home. About once a week, I sit down and practice typing what I hear. I'm not nearly as fast as I used to be in the Navy, but it's good brain exercise. And I still like to hunt and fish. Whenever I catch a salmon, I cut that sucker down the middle to see if he's got the wallet I lost in the latrine on the way to Treasure Island. In the fall, I go deer hunting with some friends along the Canadian border. At the end of the day, we come back to the cabin and play poker all night. I enjoy the game as much as I did in the Navy, but I have never been dealt another royal flush like I got on the *Algonquin.* I guess that only happens once in a lifetime.

I would have traveled coast to coast for a reunion with Scoop or Spic after the war, but I never saw either one of them after we parted company at the submarine base after the attack on Pearl Harbor. I did talk to Scoop's brother. He told me Scoop ended up working for the city of Fresno as an electrical inspector, and that's where he took up golfing. He was in his sixties when he had a heart attack on the golf course and died. What a way to go. I'm glad he was doing something he loved. His brother didn't

The Asiatic-Pacific Campaign Medal. Most U.S. military personnel who served in this geographic region from December 7, 1941, through March 2, 1946, were authorized to receive this medal. COURTESY OF CAROL EDGEMON HIPPERSON COLLECTION (PHOTO BY TINA MCGOVERN).

know how Scoop got his nickname until I told him about the poker games in the barracks at Pearl Harbor. I have no idea what happened to Spic. If he survived the war, I think he would have ended up in one of the technical fields, maybe as a teacher. He had such an analytical mind. Most of my other closest friends in the Navy died in combat.[4]

I suppose everybody has nightmares from the war. Sometimes I wake up on the floor. Adeline always asks why I'm thrashing around and talking in my sleep, but that particular nightmare doesn't come with many details. All I know is, I'm inside the *Dolphin,* and we're crash-diving. There's a Japanese destroyer dropping depth charges on us, and the boat is filling up with water, and I can't get out. Most of my nightmares come from the attack on Pearl Harbor. I'm on the roof of the administration building, the water is on fire, and the air is full of enemy planes and black smoke. I wish I had a nickel for all the times I've dreamed about that Japanese pilot. I know he's dead, but his eyes are open, and he's coming for me. I try to run away, but I can't move my legs. I used to wake up screaming from that one at least once a week. It's been better lately—more like twice a year. I don't know if the nightmares will ever stop altogether.[5]

The Navy Good Conduct Medal. This medal was typically awarded to anyone who received an honorable discharge from the U.S. Navy. (The U.S. Army, Army Air Force, Marines, and Coast Guard issued a similar medal to honorably discharged personnel at the end of World War II.) COURTESY OF CAROL EDGEMON HIPPERSON COLLECTION (PHOTO BY TINA MCGOVERN).

When I first joined the Pearl Harbor Survivors Association, there were over a hundred of us in eastern Washington and northern Idaho. In the late fifties, we started getting together for lunch every other month. Our motto is "Remember Pearl Harbor—Keep America Alert—Eternal Vigilance Is the Price of Liberty." But we never sat around and talked about our memories from December 7, 1941, and we still don't. For me, it's just good to be with people who know exactly how I feel about that day. Our chapter's membership is down to about twenty-five now. In 2005, we started meeting every month instead of every other, and we don't reserve the banquet room in the restaurants anymore. Six or seven of us is considered a big turnout these days. I'm sure that the rest of the chapters around the country are getting smaller, too. In 2008 our youngest member was eighty-three.[6]

I never thought anything like the attack on Pearl Harbor could ever happen again, but it did. September 11 hit me like a mule kick in the gut. I could not hold back the tears. I had flashbacks to Pearl Harbor, and all that fear and anger came flooding through me like it happened yesterday. I got on the phone, called some of the other Pearl Harbor survivors and a few close friends from my church. We prayed for the people who survived the attack on the

The World War II Victory Medal. All U.S. armed forces personnel (as well as those of the Philippines government) who were on active duty at any time between December 7, 1941, through December 31, 1946, were eligible for this medal. COURTESY OF CAROL EDGEMON HIPPERSON COLLECTION (PHOTO BY TINA McGOVERN).

World Trade Center and the Pentagon. I'm guessing they will have nightmares for the rest of their lives, too.[7]

I did not cancel my plane reservation to Hawaii after 9/11. It made me more determined than ever to make it to the sixtieth anniversary ceremonies at Pearl Harbor in 2001. I didn't really want to see my friend George Maybee's name carved in stone on the *Arizona*. For all those years, I think I had myself talked into believing that maybe he survived. It was hard to face the fact that he did not. I didn't cry until somebody handed me a bouquet of roses. One by one, I dropped them all in the water for George. The *Arizona* was his grave.[8]

After the ceremony on the *Arizona*, I saw a small group of Japanese men on shore. They appeared to be about the same age as me. I was told that these were some of the pilots and gunners from the six carriers that attacked us. I guess they needed to come back to Pearl Harbor, too. No one introduced me to them. If they had, I would have been cordial. Sixty years ago, Japan was the U.S. Navy's most powerful enemy, and we would have killed each other on sight. I'm glad that's History. Japan is one of our best friends and most powerful allies in the whole world

The Purple Heart Medal. Anyone in the U.S. armed forces who was wounded or killed by enemy action, died later from wounds caused by enemy action, or sustained illness or injury while a prisoner of war is eligible for the Purple Heart, the nation's oldest military medal. At least 800,000 Purple Hearts have been awarded to World War II veterans or their next of kin to date. COURTESY OF CAROL EDGEMON HIPPERSON COLLECTION (PHOTO BY TINA MCGOVERN).

now. I also know that the attack on Pearl Harbor was not the biggest battle of World War II. Far from it. But to me it will always be the worst, because it was the first, and I was there.

I have never met a Pearl Harbor Survivor who looks forward to December 7 of any year. None of us enjoy recalling what happened that day, but my chapter considers it a duty and a privilege to show up whenever the schools invite us to their assemblies. Sometimes the teachers ask us to come into the classroom and tell the students what we saw. I don't enjoy that either, but I do it anyway. The kids are always very respectful, and they ask a lot of questions. I tell them what I remember, I tell them I was scared to death, and I tell them not to call me a hero. I'm a survivor, and that's all I ever claimed to be.

I just hate it when somebody asks me how many enemy soldiers or sailors I killed during the war. I don't know how to answer that one. I did not pull the trigger on the machine gun on the roof of the administration building at Pearl Harbor. I did locate targets for the *Yorktown*'s pilots, and, yes, I painted my mother's name on some of the bombs and torpedoes that our planes used to sink all those Japanese carriers in the Coral Sea and at Midway. But it wasn't my hand on the release lever that dropped them. And, yes, I flew a lot of search-and-destroy missions in the Aleutian Islands,

Pearl Harbor survivor Ray Daves, March 2008. COURTESY OF ANGELA V. DAVES-BOYETTE.

but I never found a Japanese sub crew in my gunsights. So, in that sense, I could say that I never killed a single living soul. But that's not really the truth, and anyone who was there knows exactly what I mean. Every one of us knows that we were partly responsible for killing hundreds or thousands or millions, depending on where you draw the line between direct and indirect action. It's pretty hard to explain that without telling the whole story of the war.[9]

I never expected any medals from the Navy, and I never filled out any paperwork to get one. But thirty or forty years after I took my discharge, I got a package full of medals in the mail. I have no idea how that happened. I received another medal during the fifty-fifth anniversary of the attack on Pearl Harbor. I didn't ask for that either. In 2001, I got a letter from President Bush. He was out of office then—his son was in the White House—but it was still pretty nice of him to sit down and write to an enlisted man. I didn't always agree with his politics, but I always respected the first President Bush because he was a World War II veteran, same as me. I never met the man, but I know that he was

Chief Radioman Ray Daves, 23, and Adeline Bentz, 24, Euclid Baptist Church, Spokane, Washington, February 26, 1944. (The "dress blue" eight-button jacket indicates chief petty officer; white sparks below eagle on left sleeve indicate specialty is "radioman"; diagonal stripe indicates at least four years' service in the U.S. Navy.) COURTESY OF RAY DAVES COLLECTION.

a carrier pilot. That's what I wanted to be. I have always envied the guys who got to fly more than I did in the Navy.

My last medal did not come in the mail. It was handed to me personally, by the commander of the Navy and Marine Corps Reserve Center in Spokane on December 7, 2002. That was the sixty-first anniversary of the attack on Pearl Harbor. At the end of that ceremony, all of the Survivors were called to step forward. There were over twenty of us that day, and television cameras everywhere. I was embarrassed when the commander called my name. I still have the scar from the shrapnel wound, but I never thought I'd get a medal for it. It would have meant more to me if I'd got the Purple Heart when I was younger. I think that and all the other medals I received from World War II are more important to my grandchildren than they ever were to me.

After a while, you get so you can push it all so far back in your mind, you can almost fool yourself into thinking you don't have any memories. For a long time, I refused to admit that I did. I was afraid of what people would think if I got all teary-eyed,

Ray and Adeline Daves, December 7, 2002, following presentation of the Purple Heart medal he earned at Pearl Harbor, December 7, 1941. COURTESY OF CAROL EDGEMON HIPPERSON COLLECTION.

like I am now. That's kind of embarrassing, too, but in a way it's not. My friends were brave men. They did what had to be done, and they deserve to be remembered as heroes. I don't understand why they got killed and I survived. I still feel guilty about that, sometimes, but I'm not sorry for telling what happened to them and to me during the war. It's a relief to pass it on. I don't have to remember anymore.

See Historical Notes, page 277.

NOTE TO THE READER

The Library of Congress is now collecting and preserving audio and video recordings of interviews with American veterans of *all* wars. Diaries, letters, and photographs dating to World War I, World War II, Korea, Vietnam, the Persian Gulf, Afghanistan, or Iraq are also included in the Veterans History Project collection at the Library of Congress, as are the recorded memories of civilian workers or volunteers who contributed to the war effort.

Any item submitted to the national Veterans History Project must be accompanied by documents contained in the free "field kit" or instruction booklet. For further details, see the Library of Congress Web site: loc.gov/vets. Other points of contact for field kits, information, and guidance available to individuals, schools, and organizations who wish to participate in the nationwide effort to collect and preserve the eyewitness accounts of American war veterans include the following:

Veterans History Project
Library of Congress

101 Independence Avenue, S.E.
Washington, DC 20540-4615

Email: vohp@loc.gov
Telephone: 202-707-4916
Fax: 202-252-2046

> *The real story of what happens when America goes to war will never be found in the memoirs of the politicians or the officers who planned and organized the battles. It's in the memories— and the nightmares—of the young men and women who fought them.*
>
> —Carol Edgemon Hipperson
> Spokane, Washington
> February 14, 2008

TIME LINES AND
HISTORICAL NOTES

CHAPTER 1: THE TREE ARMY

June 1936–September 1937 Time Line

July 12: Sachsenhausen Concentration Camp opens in Germany. *Second of the six large prisons built for Nazi party opponents prior to World War II.*

July 15: League of Nations lifts economic sanctions against Italy. *The fore-runner of the United Nations is unable to stop Italy's invasion of Ethiopia.*

July 17: The Spanish Civil War begins. *Germany and Italy support Spanish fascists' efforts to overthrow Spain's Republican government.*

August 1: The Summer Olympics open in Berlin. *Germany discourages all anti-Jewish speeches and signs during the games.*

August 9: Jesse Owens wins his fourth gold medal in Berlin. *African American track star shows the world that Hitler's claim of Aryan supremacy is a myth.*

August 11: United States declares neutrality toward Spanish Civil War.

October 15: Jewish teachers in Germany are forbidden to teach Aryan chil-dren. *This was one of many Nuremberg Laws passed by Nazi ruling party prior to World War II.*

October 25: Italy and Germany announce alliance, later known as the Rome-Berlin Axis.

November 4: U.S. voters elect Roosevelt to a second term as President. *FDR carried forty-six of the forty-eight states against Republican nominee Alf Landon.*

December 11: British King Edward VIII (1894–1972) abdicates the throne.

December 12: Chinese leader Chiang Kai-shek (1887–1975) declares war on Japan.

1937

May 6: German dirigible *Hindenburg* explodes during landing at Lindenhurst, New Jersey.

May 12: New British King George VI (1895–1952) is crowned at Westminster Abbey.

May 28: Neville Chamberlain becomes Prime Minister of Great Britain.

June 3: Duke of Windsor (former British King Edward VIII) marries Wallis Simpson in France.

July 2: Amelia Earhart, first famous American woman pilot, disappears in the South Pacific. *U.S. Navy ships searched for but never found the plane or her remains.*

July 28: Japanese troops occupy China's capital city, Peking (Beijing.)

August 13: Germany requires all who know a foreign language to register with the government.

Historical Notes

1. The Civilian Conservation Corps, or CCC, was also known as "Roosevelt's Tree Army." This was the first and most popular of President Roosevelt's many New Deal programs. Franklin D. Roosevelt (1882–1945), America's thirty-second president, was often referred to as FDR.

2. Camp Peone in northern Idaho was one of about 4,500 such camps in America. From 1933 to 1942, CCC workers planted approximately 3 billion trees across the nation.

3. The Depression was a worldwide economic crisis, 1929–1939. America's unemployment rate during the Depression years peaked at 24.9 percent in 1933. The CCC employed about 3 million Americans—primarily

young men—until this federal jobs program ended for lack of funding from Congress in 1942.

4. No major army in the world was fully mechanized prior to World War II. The last U.S. Army mule was not retired until 1956, well after the war ended.

5. The invasion of Manchuria by Japanese troops based in Korea was widely reported by the international press in 1931. (Korea was annexed to Japan in 1910.) Japan's civilian government had no prior knowledge of their Army's attack on Chinese territory, which resulted in further loss of civilian control over the Japanese military and Japan's withdrawal from the League of Nations. This Manchurian Incident was the first in a series of international conflicts and events that drew the United States into World War II, the world's first truly global war.

6. "Nazi" is the common shortened form for the National Socialist German Workers Party, formed in Munich, 1919. By 1933, this was the dominant political party in Germany. Nazis blamed the Depression on German Jews, communists, and foreigners. (The series of anti-Jewish laws that were passed in Germany in 1935 are called the Nuremberg Laws.)

7. Former artist and veteran of the defeated German Army of World War I, Adolf Hitler (1889–1945), was elected chairman of the Nazi party in 1921. He was appointed Chancellor of Germany in 1933.

8. H. V. Kaltenborn (1878–1965), was the first major radio network personality to comment, analyze, and give his own opinions on national and international news events. His program was a regular feature on CBS radio from 1927 until he moved to NBC radio in 1940.

9. The British king was Edward VIII (1894–1972). Both the Church of England and Parliament opposed his plan to marry the twice-divorced American woman, Wallis Warfield Simpson. When polls showed that his subjects would not accept her as queen, he announced his decision to give up the throne for "the woman I love." Months later, his younger brother was crowned King George VI.

CHAPTER 2: JOINING THE NAVY

September 1937–mid-April 1939 Time Line

September 30: Aircraft carrier *Yorktown* (CV-5) is commissioned into the U.S. Navy.

December 11: Italy withdraws from the League of Nations. *Germany and Japan withdrew from the League of Nations in 1933.*

December 12: Japanese aircraft bomb and sink U.S. Navy gunboat *Panay* (PR-5) in Yangtze River. *The craft was evacuating neutral American civilians from Nanking, China.*

December 13: The Rape of Nanking. *At least 200,000 Chinese civilians were killed by the invading Japanese Army.*

1938

January 28: President Roosevelt calls for increases in U.S. armed forces.

February 20: Adolf Hitler announces German support for Japan's invasion of China.

March 12: The Anschluss (unification of Austria and Germany) begins. *German forces crossed the border unopposed.*

May 12: Aircraft carrier *Enterprise* (CV-6) is commissioned into service with the U.S. Navy.

May 17: Congress passes Naval Expansion Act, a major increase of U.S. Navy ships and personnel.

June 22: African American heavyweight boxer Joe Louis wins title from German Max Schmeling.

August 8: First Nazi concentration camp in Austria opens at Mauthausen.

September 30: British Prime Minister Neville Chamberlain says, "peace for our time." *The Munich Agreement allows German conquest of Czechoslovakia, unopposed.*

October 1: Germany seizes one-third of Czechoslovakia, the Sudetenland.

October 21: Canton, China, falls to invading Japanese Army.

October 30: "War of the Worlds," a radio drama, causes panic. *Many Americans believe they are under attack by space ships from Mars.*

November 9–10: Kristallnacht (night of glass). *Nazis destroy Jewish shops and synagogues in Germany and Austria.*

November 10: "God Bless America." *Singer Kate Smith gives first public performance of this Irving Berlin song.*

December 9: First modern radar equipment is installed on a U.S. Navy ship, the battleship *New York* (BB-34).

1939

March 15: Germany invades and occupies the rest of Czechoslovakia.

March 20: Naval Research Laboratory requests funding for research on atomic energy. *U.S. Navy seeks it as an alternative to diesel as fuel for ships.*

March 31: Great Britain threatens war if Germany invades Poland.

April 1: Spanish Civil War ends. *General Francisco Franco's Nationalist forces defeat Spanish Republicans.*

April 7: Italy invades Albania.

Historical Notes

1. The Ford Motor Company produced about 4.5 million Model A cars from 1927 to 1931. At the Model A's normal 40 mph highway speed (top speed was slightly above 60 mph), fuel consumption averaged 40 miles per gallon. A new Model A of this generation cost from $385 to $570, depending on optional equipment.

2. Although most U.S. states (39 of 48) were issuing driver's licenses by 1935, Arkansas did not begin to require drivers to be licensed until mid-1937.

3. Oregon was one of the few states with minimum wage laws for workers in 1937. The federal minimum wage of twenty-five cents per hour—roughly equal to the purchasing power of $3.68 per hour in 2008—was not required in all states until mid-1938.

4. All applicants to the U.S. Navy were supposed to provide proof of age (at least seventeen), and parental permission was required for anyone under twenty-one. The degree to which these rules were enforced varied a great deal among recruiting locations across the country prior to World War II.

5. The Social Security Act of 1935 was another New Deal program, chiefly intended to provide retirement income for older Americans. It also appropriated some funds to the states for distribution to unemployed workers, mothers and children, crippled children, injured, disabled, or

blind Americans, and public health services. Although the first Social Security cards were issued in 1936, many Americans were still unaware of the program's existence in 1938.

6. China and Japan were U.S. allies during World War I (1914–1918), and both were major trading partners with the United States prior to World War II. America joined the League of Nations protest against Japan's invasions of Chinese territory and supported China in its subsequent war with Japan.

7. In response to increasing global tensions with Germany, Italy, and Japan in 1938, Congress granted President Roosevelt's request for $800 million to increase the size and strength of the U.S. Navy by 20 percent. More than a hundred new warships were under construction in 1939, so the Navy required about 20,000 additional sailors at this time.

8. Prior to World War II, the Naval Training Center at San Diego occupied about 235 acres, with housing and basic training facilities for approximately 7,000 recruits per boot camp session (30,000 recruits per year). At this time in 1939, most U.S. warships in the Pacific were based at San Diego and other West Coast cities.

CHAPTER 3: BASIC TRAINING

Mid-April–August 1939 Time Line

April 27: U.S. Congress debates halting all trade with Japan because of its invasion of China.

May 8: Spain withdraws from the League of Nations.

May 20: World's first commercial transatlantic flight. *A Pan-American Airlines Yankee Clipper flies from New York to Portugal.*

July 23: Americans say no to war with Japan. *Gallup Poll shows only 6 percent favor a war to protect U.S. business interests in China.*

July 26: United States announces trade agreements with Japan will end in six months.

August 23: Germany and the USSR (Russia) sign treaty, agree not to invade each other.

August 25: Great Britain and Poland sign treaty, agree to defend each other.

Historical Notes

1. By the end of 1939, the Navy's basic training was reduced to twelve weeks, then eight. After the United States entered World War II, recruits trained for three to seven weeks at San Diego and other naval bases in the United States. (Since 1994, the nine-week boot camp for new sailors has been offered at only one base near Chicago, the Great Lakes Naval Recruit Training Command.)

2. Although there is no official record of how or when the term "boot camp" originated, it may have been an acronym for the Navy's Basic Orientation and Organizational Training program.

3. This was one of the last basic training classes in San Diego that was required to sleep in hammocks. By 1940 the barracks were furnished with bunk beds. (Hammocks were still found on many U.S. ships during World War II.)

4. John Paul Jones (1747–1792) was the U.S. Navy's first hero. During the Revolutionary War, while commanding *Bonhomme Richard,* John Paul Jones declined the British captain's invitation to surrender with the famous words: "I have not yet begun to fight!" and subsequently captured the British ship. His grave at Annapolis, Maryland, is a national shrine.

5. The World War I–era Springfield rifle was still in use before and during World War II, even after the semiautomatic M-1 Garand and Browning automatic rifles became more widely available. It was also the snipers' weapon of choice for some U.S. Marines during the later wars in Korea and Vietnam. ("Thirty-ought-six" refers to the Springfield's 30.06-caliber cartridges.)

6. At this time in 1939, U.S. military strategists were drafting and developing the famous color-coded Rainbow series of five different war plans in the event of war with Japan or Germany or both. (Rainbow 5 was the code name for the plan that was accepted by both the Army and Navy and in effect when the United States entered World War II.)

7. Lt. Cmdr. Charles W. Flusser (1832–1864) was commanding the U.S. Navy gunboat *Miami* when he was killed in action during the Civil War. The destroyer *Flusser* (DD-368) was the fourth naval vessel named after him.

CHAPTER 4: THE DESTROYER

September 1939–May 1940 Time Line

September 1: Germany invades Poland; Italy announces neutrality.

September 3: World War II begins. *Great Britain, France, Australia, and New Zealand declare war on Germany.*

September 5: Neutrality Patrol: U.S. Navy will begin monitoring foreign warships in the Atlantic.

September 8: Limited National Emergency: *President Roosevelt orders major increases in personnel for all U.S. armed forces.*

September 10: Canada declares war on Germany.

September 17: USSR invades eastern Poland.

September 27: Poland surrenders to German and Soviet invading armies.

September 29: Poland is divided between German and Soviet occupying forces.

October 2: Germany announces intention to board and search U.S. cargo vessels in the Atlantic.

October 5: U.S. Navy forms a Hawaiian Detachment. *Two years later, this portion of the United States Fleet is renamed the Pacific Fleet.*

October 11: President Roosevelt receives letter signed by physicist Albert Einstein (1879–1955). *Letter urges funding for research on nuclear fission, warns of German research in this field.*

November 30: USSR invades Finland

December 14: League of Nations expels the USSR.

1940

January 6: Adm. James O. Richardson is named Commander in Chief, United States Fleet.

April 2: U.S. Fleet in the Pacific departs West Coast bases for maneuvers and war games near Hawaii.

April 9: Germany invades Denmark and attacks Norway.

April 25: Aircraft carrier *Wasp* (CV-7) is commissioned into the U.S. Navy.

The normal thirty-two months needed to construct a ship of this size is reduced to fifteen months during World War II.

Historical Notes

1. During his twelve years as President of the United States, Franklin D. Roosevelt gave thirty radio speeches called Fireside Chats that he used to inform Americans of major policies or decisions by the federal government. In his fourteenth Fireside Chat, September 3, 1939, he announced that the United States would remain neutral toward the war in Europe.

2. *Flusser* (DD-368) was 341' 4" long and 35' wide, typical of the destroyers used by the U.S. Navy prior to and during the early years of World War II. Standard crew was 158, including officers and enlisted men.

3. About 44,000 of the total 350,000 Native Americans in the United States served in the U.S. armed forces during World War II. Before World War II, many destroyers were assigned to South China Patrol to protect American civilian and merchant vessels from pirates.

4. Prior to World War II, it was Navy custom to admit a hundred enlisted men from the Navy and Marines for officer training and education at Annapolis, each year. In addition to the entrance exam, the enlisted man was required to serve at least nine months sea duty before he could be admitted to the Naval Academy at Annapolis, Maryland.

5. Most Americans did not consider smoking dangerous or socially unacceptable prior to or during World War II. The *Surgeon General's Report on Smoking and Health*, which warned of cigarette-related diseases, was not published until nearly twenty years after the war, in 1964.

6. On September 24–25, 1939, an eastern Pacific tropical cyclone moved ashore at Long Beach, California, with sustained winds of 50 mph. This is the only storm of that origin, type, and strength known to have touched the coast of southern California in recorded weather history.

7. In 1939–1940, Rear Adm. Robert A. Theobold commanded Destroyer Flotilla One, which included several squadrons and divisions of destroyers in the Pacific. *Flusser* was assigned to Division Nine, along with *Drayton* (DD-366), *Lamson* (DD-367), *Mahan* (DD-364), and *Porter* (DD-356). As a Rear Admiral, Theobold's flag would have had two stars. Vice Admirals' flags had three stars; Admirals had four stars. (The five-star Admiral of the Fleet rank did not exist prior to World War II.)

8. Speed at sea is measured in knots, or nautical miles an hour. A nautical mile is 6,080 feet, equal to 1.15 miles on land. At their top, or flank, speed of 37 knots, *Flusser* and other destroyers in this maneuver were making sudden turns at the equivalent of 43 mph on land.

9. The 400-room Royal Hawaiian Hotel, which opened in 1927, was the largest hotel on Waikiki Beach. Prior to World War II, it was normally occupied by American tourists who traveled to Hawaii on cruise ships. (The weekly "hula shows" began broadcasting in 1937 and continued as a popular beach attraction until 2002.)

10. Other Navy installations on Oahu prior to World War II were the naval air stations at Ford Island and Kaneohe. Army facilities included the airfields Hickham, Bellows, Wheeler, and Haleiwa, as well as Forts Shafter, Armstrong, DeRussy, Ruger, Kamehameha, Weaver, Barrette, and Schofield Barracks. Ewa and Hase were Marine air stations.

11. John Wayne (1907–1979) began his career in low-budget action and western cowboy movies in 1928. He became internationally famous after his starring role in the 1939 John Ford–directed *Stagecoach*.

12. John 3:16 refers to John, chapter 3, verse 16, in the New Testament. This particular verse ("For God so loved the world that he gave his only Son, that whoever believes in Him should not perish but have eternal life") is considered central to the Christian faith.

13. Adm. Joseph Richardson, then Commander in Chief of the United States Fleet, also preferred Maui's Lahaina Roads to the more crowded (and more difficult to escape from) Pearl Harbor at Oahu. His vocal and written objections to the Navy's continued presence at Pearl Harbor probably led to his loss of command to Adm. Husband Kimmel in early 1941.

14. "Blackfish" was the common name for many types of whales and dolphins found in Hawaiian waters prior to World War II. The size and characteristics of this one are consistent with the false killer whale and the short-finned pilot whale. Both are actually dolphins.

15. *Flusser* carried four 5-inch guns. The size and number of antiaircraft guns and depth charges varied on this and other destroyers during World War II. Torpedoes cost about $10,000 each (in 1940 dollars), which is why the U.S. Navy seldom used them in live training exercises prior to World War II.

CHAPTER 5: RADIO SCHOOL

May–August 30, 1940 Time Line

May 7: U.S. Fleet in the Pacific is ordered to base at Pearl Harbor.

May 9–10: Germany invades Belgium, Luxembourg, and Holland.

May 10: Winston Churchill replaces Neville Chamberlain as Prime Minister of Great Britain.

May 14: Holland surrenders to Germany.

May 26–June 3: The Miracle at Dunkirk: *300,000 British and French soldiers evacuate France. British civilian vessels assisted their escape from capture by the approaching German Army.*

May 28: Belgium surrenders to Germany.

June 10: Norway surrenders to Germany. Italy declares war on Great Britain and France. Canada declares war on Italy.

June 14: German forces enter Paris.

June 14: First prisoners arrive at Nazi concentration camp Auschwitz.

June 22: France surrenders to Germany. *The Vichy French government in Bordeaux begins cooperating with the Nazi occupation.*

June 22: Japanese Army General Hideki Tojo becomes Japan's Minister of War.

June 23: Adolf Hitler tours Paris, now under Nazi occupation.

June 28: Great Britain recognizes the Free French government. *Charles de Gaulle leads French citizens who oppose the German occupation.*

June 28 U.S. Congress passes the Alien Registration Act. *All noncitizens must report to post offices for interviews and fingerprinting.*

July 5: Vichy French government breaks off all diplomatic relations with Great Britain.

July 5: United States stops selling aircraft parts to Japan.

July 10: The Battle of Britain begins, the first major air battle in world history. *Royal Air Force defends British ships, airfields, and factories from German bombers.*

July 19: Adolf Hitler announces Germany's intention to invade and occupy England.

July 19: U.S. Congress's Two Ocean Navy bill funds a 70 percent increase in the size of U.S. Navy.

July 26: United States stops selling aviation fuel to Japan.

August 3–4: Italy invades British Somaliland (Somalia), Africa.

August 23–24: First German bomber attacks on Central London. *Total British civilians killed by German bombing raids during World War II: 43,000.*

August 25: First British bomber attacks on Berlin.

August 30: Vichy France consents to Japan's occupation of northern Indochina (North Vietnam).

Historical Notes

1. By mid-1940, the entire coast of China was occupied by Japanese troops. The city of Shanghai was also under Japanese control, except for the International Settlement, for businesses from several nations, including the United States. These China Marines were probably returning from duty as guards for the American embassy and civilian businesses in Shanghai.

2. Most U.S. warships in the Pacific were no longer based at San Diego or any other West Coast city at this time. After the 1940 spring maneuvers in Hawaiian waters, they were ordered to remain at Pearl Harbor.

3. The major effect of the European war upon American sailors in the Pacific in the spring of 1940 was the decision to base the fleet at Pearl Harbor, which reduced the sailing distance to territories in the South Pacific by about two thousand miles. Military strategists believed the presence of U.S. warships in Hawaii would deter Japan from attacking British, French, and Dutch colonies in the Pacific while the Europeans were at war with Germany.

4. When America entered the war, actor John Wayne was thirty-four, married with four children, and classified 3-A ("deferred for dependency reasons") by the Selective Service. Although he did begin the paperwork to change this classification in order to join the U.S. Navy, his application was never completed or filed. John Wayne did, however, star in many war-action films during World War II, including *Flying Tigers* (1942), *Fighting Seabees* (1944), *They Were Expendable* (1945), and *Back to Bataan* (1945).

5. Some scenes in *Shepherd of the Hills* (released in 1941) were filmed at Big Bear Lake, California, during the summer of 1940. Of John Wayne's 152 films, 1928–1976, this was his seventy-seventh.

6. Pensacola, Florida, became the U.S. Navy's first air base in 1914. By 1940, most of those who received flight training at Pensacola were Annapolis graduates, but the Navy did accept some enlisted men as pilot trainees before and during World War II.

7. In 1940, base pay for a Navy enlisted man with service school training, followed by the usual promotion to third class petty officer, was $60 per month. Submarine duty was considered more hazardous, thus paid an additional five dollars per month. (After six months on a submarine, an enlisted man could take another exam that would increase his pay by twenty dollars per month.)

8. The *Richmond* (CL-9), commissioned in 1923, was the fourth U.S. Navy ship named after the capital of the state of Virginia. It was a light cruiser, with fewer and smaller guns than a heavy cruiser.

CHAPTER 6: THE CRUISER

September 1940 Through March 1941 Time Line

September 2: Destroyers-for-Bases agreement. *U.S. Navy trades fifty World War I–era destroyers for ninety-nine-year leases on British bases in the Caribbean.*

September 7: The Blitz. *German bombers begin nightly attacks on British cities.*

September 13: Italy invades Egypt.

September 14: First peacetime draft in U.S. history: Congress passes the Selective Service Act. *All American males, 21–35, are required to register for possible military service.*

September 27: Japan joins the Axis, signs Tripartite Pact with Italy and Germany.

September 30: United States stops selling all iron and steel scrap metal to Japan.

October 8: Japan protests United States refusal to sell scrap metal and aviation fuel.

October 12: First launch of U.S. Army planes from a Navy aircraft carrier. *Twenty-four P-40 Warhawk fighter planes took off from the carrier* Wasp (CV-7).

October 28: Italy invades Greece.

November 5: Franklin D. Roosevelt is elected to a third term as President. *Republican challenger was Wendell Willkie.*

November 11: World's first aircraft carrier strike on enemy warships at anchor. *Planes from the British carrier* Illustrious *sink five Italian warships in harbor at Taranto, Italy.*

November 15: First 75,000 U.S. draftees must report for military service.

November 16: Nazis force Polish Jews to relocate to the Warsaw Ghetto.

November 20–24: Hungary, Romania, and Slovakia join the Axis powers.

December 9–10: British offensive against Italian forces in North Africa begins.

1941

January 25: Construction begins on *Wisconsin* (BB-64). *It will be the last battleship built for the U.S. Navy.*

January 27: First warning of Japanese plan to attack Pearl Harbor. *The U.S. ambassador to Japan reports rumors that are not taken seriously.*

January 30: Germany announces it will attack U.S. ships carrying aid to England.

February 1: U.S. Navy reorganizes into: Pacific, Atlantic, and Asiatic Fleets. *Adm. Husband E. Kimmel assumes command of the Pacific Fleet, now based at Pearl Harbor.*

February 4: The United Service Organizations (USO) is incorporated in New York.

February 12: German Lt. Gen. Erwin Rommel, the "Desert Fox," arrives in North Africa.

February 14: First German Afrika Korps tanks arrive in North Africa.

March 1: Bulgaria joins the Axis powers.

March 11: U.S. Congress passes the Lend-Lease Act. *FDR can now sell, trade, or lend U.S. weapons to warring countries.*

March 15: First unit of U.S. Fleet Marine Force deployed to the southern hemisphere during World War II. *They arrived at Pago Pago, American Samoa.*

Historical Notes

1. Mae West (1892–1980) was Hollywood's first superstar sex symbol and "blonde bombshell," said to be the highest paid woman in America prior to World War II. The Type B-4 inflatable cotton life preserver worn by Allied flight crews was nicknamed for her.

2. *Richmond* (CL-9) did return to the Atlantic in the fall of 1940. After fleet exercises, this ship was transferred back to Pearl Harbor in January 1941. (*Richmond*'s first World War II combat actually occurred in the Pacific, against the Japanese Imperial Navy in Alaskan waters, during the Battle of the Komandorski Islands, 1943).

3. Enlisted men's shifts could vary in different sections of the ship, but the typical noncombat day was divided into seven watches: midwatch (midnight to 4:00 A.M.), followed by morning watch (4:00-8:00 A.M.), forenoon watch (8:00 A.M. to noon), afternoon watch (noon to 4:00 P.M.), first dogwatch (4:00-6:00 P.M.), second dogwatch (6:00-8:00 P.M.), and evening watch (8:00 P.M. to midnight).

4. *Richmond* became the flagship for Rear Adm. Thomas Withers when he assumed command of the Pearl Harbor–based Submarine Scouting Force on January 17, 1941.

5. Weapons on *Richmond* included twelve 6-inch guns, four 3-inch guns, six 21-inch torpedo-launching tubes, plus varying numbers and sizes of antiaircraft guns. (Cruisers designated as "heavy" carried the larger-sized 8-inch and 5-inch guns.)

6. The destroyers *Aylwin* (DD-355) and *Farragut* (DD-348) collided during night exercises in Hawaiian waters, March 19, 1941. One man on *Aylwin* died.

7. In early 1941, the Mitsubishi A6M Type 0 (commonly known as the Zero) was believed to attain speeds up to 380 mph at higher altitudes, compared to the Grumman F4F-3 (later known as the Wildcat) fighter plane's maximum speed of 330 mph at 21,000 feet. Although the Zero's speed may have been exaggerated, its climb rate and maneuverability in aerial combat was indisputably superior to the Wildcat's.

8. In the spring of 1941, the Imperial Japanese Navy outnumbered the U.S. Navy's Pacific Fleet in all five types of warships: aircraft carriers, 10 to 3; battleships, 10 to 9; cruisers, 35 to 21; destroyers, 111 to 67; submarines 64 to 27.

CHAPTER 7: THE SUBMARINE BASE

April 1941–7:55 A.M., December 7, 1941 Time Line

April 3: Pro-Nazi government takes control in Iraq.

April 6: Germany invades Yugoslavia and Greece; Italy declares war on Yugoslavia.

April 9: Denmark accepts U.S. offer to assume responsibility for defense of Greenland.

April 10: First combat between U.S. and German warships during World War II. *American destroyer depth-charges a German submarine in the Atlantic.*

April 13: Japan and USSR (Russia) pledge neutrality toward each other.

April 17: Yugoslavia surrenders to Germany.

April 23: Greece surrenders to Germany and Italy.

April 27: German troops occupy Athens.

May 2: Fighting breaks out in Iraq; British battle pro-Nazi Iraqi forces.

May 21: First U.S. Merchant Marine ship is sunk by German submarine during World War II.

May 26: Rainbow 5 is code name for U.S. Navy strategy in case of war with Japan.

May 27: President Roosevelt declares Unlimited National Emergency. *FDR says conflict in Europe has become a "world war for world domination."*

May 27: Sinking of the *Bismarck*: the German battleship is torpedoed by British carrier planes.

May 31: British and Iraqi fighting ends with armistice signed in Baghdad.

June 3: Gallup Poll shows 83 percent of Americans oppose entering the war in Europe.

June 4: Pro-Allied government forms in Iraq.

June 12: U.S. Naval Reserve is called to active duty.

June 14: United States freezes all German and Italian assets in America.

June 21: Hitler seeks continued U.S. neutrality, orders German Navy to avoid American warships.

June 22: Germany invades USSR; Italy declares war on USSR.

June 25: FDR announces United States will send supplies and weapons to USSR. *In October, Congress approves $1 billion in lend-lease aid to USSR.*

July 7: Roosevelt announces Iceland accepts U.S. offer to assume responsibility for Iceland's defense.

July 12: British and USSR agree to treaty of mutual assistance against Germany and Italy.

July 18: Japan's Prince Konoye forms a new civilian government.

July 25: Vichy France allows Japanese occupation of southern French Indochina (South Vietnam).

July 26: United States protests Japan's occupation of French Indochina. *Roosevelt orders freeze of Japanese assets, stops all oil sales to Japan.*

July 26: British cancel all commercial agreements with Japan.

July 28: Dutch East Indies (Indonesia) stops all oil exports to Japan.

July 28: Japan freezes all American assets in Japan.

July 29: Japan freezes all Dutch assets in Japan.

August 6: Japan issues first formal demand for United States to resume oil sales.

August 9–12: The Atlantic Charter Conference. *Roosevelt and Churchill meet for the first time at Argentia, Newfoundland.*

August 17: United States threatens war if Japan invades oil-rich Indonesia or Malaysia.

August 25: Soviet and British troops invade and occupy Iran.

September 1: Nazis order Jews to wear a yellow star of David for identification in public.

September 3: First use of gas chambers for mass killing by Nazis at Auschwitz.

September 8: The siege of Leningrad begins; German forces surround the city.

September 11: Construction begins on the Pentagon, future War Department headquarters.

September 18: U.S. Navy warships are used to escort British ships across the Atlantic for the first time of the U.S. War Department.

September 26: Kiev, Ukraine, falls to German Army.

October 5: Japanese Navy selects carrier pilots for planned attack on U.S. bases in Hawaii.

October 16: General deportation of all German Jews to concentration camps begins.

October 16: Prince Konoye, Japan's civilian Prime Minister resigns.

October 18: Japanese Army General Hideki Tojo becomes Premier and Minister of War.

October 20: United States offers to resume oil sales if Japan withdraws all troops from China and French Indochina (Vietnam).

October 20: Aircraft carrier *Hornet* (CV-8) is commissioned into U.S. Navy.

October 31: First U.S. Navy warship sunk by enemy action during World War II. *German submarine torpedoes destroyer* Reuben James (DD-245) *near Iceland.*

November 1: U.S. Coast Guard is transfers from Treasury Department to the Navy. *This was standard procedure in time of war or national emergency.*

November 14: United States orders all Marines out of Shanghai, Tientsin, and Peiping.

November 17: U.S. Merchant Marine ships are permitted to begin arming themselves.

November 18: British begin offensive against German Afrika Korps in Libya.

November 20: Japan rejects U.S. peace proposal, demands oil and the end of all U.S. aid to China.

November 24: First war warning given to U.S. admirals at Pearl Harbor and the Philippines. *Both locations are advised that Japan might strike "in any direction" at any time.*

November 25: Japanese troop carriers are sighted near Formosa (Taiwan).

November 26: United States again offers oil for Japan's withdrawal from China and Indochina.

November 26: Six-carrier Japanese task force departs secretly from harbors in Kurile Islands. *If final peace negotiations should fail, their orders are to destroy the U.S. Pacific Fleet in Hawaii.*

November 27: United States issues war warning to commanders of Pacific and Asiatic Fleets. *Both were told to prepare for possible Japanese attack on Philippines or Thailand.*

November 28: Carrier *Enterprise* (CV-6) departs Pearl Harbor on mission to Wake Island.

November 30: Tojo tells Japanese civilian press that negotiations with the United States are continuing.

December 1: Japan's Cabinet Council consents to war with the United States, Great Britain, and the Netherlands.

December 2: First U.S. Naval Armed Guards are assigned to a Merchant Marine ship.

December 2: Tojo orders Japanese embassy in Washington, D.C., to burn code books.

December 5: U.S. carrier *Lexington* (CV-2) departs Pearl Harbor on mission to Midway Islands.

December 6: Japan's Emperor Hirohito does not answer FDR's request for further peace talks. *He may have feared the loss of his throne had he opposed the military's decision to go to war.*

December 6: Tokyo informs Japanese carriers that no U.S. carriers are present at Pearl Harbor. *Target list is revised; chief targets are now American battleships and planes.*

December 7: Six Japanese aircraft carriers are 275 miles north of Oahu.

6:00 A.M.: First Japanese carrier planes launch for strike on Oahu.

6:45 A.M.: U.S. destroyer spots and sinks a Japanese minisub near the entrance to Pearl Harbor.

7:02 A.M.: U.S. radar on Oahu shows incoming planes. *Inexperienced operators mistake them for expected U.S. planes.*

7:51 A.M.: Japanese carrier planes strike U.S. Naval Air Station at Kaneohe.

7:55 A.M.: First formations of Japanese planes appear over Pearl Harbor.

Historical Notes

1. The barracks described here served as living quarters for all 700 enlisted men assigned to the submarine base at this time. By December 1941, twenty-seven of the Navy's fifty-five submarines in the Pacific were

based at Pearl Harbor. (A fourth floor was added to the barracks in 1943 to house the increase in base personnel during the war.)

2. The Submarine administration building at Pearl Harbor was also headquarters of CinCPac—Commander in Chief, Pacific Fleet— during World War II. The office of Adm. Husband Kimmel, who commanded the Pacific Fleet at this time, was located on the second floor.

3. In July 1941, President Roosevelt ordered an end to all U.S. trade with Japan, including the sale of oil, until they withdrew their troops from China and French Indochina (Vietnam). This reduced Japan's total oil imports, for both military and civilian uses, by about 80 percent.

4. The Pali cliff, overlooking Oahu's Nuuanu Valley, is the site of the 1795 battle in which Hawaii's first king, Kamehameha the Great, is said to have forced a rival's army to jump to their deaths.

5. The minimum age for American voters in 1941 was twenty-one. States were not required to permit absentee voting by military personnel on active duty until Congress passed the Soldier Voting Act of 1942.

6. Both officers and enlisted men in the U.S. Navy brought their families to Hawaii when the Pacific Fleet moved to Pearl Harbor in 1940. By late 1941, approximately 10,000 dependents of the total 46,000 Navy personnel in Hawaii resided on or near the base at Pearl Harbor. (Comparative total U.S. Army and Army Air Force personnel in Hawaii in early December 1941: 43,000.)

7. Joe DiMaggio (1914–1999), center fielder for the New York Yankees, achieved a 56-game hitting streak from May 15 through July 16, 1941. Ted Williams (1918–2002) of the Boston Red Sox ended the 1941 season with a .406 batting average. Neither of these major-league baseball records has been matched or surpassed.

8. On November 24, 1941, a message from U.S. Chief of Naval Operations to Adm. Kimmel at the submarine base in Pearl Harbor warned of an expected Japanese attack on the Philippines or Guam. A similar war warning on November 27 added Thailand and Borneo as likely targets.

9. On the night of December 6, 1941, the destroyer *Flusser* (DD-368) was with the carrier *Lexington* (CV-2) task force, on the mission to deliver more planes to defend the U.S. base on Midway Island. The cruiser *Richmond* (CL-9) was on patrol against German submarines off the coast of South America.

CHAPTER 8: THE ATTACK ON PEARL HARBOR

Sunday Morning, December 7, 1941 Time Line

7:55 A.M.: Japanese carrier planes strafe U.S. Marine Air Station at Ewa.

7:55 A.M.: First bomb falls on U.S. Army's Hickam Field.

7:55 A.M.: First bomb falls on Ford Island.

7:56 A.M.: First torpedo strikes battleship *West Virginia* (BB-48).

7:58 A.M.: Radio message from Ford Island to Pacific Fleet: "Air Raid, Pearl Harbor—This is no drill."

8:00 A.M.: U.S. ships begin firing antiaircraft guns at Japanese planes. *Total U.S. Navy ships inside Pearl Harbor at this time: 70 warships, 24 auxiliary-type ships.*

8:02 A.M.: First bombs fall on U.S. Army planes at Wheeler Field, Oahu.

8:05 A.M.: Battleship *California* (BB-44) is hit by two torpedoes.

8:10 A.M.: Battleship *Oklahoma* (BB-37) capsizes.

8:12 A.M.: Target ship (former battleship) *Utah* (AG-16/BB-31) capsizes.

8:15 A.M.: Battleship *Arizona* (BB-39) explodes.

8:17 A.M.: Destroyer *Helm* (DD-388) attacks Japanese minisub near harbor entrance. *None of the twenty full-size or five minisubmarines damaged any U.S. ship at Pearl Harbor.*

8:20 A.M.: First planes from U.S. carrier *Enterprise* (CV-6) arrive over Oahu.

8:27 A.M.: First U.S. warship gets under way, destroyer *Monaghan* (DD-354).

8:35 A.M.: *Enterprise* planes, mistaken for Japanese, are fired on by antiaircraft gunners.

8:40 A.M.: Last planes launched by Japanese carriers arrive over Pearl Harbor.

8:43 A.M.: *Monaghan* depth-charges and sinks Japanese minisub inside Pearl Harbor.

9:00 A.M.: Destroyer *Shaw* explodes in dry-dock area.

9:00 A.M.: Japanese planes drop incendiary bombs on destroyers in dry-dock area.

9:00 A.M.: Japanese plane explodes and crashes near submarine docks.

9:00 A.M.: Japanese fighter planes strafe Bellows Field.

9:06 A.M.: Japanese dive bombers attack battleship *Pennsylvania* (BB-38) in dry-dock area.

9:07 A.M.: Antiaircraft gunners cease fire on U.S. heavy bombers attempting to land at Hickam Field. *These were the B-17 Flying Fortresses expected from the mainland that morning, for which the first incoming Japanese carrier planes were mistaken by the radar operators on Oahu.*

9:40 A.M.: Battleship *Nevada* (BB-36) runs aground south of Ford Island. *This was the only battleship able to get under way during the attack.*

9:45 A.M.: Japanese planes, low on fuel and ammunition, begin returning to the six carriers.

10:00: A.M.: Light cruiser *St. Louis* (CL-49) sinks a minisub outside Pearl Harbor entrance.

Historical Notes

1. Of the 1,512 men who were aboard the battleship *Arizona* (BB-39) at this time, only 335 survived. *Arizona* had the highest number of casualties of any ship present at Pearl Harbor on December 7, 1941.

2. U.S. Navy guns fired 300,000 rounds at the attacking planes. Most of the rounds came from .30 and .50-caliber machine guns. Twenty-nine Japanese planes were shot down or crashed by accident during this attack on Pearl Harbor and other bases on Oahu.

3. The precise number and types of Japanese planes remained unknown until after the war. According to postwar interviews with Japanese military leaders, the six carriers launched a total of 360 planes: 40 torpedo bombers, 100 high-level or horizontal bombers, 130 dive bombers, 90 fighter planes. They sank four large U.S. warships and damaged ten.

4. The three submarines were *Narwhal* (SS-167), *Tautog* (SS-199), and *Dolphin* (SS-169). A fourth submarine, *Cachalot* (SS-170), was also in port, but tied in the dry-dock area, thus not visible from the roof of the administration building. No U.S., submarines were damaged during the attack on Pearl Harbor.

5. Total Japanese pilots and other personnel killed during the attack on Pearl Harbor and other U.S. bases on Oahu: 64. Total Japanese Navy personnel killed or missing during World War II: 414,900.

6. All four of the warships in dry dock were struck by bombs on December 7, 1941: battleship *Pennsylvania* (BB-38) and destroyers *Shaw* (DD-373), *Cassin* (DD-372), and *Downes* (DD-375). The largest explosion happened on *Shaw*, where bombs ignited weapons and ammunition on the bow.

7. Prior to the attack, the U.S. military had 345 planes in flyable condition on Oahu bases: 202 Navy and Marine and 143 Army Air Force. After the attack, the Navy and Marines had only 52 flyable planes, the Army Air Force had 87. Most of the planes were destroyed on the ground within the first few minutes of the two-hour attack.

8. The attack on Pearl Harbor was a preemptive strike, intended to disable the Pacific Fleet for at least six months, long enough to prevent American interference with the Japanese military's plan to invade and occupy the Philippines and European territories in the Pacific, particularly the oil-rich Dutch East Indies (Indonesia).

9. Of the total 2,403 Americans reported killed, missing, or died from wounds suffered during the attack, 2,008 were Navy personnel. The Army and Army Air Force reported 218 dead; Marines reported 109. There were also 68 civilian deaths.

CHAPTER 9: AFTERSHOCKS

10:00 A.M., December 7–December 24, 1941 Time Line

December 7: Japan declares war on the United States. *Formal documents are delivered hours after the carrier strike on Pearl Harbor.*

December 7: At 1:30 P.M., Japanese six-carrier task force departs Hawaiian waters.

December 7: Hawaii's territorial governor declares martial law.

December 7: Canada and Dutch East Indies declare war on Japan.

December 8: Japan attacks Philippines, Hong Kong, Guam, Malay Peninsula, Thailand.

December 8: Japan invades Shanghai International Settlement, captures U.S. China Marines.

December 8: First (and only) surrender by a U.S. Navy ship during World War II. *Japanese forces capture the gunboat* Wake (PR-3), *Shanghai, China.*

December 8: United States and Great Britain declare war on Japan.

December 8: Nicaragua, Honduras, El Salvador, Guatemala, Haiti, Dominican Republic, Panama, the Netherlands, and Free French (in exile), declare war on Japan.

December 9: FDR's Fireside Chat following the attack on Pearl Harbor. *"It will be not only a long war, it will be a hard war."*

December 9: Japanese troops occupy Bangkok, Thailand.

December 9: Tarawa and Makin, Gilbert Islands, fall to Japan.

December 9: Australia, South Africa, New Zealand declare war on Japan.

December 9: China declares war on Japan, Germany, and Italy.

December 9: Civilian press reports Japanese carrier planes are approaching Golden Gate Bridge. *False alarm broadcast by a San Francisco radio station fuels fear of Japanese Americans.*

December 10: Cuba declares war on Japan.

December 10: First Japanese aircraft confirmed destroyed by a U.S. Navy plane in World War II. *A PBY shot down a Zero near the Philippines.*

December 10: Guam, only U.S. base in the Marianas Islands, surrenders to Japan.

December 10: First large Japanese submarine sunk during World War II.

I-170 was destroyed by planes from U.S. carrier Enterprise (CV-6) *near Hawaii.*

December 10: First Allied battleships attacked at sea by carrier planes during World War II. *Japanese planes sank the British* Prince of Wales *and* Repulse *near Singapore.*

December 10: Costa Rica declares war on Japan.

December 11: Japan attacks Burma.

December 11: Vandals chop down four Japanese cherry trees in Washington, D.C. *The surviving trees, gifts from Japan in 1912, are renamed Oriental flowering cherries.*

December 11: U.S. Congress authorizes the Navy to retain all men beyond their original enlistments.

December 11: Germany and Italy declare war on the United States.

December 11: United States declares war on Germany and Italy; most Central American countries follow.

December 15: Japanese submarine shells Kahului, Maui, Hawaii.

December 17: Japanese troops land on Borneo, British East Indies (Malaysia).

December 17: Adm. Chester W. Nimitz is named Commander-in-Chief, Pacific Fleet.

December 18: First investigation into U.S. military's failure to protect Pearl Harbor begins. *A former U.S. Supreme Court justice heads the Roberts Commission.*

December 20: U.S. Flying Tigers begin air attacks on Japanese forces in China. *Claire Chennault commands these American pilots in China-Burma-India Theater.*

December 21–22: Japanese carrier planes attack U.S. base on Wake Island.

December 22: History's closest military alliance in wartime begins.

British Prime Minister Churchill arrives in the United States for meetings with President Roosevelt.

December 22: Japanese troops land on Luzon, main island of the Philippines.

December 23: U.S. base on Wake Island surrenders to Japan. *The surviving 470 military personnel and 1,146 civilian workers become prisoners of war.*

Historical Notes

1. All medical facilities at or near Pearl Harbor were overwhelmed by the number needing care after this attack. Total Americans wounded were: 710 Navy, 364 Army and Army Air Force, 69 Marines, and 35 civilians. (Total U.S. military personnel wounded during World War II: 670,846.)

2. Within the first two hours after the attack on Pearl Harbor, U.S. scout planes reported enemy troops in blue coveralls with red emblems on the north shore of Oahu. American planes and ships also reported Japanese paratroopers and troop-carrying ships at Barbers Point, on the south shore. All such sightings were later proved false.

3. The six-carrier Japanese task force set out with a total of thirty ships from Japan's Kurile Island bases in the North Pacific. They were not

detected because all U.S. scout planes were deployed south and west of Oahu, due to the belief that any attack on Pearl Harbor would have to start from Japan's naval bases in the Marshall Islands in the *South* Pacific. (A northern approach was considered too difficult and, therefore, too unlikely to justify additional aviation fuel for scouting in that direction.)

4. Japan had no plan to invade or capture any U.S. facility on Oahu, including the fuel tanks. When the Japanese planes returned to their carriers to refuel and rearm for another strike on secondary targets, such as the submarine base, the Japanese admiral chose to leave Hawaiian waters immediately rather than risk a counterattack on his carriers by the American carriers whose locations were unknown to him at that time.

5. About one-fourth of the U.S. Navy's dead at Pearl Harbor were buried in the Nuuanu Cemetery on Oahu; others were interred near Halawa, on the naval reservation known as Red Hill. After World War II, the Red Hill graves were among the first to be relocated to the National Cemetery of the Pacific, in the crater north of Honolulu, often referred to as the Punchbowl.

6. The Japanese carrier planes' attack on Pearl Harbor sank 6 U.S. Navy ships: 4 battleships (*Arizona* [BB-39], *Oklahoma* [BB-37], *California* [BB-44], *West Virginia* [BB-48], 1 mine layer (*Ogala* [CM-4]); 1 former battleship (*Utah* [BB-31/AG-16]). Another 12 ships were damaged but not classified as "sunk": 4 battleships, 3 cruisers, 3 destroyers, 1 seaplane tender, 1 repair ship. Only *Arizona, Oklahoma,* and *Utah* never returned to service during World War II.

7. *Oklahoma* turned over and sank so quickly after it was torpedoed on December 7, 1941, many of its 1,354 crew were trapped on the lower decks. Although rescuers did free 32 men by cutting holes in the ship's hull, some of the 415 reported killed or missing were probably alive for days or weeks until they drowned or suffocated.

8. Within two days of the attack on Pearl Harbor, 370 Japanese, 98 Germans, and 14 Italians were arrested in Hawaii. In the months that followed, about 110,000 Japanese Americans on the West Coast were forced into internment camps called "relocation centers." A few CCC camps were converted to that purpose; other CCC camps were used to house German and Italian prisoners of war.

CHAPTER 10: THE SUBMARINE

December 24, 1941–February 3, 1942 Time Line

December 24: First Japanese submarine attacks on U.S. merchant ships near Los Angeles.

December 25: British crown colony Hong Kong surrenders to Japan.

December 31: Japanese submarines shell three Hawaiian Islands: Kauai, Maui, Hawaii.

December 31: Adm. Nimitz assumes command of the U.S. Pacific Fleet.

1942

January 1: United Nations Declaration: Twenty-six Allied countries pledge to defeat the Axis powers.

January 2: Manila, Philippines, falls to Japan.

January 9: First Japanese attack on U.S. and Filipino forces on the Bataan Peninsula, Philippines.

January 11: First enemy attack on a U.S. aircraft carrier during World War II. Saratoga (CV-3) *was damaged by torpedo from a Japanese submarine near Oahu.*

January 11: Japan declares war on the Netherlands and invades Dutch East Indies (Indonesia).

January 12: German submarines begin attacking Allied ships off the U.S. East Coast.

January 12: U.S. Congress authorizes a 66 percent increase in Navy personnel.

January 15: American, British, Dutch, and Australian navies unite as ABDA force against Japan. *National differences in training, weapons, and combat maneuvers lead to further Allied losses.*

January 16: Japan invades Burma.

January 20: The Final Solution begins. *At Wannsee Conference, Nazi leaders coordinate plans to kill European Jews.*

January 23: Japan invades the Solomon Islands.

January 24: First major surface battle for U.S. Navy warships during WWII. *The Battle of Balikpapan, Dutch East Indies.*

February 1: First U.S. aircraft carrier attack on an enemy base during WWII. Yorktown *and* Enterprise *planes struck Japan's bases in the Marshall and Gilbert Islands.*

Historical Notes

1. The Marshall Islands, about 2,100 miles southwest of Pearl Harbor, are two parallel chains of islands and atolls that Japan acquired after Germany's defeat in World War I (1914–1918). In December 1941, the Marshall Islands were the closest land-based threat to Hawaii. An additional purpose for this mission was to detect and warn of another Japanese attack on Pearl Harbor.

2. The "Execute Unrestricted Submarine Warfare Against Japan" order was received at Pearl Harbor, midafternoon, December 7, 1941. All Japanese cargo and transport vessels, military or civilian, were subsequently targeted by all Allied submarines. Of the 273 U.S. submarines deployed during World War II, 50 were destroyed or missing in the Pacific, 1 vanished in the Caribbean, 1 was lost in training off the coast of Florida.

3. Sonar is an acronym for sound navigation and ranging. Many radiomen doubled as sonar operators until sonar interpretation became a separate specialty, or rating, in 1943. The detectable differences in sonar pings caused by an observed object, such as a whale or a ship, results from the principle of physics commonly known as the Doppler effect.

4. The Big Band Era in American popular music, 1936–1945, is subdivided into two stylistic forms. Although some bands had major hits in both categories, most were classified as either swing bands, such as Benny Goodman's, or sweet bands, such as Glenn Miller's. The sweet band style was the more popular of the two during the war years.

5. *Dolphin* (SS-169), commissioned in 1932, was 319' 1" long, 27' 11" wide, with a standard crew of fifty-seven. The custom of referring to all submarines as "boats" probably dates to the smaller submarines of the eighteenth and nineteenth centuries. The U.S. Navy's first twentieth-century submarine was the 54-foot-long *Holland* (SS-1), commissioned in 1900.

6. *Dolphin*'s executive officer for this mission was Lt. Commander Bernard A. Clarey (1912–1996), later noted for his skill and aggres-

siveness in submarine warfare and reconnaissance as commanding officer of *Pintado* (SS-387). After the war, Clarey became an admiral. In 1970, he was named Commander-in-Chief, Pacific Fleet (CinCPac).

7. Kwajalein, the world's largest coral atoll, is located in the geographic center of the Marshall Islands. Prior to and during World War II, it was one of Japan's largest air and naval bases in the region.

8. *Dolphin*'s radio reports from the Marshall Islands were received at CinCPac headquarters, Pearl Harbor, January 27, 1942. Although three other submarines were on similar missions in this region, it was *Dolphin*'s detailed analysis of "light" defenses at Kwajalein that caused the base to be added to the target list for the first strike by U.S. carriers.

9. The *Enterprise* (CV-6) task force was en route to meet the *Yorktown* (CV-5) task force near the Marshall Islands. Planes from both carriers attacked Japanese bases in this region on February 1, 1942. This was the first U.S. carrier-plane attack on any enemy base during World War II.

10. Although *Dolphin*'s executive officer described it as a "deathtrap," this submarine completed two more missions in 1942 before it was retired to service as a training vessel. The captain was reassigned to administrative duties ashore. By the end of 1942, nearly one-third of the U.S. Navy's submarine captains were replaced for similar reasons: "unproductive" missions.

11. Within ten days of the attack on Pearl Harbor, President Roosevelt named Adm. Chester W. Nimitz to command the U.S. Pacific Fleet. Nimitz officially replaced the prewar Commander-in-Chief, Adm. Husband Kimmel, during ceremonies at the submarine base, December 31, 1941.

CHAPTER 11: THE AIRCRAFT CARRIER

February 3–April 27, 1942 Time Line

February 6: The Combined Chiefs of Staff, comprising U.S. and British officers, plan joint military operations.

February 15: Japan captures oil refineries on Sumatra, Dutch East Indies (Indonesia).

February 15: Singapore, the largest British air and naval base in the Pacific, surrenders to Japan.

February 19: Four Japanese aircraft carriers strike Port Darwin, Australia, and sink three U.S. ships.

February 19: Executive Order 9066 authorizes the removal of Japanese Americans from the West Coast.

February 20: First U.S. Navy ace of World War II is *Lexington* (CV-2) fighter pilot "Butch" O'Hare. *He shot down five Japanese bombers in one day; Chicago's international airport is named for him.*

February 23: One Japanese submarine surfaces and shells California coast and oil refinery. *As many as fifteen Japanese submarines were patrolling between the United States West Coast and Hawaii at this time.*

February 27: Battle of Java Sea: The Japanese Navy defeats ABDA near Dutch East Indies. *American, British, Dutch, and Australian warships cannot stop the Japanese invasion.*

March 5: Seabees is now the authorized name for the U.S. Navy's Construction Battalions.

March 8: Rangoon, Burma falls to Japan.

March 9: Java, Dutch East Indies (Indonesia) surrenders to Japan.

March 11: U.S. Army Lt. Gen. Douglas MacArthur is evacuated from the Philippines. *Ten days later, in a radio message from Australia, he says, "I came through and I shall return."*

March 17: Allies designate U.S. military to defend all areas of the Pacific, including Australia. *British take responsibility for Middle East and Indian Ocean regions.*

March 21: First Japanese Americans arrive at Manzanar "relocation center" in California. *More than 100,000 Japanese Americans lived in ten such camps during WWII.*

March 30: MacArthur is designated to command Southwest Pacific Area.

April 3: Adm. Nimitz is designated to command U.S. Pacific Fleet and Pacific Ocean Area. *He is now responsible for all air, sea, and land forces in the North, South, and Central Pacific.*

April 7: U.S. Navy authorizes training of African American men in all specialties. *African American sailors are no longer limited to food preparation and service.*

April 9: 76,000 U.S. and Filipino troops surrender to Japan on Bataan Peninsula, the Philippines. *About 10,000 died during the subsequent sixty-five-mile Bataan Death March to POW camps.*

April 18: The Doolittle Raid is the first air attack on Japan's home islands during World War II.

April 27: U.S. carrier *Yorktown* (CV-5) departs Tonga Islands for the Coral Sea.

Historical Notes

1. *Yorktown* (CV-5), commissioned in 1937, was 809' 6" long, 83' 1" wide. Standard crew was 2,919, with up to 85 planes. *Yorktown* was one of four carriers in the Atlantic Fleet until it departed from the East Coast for service with the Pacific Fleet on December 16, 1941.

2. The TBD Devastator, first monoplane to appear on U.S. aircraft carriers, was considered obsolete when America entered World War II. Most were destroyed in combat in the Pacific in the first six months of the war. By mid-June 1942, the TBF Avenger torpedo plane was in service on all American aircraft carriers for the rest of the war.

3. *Yorktown*, escorted by three cruisers and four destroyers, left Pearl Harbor on February 14, 1942, as the flagship for Task Force 17. *Yorktown*'s maximum speed was 32 knots. None of the six battleships repaired and returned to service after the attack on Pearl Harbor could exceed 21 knots. (Typical distance per day for U.S. carrier task forces during World War II: 300–400 miles.)

4. Pago Pago is a port city on the island of Tutuila, one of the seven islands in American Samoa, a U.S. territory since 1899. *Yorktown*'s first mission during World War II was to provide air cover for ships carrying Marines to Pago Pago in January 1942.

5. On March 8, 1942, Japan invaded New Guinea (the world's second largest island) with landing forces at two harbors, Lae and Salamaua. Both had been Australian ports and air bases until they fell to Japanese ships, planes, and troops. *Yorktown* and *Lexington* (CV-2) were in the Gulf of Papua at this time.

6. On March 10, 1942, *Yorktown* and *Lexington* launched 104 planes, and they sank or damaged thirteen Japanese ships. This was the first carrier strike of World War II on Japanese-occupied New Guinea. When FDR received news of the outcome, he wrote to Winston Churchill, British Prime Minister, "It was by all means the best day's work we have

had." (*Lexington* lost one plane to antiaircraft fire and returned to Pearl Harbor on March 26.)

7. Sixteen B-25 (medium) bombers, led by Lt. Col. James Doolittle, were launched from the carrier *Hornet* (CV-8), April 18, 1942, and bombed Tokyo, Nagoya, and Kobe. One plane landed in Soviet territory; the rest landed on or near the coast of China. Most of the seventy-one crew members who survived the mission were found and rescued by Chinese civilians.

8. Crux, commonly known as the Southern Cross, is a prominent feature in the night sky at this latitude in the South Pacific. When *Yorktown* arrived at Tongatabu on April 20, 1942, this famous constellation would have appeared at approximately 40 degrees above the horizon.

9. Two of the three Japanese carriers entering the Coral Sea at this time had been with the task force that attacked Pearl Harbor. By mid-April, 1942, U.S. codebreakers at Pearl Harbor had deciphered much of the Japanese Navy's JN-25 code. Adm. Nimitz was informed of their carriers' movements from that point on.

CHAPTER 12: THE BATTLE OF THE CORAL SEA

April 27–May 27, 1942 Time Line

April 28: President Roosevelt says the war is now costing U.S. taxpayers $100 million per day.

May 3: Japanese forces invade, occupy Tulagi, Solomon Islands.

May 4: U.S. carrier *Yorktown* strikes Japanese forces at Tulagi.

May 4: Sugar rationing begins in United States. *War reduces sugar imports from islands in the South Pacific.*

May 4: First use of gas chambers to kill Jews at concentration camp Auschwitz. *Number of people executed by Nazis at Auschwitz and Birkenau: 1.5–2 million.*

May 6: All remaining U.S. troops in the Philippines surrender to Japanese forces at Corregidor. *About 30 percent of the 17,000 Americans captured in the Philippines died in captivity.*

May 7: First Japanese aircraft carrier sunk during World War II: *Shoho*, in the Coral Sea.

May 8: First American aircraft carrier sunk during World War II: *Lexington* (CV-2), Coral Sea.

May 12: Battleship *Massachusetts* (BB-59) is commissioned into the U.S. Navy. *"Big Mamie" was the fifth of ten new battleships added during World War II.*

May 15: The Women's Army Auxiliary Corps (WAAC) is established. *The WAAC was later renamed Women's Army Corps (WAC).*

May 22: Mexico declares war on Germany, Italy, and Japan.

May 27: *Yorktown* arrives at Pearl Harbor for repairs after the Battle of the Coral Sea.

Historical Notes

1. The unusual number of coral atolls in this region of the Pacific Ocean is caused by its proximity to the world's largest deposit of coral off the northeastern coast of Australia (The Great Barrier Reef).

2. *Yorktown*'s (CV-5) strike on Japanese invasion forces at Tulagi, Solomon Islands, sank at least seven maru or auxiliary ships (minecraft and landing barges) and damaged two enemy destroyers. *Yorktown* lost two fighter planes and one torpedo bomber in this attack. (Total number of U.S. planes lost in combat and accidents in the Pacific during World War II: 22,951.)

3. Rear Adm. Frank Jack Fletcher was aboard *Yorktown* and in command of both U.S. aircraft carriers in the Coral Sea at this time. Rear Adm. Aubrey Fitch was aboard *Lexington* (CV-2) when the two carriers physically joined task forces on May 5, 1942.

4. *Neosho* (AD-23) and its destroyer escort, *Sims* (DD-409), were attacked by Japanese carrier planes in the Coral Sea on the morning of May 7, 1942. *Sims* sank almost immediately; fifteen men survived. *Neosho* lingered and was sunk on May 11. There were 108 survivors, about one-third of the men on board.

5. The aircraft carrier *Shoho* was approximately 160 miles from *Yorktown* when it was attacked and sunk by ninety-three planes from *Yorktown* and *Lexington*. (Total Japanese carriers of all sizes sunk during World War II: 19.)

6. *Shoho* was a light (small) Japanese carrier of about twenty planes, none of which were involved in the attack on *Neosho*. *Shoho*'s mission

was to provide air cover for the eleven Japanese troopships en route to invade the Australian base at Port Moresby, New Guinea.

7. Six planes from Japanese carriers *Zuikaku* and *Shokaku* attempted to land on the *Yorktown* 7:00–7:30 P.M., May 7, 1942. (One was shot down by *Yorktown* antiaircraft gunners; eleven others splashed due to lack of fuel while looking for their own carriers in the dark.)

8. On the second day of the Battle of the Coral Sea, *Yorktown* launched an attack group of forty-one planes; *Lexington* launched forty-three.

9. Thirty planes from *Shokaku* and *Zuikaku* were shot down by U.S. fighter planes and antiaircraft gunners defending *Yorktown* and *Lexington,* May 8, 1942.

10. *Yorktown* avoided eight torpedoes and six bombs, all aimed at the ship's island-bridge area. The only direct hit on *Yorktown* was an 800-pound armor-piercing bomb that penetrated the flight deck, fifteen feet from the island, and exploded on deck level four.

11. *Shokaku* did not sink, but it was heavily damaged and out of action for two months. *Zuikaku* was not seen by U.S. planes because of cloud cover. *Zuikaku* was also out of action until mid-June 1942, because it lacked planes and pilots to replace those lost during the Battle of the Coral Sea.

12. *Lexington* was hit by two Japanese torpedoes, which indirectly led to several internal explosions. The destroyer *Phelps* (DD-361) sank *Lexington* with two torpedoes. (This was ordered to prevent the abandoned carrier's capture by the Japanese.)

13. Forty *Yorktown* sailors were killed in action on May 8, 1942, primarily by the bomb explosion on deck four. (Total U.S. Navy personnel killed or missing during World War II: 36,900.)

14. *Yorktown* lost two fighter planes and seven dive-bombers in combat on May 8, 1942. Six pilots and six aviation radiomen (gunners) were reported missing in action, presumed dead. (Total U.S. military personnel classified MIA during World War II: 78,000.)

15. Adolf Hitler also proclaimed the Battle of the Coral Sea a Japanese victory. *The New York Times* inaccurately reported the opposite, claiming nearly two dozen Japanese ships were sunk or crippled, and the "enemy in flight, pursued by Allied warships." (The U.S. Navy did not announce the sinking of *Lexington* to the American public until weeks later.)

16. The Battle of the Coral Sea was the world's first battle between aircraft carriers. It was also the first time Japan was stopped from a planned invasion of Allied territory. (The troopships headed for Port Moresby, New Guinea, returned to Japan, thus ending the threat to northern Australia.)

17. *Yorktown* was recalled to Pearl Harbor on or about May 14, 1942. Navy codebreakers had discovered that the Japanese were planning a major carrier strike on the U.S. naval air station located at the farthest northern tip of the Hawaiian island chain: Midway.

18. *Oklahoma* (BB-37) remained where it sank until 1943, then was lost while being towed to the West Coast for repairs. No attempt was ever made to raise *Arizona* (BB-39) or the former battleship *Utah* (BB-31/AG-16). All other ships damaged or sunk during the attack on Pearl Harbor were repaired and returned to service during World War II.

CHAPTER 13: THE BATTLE OF MIDWAY

May 27–noon, June 4, 1942 Time Line

May 27: Four aircraft carriers depart Japanese ports for the planned attack on Midway.

May 28: *Enterprise* (CV-6) and *Hornet* (CV-8) depart Pearl Harbor to defend Midway.

May 30: First 1,000-bomber British Royal Air Force attack strikes Cologne, Germany.

May 30: *Yorktown* (CV-5) departs Pearl Harbor to defend Midway.

June 2: *Yorktown* combines task forces with *Hornet* and *Enterprise* near Midway.

June 3: First Japanese attack on Alaska during World War II. *Light carrier* Ryujo*'s planes bomb and strafe U.S. military bases on Alaska's Aleutian Islands.*

June 4: Early morning strike by Japanese carrier planes on U.S. Naval Air Station at Midway.

June 4: Midmorning strike by U.S. carrier planes destroys three Japanese carriers near Midway.

June 4: At noon, Japanese carrier planes attack *Yorktown* near Midway.

Historical Notes

1. *Hornet* (CV-8), seventh ship of that name, was commissioned in October 1941 but did not join the Pacific Fleet until March 1942. *Hornet* and *Enterprise* (CV-6) were at Pearl Harbor from May 26–28, 1942. *Saratoga* (CV-3) was on the West Coast for repairs. Thus *Hornet, Enterprise,* and *Yorktown* (CV-5) were the only aircraft carriers in service with the Pacific Fleet at this crucial time.

2. Midway, an atoll with two small islets, is 1,135 miles northwest of Pearl Harbor. This was the westernmost U.S. military installation in the Pacific at this time. Midway Naval Air Station, established in 1941, was guarded by U.S. Marines.

3. In 1942 alone—America's first full year of involvement in World War II—the U.S. military lost a total of 344 planes in combat or "operational accidents" such as this one on *Yorktown.*

4. There were 93 warships in the Japanese task force which was assigned to attack, invade, and occupy Midway: 4 large carriers, 2 light carriers, 4 seaplane carriers, 7 battleships, 14 cruisers, 46 destroyers, 16 submarines.

5. The U.S. task force sent to defend Midway from the approaching Japanese Imperial Navy was outnumbered in every surface warship type. The 47 American warships included 3 carriers—*Hornet, Enterprise,* and *Yorktown*—8 cruisers, 17 destroyers, and 19 submarines.

6. Adm. Nimitz's advance knowledge of the Japanese plan to attack Midway was provided by the Navy Combat Intelligence Unit at Pearl Harbor. By June 1942, U.S. cryptographers were able to decipher most of the code used to communicate with and among all admirals in the Imperial Japanese Navy.

7. Postwar interviews with Japanese military leaders indicated no plan for a second attack on Pearl Harbor, nor did Japan plan a carrier strike on the West Coast in June 1942. The Japanese military believed this attack on Midway would lure the Pacific Fleet's last three serviceable carriers into a battle where they would be outnumbered and destroyed.

8. Japan originally planned to send six large carriers to attack Midway, as they did Pearl Harbor, but *Zuikaku* and *Shokaku* were still out of service after damage and losses sustained in the Battle of the Coral Sea. Thus, Japan's Midway task force included the only four large carriers available at that time: *Kaga, Akagi, Soryu,* and *Hiryu.*

9. *Yorktown's* dive-bomber squadron caught *Soryu* in the act of refueling and rearming planes which had just returned from bombing the naval air station on Midway. *Soryu* sank a few hours later, in the afternoon of June 4, 1942.

10. *Akagi* and *Kaga* were also refueling and rearming their planes when they were attacked by dive-bombers from *Enterprise. (Kaga* sank later that night; *Akagi* was so badly damaged, Japanese destroyers torpedoed and sank it the next day.)

11. The eighteen Japanese dive-bombers and four fighter planes approaching *Yorktown* at this time were from *Hiryu,* fourth and last of the large Japanese carriers present during the Battle of Midway.

12. The Tokyo Rose radio programs, directed toward U.S. forces in the Pacific, often included taunts and inaccurate reports of Allied losses. Although many English-speaking women were employed at Radio Tokyo for this purpose, only one Japanese-American woman was ever tried and convicted for treason as Tokyo Rose. She was pardoned by President Gerald Ford in 1977.

13. *Yorktown* was hit by three bombs during this attack. The second bomb exploded in or near the carrier's smokestack and disabled its engines.

CHAPTER 14: ABANDON SHIP

12:20 P.M.–afternoon, June 4, 1942 Time Line

12:20 P.M.: Yorktown comes to full stop due to bomb damage by Japanese carrier planes.

12:40 P.M.: Bomb damage to *Yorktown's* flight deck is repaired.

1:13 P.M.: Rear Adm. Fletcher leaves *Yorktown,* transfers to cruiser *Astoria* (CA-34).

1:40 P.M.: Yorktown's engines re-start.

2:02 P.M.: Yorktown's speed is 5 knots (20 knots is necessary to resume flight operations).

2:10 P.M.: Yorktown receives radar warning of incoming Japanese carrier planes.

2:32 P.M.: Twelve *Yorktown* fighter planes engage ten Japanese torpedo bombers and six fighter planes.

2:40 P.M.: U.S. cruisers and destroyers open fire on Japanese planes approaching *Yorktown.*

2:44 P.M.: First of two Japanese torpedoes strike *Yorktown,* port side.

2:45 P.M.: *Yorktown* search planes report location of a fourth, still-undamaged Japanese carrier.

2:50 P.M.: *Yorktown* is at full stop, listing 26 degrees.

2:55 P.M.: Capt. Elliott Buckmaster orders all surviving *Yorktown* crew to abandon ship.

Historical Notes

1. Fifty-two antiaircraft gunners were killed (twenty-five wounded) by the Japanese attack on *Yorktown* (CV-5) at Midway.

2. The three U.S. carriers launched a total of forty-one TBD Devastator torpedo planes on June 4, 1942. Thirty-five were shot down by Japanese fighter planes or antiaircraft guns. Two of the surviving six were from a *Yorktown* squadron. Both ran out of fuel and splashed on the way back to the carrier.

3. U.S. Navy Lt. Cmdr. J. S. "Jimmy" Thach invented and taught the aerial combat tactic known as the Thach weave, which compensated for the superior maneuverability of the Japanese fighter planes. He was one of *Yorktown*'s fighter pilots at Midway.

4. American fighter planes and antiaircraft fire shot down five Japanese torpedo planes and three Zeroes during this second attack on *Yorktown.* (Total Japanese military aircraft lost in combat or to accidents during World War II: 49,485.)

5. Rear Adm. Frank Jack Fletcher was accompanied by his personal staff and several enlisted men from *Yorktown* when he transferred his flag to the heavy cruiser *Astoria* (CA-34).

CHAPTER 15: RESCUED AT SEA

Mid-afternoon, June 4–June 9, 1942 Time Line

3:00 P.M.: U.S. destroyers begin rescuing *Yorktown*'s crew near Midway.

4:00 P.M.: Second Japanese carrier plane attack on Alaska's Aleutian Islands.

4:03 *P.M.*: Rear Adm. Frank Jack Fletcher passes command to Adm. Raymond A. Spruance on *Enterprise*. *All subsequent decisions for entire U.S. task force at Midway are made by Spruance.*

5:00 *P.M.*: U.S. carrier planes attack *Hiryu*, fourth largest Japanese carrier at Midway.

7:20 *P.M.*: Japanese carrier *Soryu* sinks, due to damage from morning attack.

7:25 *P.M.*: Japanese carrier *Kaga* sinks, due to damage from morning attack.

June 5, 1942

12:20 *A.M.*: Japanese Adm. Isoroku Yamamoto calls off the invasion of Midway.

Dawn: Japanese carrier *Akagi* sinks, due to damage from June 4 attack.

9:00 *A.M.*: Japanese carrier *Hiryu* sinks, due to damage from June 4 attack. *Total Imperial Japanese Navy warships sunk by Allies during World War II: 686.*

June 6, 1942

1:30 *P.M.*: Japanese submarine *I-168* fires torpedoes at abandoned *Yorktown*.

June 7, 1942

U.S. aircraft carrier *Yorktown* sinks at 6:00 A.M., due to June 6 attack by Japanese submarine.

U.S. Navy announces victory at Midway, declines to state American losses or casualties. *Actual losses: 349 killed or missing, 98 carrier planes, 38 land-based planes, 2 warships.*

Japanese troops invade and occupy Attu and Kiska, Aleutian Islands, Alaska.

June 9, 1942

Japanese officials and Tokyo Rose claim Midway victory, but admit that 35 planes and 2 ships were lost. *Actual losses: 2,155 killed or missing, 250 carrier planes, 5 ships (4 large carriers; 1 cruiser).*

American commanders of newly created U.S. Eighth Air Force arrive in England.

Kodiak is established as an operating base for U.S. Navy ships and submarines in Alaska. *This island in the Gulf of Alaska had previously served as a base for military planes.*

Historical Notes

1. All of the *Yorktown*'s (CV-5) 2,270 known survivors were rescued by U.S. destroyers within three hours after the carrier was disabled and abandoned near Midway.

2. *Enterprise* (CV-6) and *Hornet* (CV-8) launched forty-one dive-bombers when the fourth enemy carrier was sighted, late afternoon, June 4, 1942. *Hiryu* was so heavily damaged by their attack, it sank the following day.

3. On the night of June 4, 1942, the destroyer *Hughes* (DD-410) was assigned to torpedo and sink the *Yorktown* only if the abandoned carrier was in danger of capture by any ship from the large Japanese task force near Midway.

4. Aviation Radioman Second Class Robert Boyd "Mike" Brazier (1916–1942) was awarded, posthumously, the Navy's Distinguished Flying Cross medal for heroism during the Battle of Midway. Two years later, a new destroyer escort ship, *Robert Brazier* (DE-345), was named for him.

5. Of the 241 in the *Hammann* (DD-412) crew, eighty-one were killed or missing. "Many" drowned after this mysterious underwater explosion, probably caused by the accidental detonation of one of the destroyer's own torpedoes. (Ninety-two of the 167 U.S. Navy and Coast Guard vessels sunk or damaged beyond repair during World War II were destroyers or destroyer escort-type ships.)

6. The Japanese submarine *I-168* did escape, with little or no damage, in spite of at least sixty-one depth charges dropped in this area by the destroyers *Hughes* (DD-410), *Gwin* (DD-433/DM-33), and *Monaghan* (DD-354).

7. The 19,800-ton *Yorktown*, landed right side up, three miles down. It was found in 1998 in its present location near Midway Island and was photographed and documented by underseas explorer Robert Ballard, who also found the passenger ship *Titanic* in the North Atlantic.

CHAPTER 16: THE SUMMER OF '42

June 10–September 1942 Time Line

June 11: First U.S. bombing raid on Japanese-occupied Aleutian Islands, Alaska. *The Army Air Force B-17 and B-24 heavy bombers flew from U.S. base at Cold Bay.*

June 12: Anne Frank receives a diary for her thirteenth birthday. *Days later, she begins writing of hiding from Nazis in German-occupied Amsterdam.*

June 18: First U.S. efforts to develop an atomic bomb. *The Army Corps of Engineers begins organizing for research on the still-theoretical weapon.*

June 21: Japanese submarine *I-25* shells Oregon beach near Fort Stevens. *This was the first and only attack on a military base on the U.S. mainland during World War II.*

June 25: European Theater of Operations is established by U.S. Army. *Maj. Gen. Dwight D. Eisenhower (1890–1969) commands.*

June 30: U.S. civilian press reports one million Jews killed by Nazis. *A brief article in* The New York Times *was buried on page 7.*

July 1: First Flying Fortress arrives in England. *The U.S. Army Air Force's B-17 was the world's first high-altitude, long-range bomber.*

July 4: First U.S. Eighth Air Force operation of World War II over Nazi-occupied Europe. *Americans flew six of the British bombers in an RAF attack on German air bases in Holland.*

July 4: Flying Tigers become part of U.S. Tenth Air Force. *American aviators continue to defend China as China Air Task Force.*

July 22: Treblinka, Poland, becomes a Nazi death camp. *Treblinka was one of the twenty-six major prison camps in Europe devoted exclusively to mass murder.*

July 30: WAVES established: Women Accepted for Volunteer Emergency Service. *About 84,000 American women served in the Navy's WAVES during World War II.*

August 4: First Jews from Belgium are deported to Auschwitz. *Of the 25,631 Belgian Jews taken to Auschwitz during World War II, 1,244 survived.*

August 7: First U.S. ground offensive of World War II. *Marines land on Japanese-occupied Guadalcanal, largest of the Solomon Islands.*

August 9: The Battle of Savo Island: Japanese Navy sinks four Allied cruisers. *U.S. Marines in battle on Guadalcanal are left without supplies or support from warships' guns.*

August 11: The atomic weapons project receives its official code name: Manhattan Engineering District. *"Manhattan Project" is the common name for secret U.S. research and development of atomic weapons.*

August 16: Battleship *Alabama* (BB 60) is commissioned into the U.S. Navy. *Average 39-month construction time for battleships reduces to 32 months during World War II.*

August 17: First U.S. bombing raid over Europe during World War II. *Twelve B-17 heavy bombers attack German-occupied France.*

August 22: Brazil declares war on Italy and Germany.

August 24: Japanese aircraft carrier *Ryujo* sinks near Guadalcanal, Solomon Islands. *It was destroyed by planes from U.S. carrier Saratoga (CV-3).*

Historical Notes

1. By July 1942, the number of enlisted men at Pearl Harbor's submarine base was 1,081, nearly twice as many as the year before. Sub base enlisted personnel peaked at 6,633 in mid-1944. (Total U.S. Navy personnel in all locations during the summer of 1942: 640,570.)

2. The Battle of Midway did not end the war, but it was a major turning point: After the loss of carriers and trained pilots at Midway, Japan was no longer the dominant air and sea power in the Pacific. This permitted the U.S. military to turn more public attention and resources to future battles with Nazi Germany and its Axis allies in Europe and North Africa.

3. The carrier *Bonhomme Richard,* under construction at this time, was renamed *Yorktown* (CV-10) and commissioned the following year. Nicknamed the "Fighting Lady," this new carrier served for the rest of the war and the two wars that followed, Korea and Vietnam. (It is currently on display at Patriots Point Naval and Maritime Museum, Charleston, South Carolina.)

4. During World War II 6,332, 000 (38.8 percent) of all U.S. military personnel were volunteers; 11,535,000 (61.2 percent) were drafted. More than 6 million additional volunteers and draftees were rejected for mental, physical, or other reasons such as age, occupation, or number of dependents.

5. U.S. military aircraft production far exceeded that of all other countries during World War II, largely because 6.5 million American women took jobs in defense-related factories. By war's end, women constituted more than one-third of the total civilian labor force. (Total U.S. planes built, 1941–1945: 295,486.)

6. Three U.S. submarines were lost in the Pacific during the summer of 1942. Of the 16,000 men who served on submarines during World War II, 22 percent were killed or missing in action. This was the highest percentage of casualties among all branches of the military during World War II.

7. Many submarines reported dud torpedoes in early 1942. The malfunctions were blamed on human error until mid-1943 when the Navy discovered that the torpedoes themselves were defective. As torpedo technology improved, submarine kills increased. Deadliest American submarine of all during World War II was *Tautog* (SS-199): it sank twenty-six enemy ships.

8. *Perch* (SS-176) had far worse trouble than dud torpedoes. After this crewman's January or February 1942 mission, *Perch* was scuttled—deliberately sunk by its crew—after being damaged by Japanese destroyers. All fifty-nine surviving crew members were taken prisoner, March 3, 1942. The Waterfront Memorial at Pearl Harbor honors all fifty-two U.S. submarines lost during World War II and the more than 3,500 submarine crewmembers killed or missing or presumed dead.

9. The U.S. Navy leased the entire Royal Hawaiian Hotel during World War II, beginning in late January 1942. For the remainder of the war, this luxury resort on Waikiki Beach was known as the "Rest and Recuperation Annex to the Submarine Base." The Royal Hawaiian Hotel did not reopen to civilian tourists until 1947.

10. Rumors of a presidential conference with Adm. Nimitz at CinCPac headquarters during the summer of 1942 were two years premature. President Franklin D. Roosevelt arrived at Pearl Harbor on the heavy cruiser *Baltimore* (CA-68), July 26, 1944.

11. By this time in 1942, Nimitz was in overall command of the Pacific Fleet and all other American military forces in the North, Central, and South Pacific. (Army Gen. Douglas MacArthur commanded the military in the Southwest Pacific.)

12. The United Service Organizations (USO) offered entertainment and assistance to U.S. military personnel in about three thousand locations during World War II. (The six founding organizations of the USO were

the YMCA, YWCA, National Catholic Community Service, National Jewish Welfare Board, National Traveler's Aid Association, and Salvation Army.)

13. The Japanese Army had 6.3 million serving in the Pacific during World War II. (The total for the U.S. Army in both Europe and the Pacific during World War II was 7.9 million.)

14. It took 11,000 Marines, 50,000 soldiers, a naval battle, and six months of combat to remove 36,000 Japanese troops from Guadalcanal, largest of the Solomon Islands. This was the first major land battle for U.S. troops during World War II. (Total U.S. Marine and Army personnel killed in action during this campaign: 1,592. Japan lost at least 14,000.)

15. In the Battle of the Atlantic, German submarines attacked all ships from any nation that carried troops and supplies to England. More American ships were sunk in June 1942 than in any other month of the entire war. (Total Allied merchant and supply ships destroyed by German subs during World War II: 5,150).

CHAPTER 17: FIRST LEAVE

September–October 1942 Time Line

September 1: U.S. Navy Seabees are inserted in a combat zone for the first time. *They build infrastructure for a new U.S. base on Guadalcanal, Solomon Islands.*

September 7: Fireside Chat calls for more U.S. civilian sacrifice on the home front. *President Roosevelt says the war will cost nearly $100 billion in 1943.*

September 8: The Allies establish a plan for "round-the-clock" bombing of Nazi-occupied Europe. *American planes will fly daylight missions; British will continue bombing at night.*

September 9: First (and only) aerial bombing attack on the continental United States during World War II. *One small plane launched by a Japanese submarine drops bomb in an Oregon forest.*

September 13: The Battle of Stalingrad turns house to house. *Total German forces killed or captured by Russians at Stalingrad: 300,000.*

September 16: U.S. carrier *Wasp* (CV-7) sinks near Guadalcanal. Wasp *was sunk by U.S. destroyers after it was heavily damaged by a Japanese submarine.*

September 25: First combined Canadian-American bombing mission of World War II. *Canada's Kittyhawk fighter planes take part in this attack on Japanese-occupied Aleutian Islands, Alaska.*

September 27: Glenn Miller's last performance as a civilian. *The world-famous musician of the big-band era joined the U.S. Army Air Force.*

Historical Notes

1. The federal government ordered all car manufacturers to stop selling vehicles to civilians in February 1942. This and many other American industries were required to retool to build and sell products chiefly to the military by the Office of Production Management.

2. Treasure Island is a man-made island, created for the Golden Gate International Exposition (1939–1940), which celebrated the completion of both the Golden Gate Bridge and the San Francisco–Oakland Bay Bridge. During World War II, Treasure Island was converted to a processing center for Navy personnel returning from—or on their way to—service in the Pacific.

3. The Zephyr was produced during the model years 1936–1942 by the Lincoln division of the Ford Motor Company. When civilian car manufacturing and sales resumed after World War II, the Lincoln Continental evolved from the prewar Zephyr.

4. By the fall of 1942, the U.S. Army had seized nineteen civilian airlines and about four hundred passenger planes for military use. This left approximately one hundred planes for all civilian travel in the United States. Thus, the shortage of seats, few nonstop flights, and increased demand for space on the nation's trains and buses during World War II.

5. *Yorktown* (CV-5) survivors were probably segregated from the general population at Treasure Island because the Navy had not yet announced the sinking of *Yorktown*. The loss was not revealed to the civilian press until mid-September 1942. Human casualties at Midway remained secret until 1943.

6. The shortage of fabric for military uniforms induced the U.S. government's War Production Board to order clothing manufacturers to shorten women's skirts. Further savings were achieved in men's fashions: trouser cuffs were eliminated, as were the traditional vests for business suits.

7. Motion picture studios in the United States released hundreds of films in 1942. *Casablanca, Yankee Doodle Dandy, Mrs. Miniver,* and Disney's

animated *Bambi* were among those that were seen for the first time in American movie theaters that year.

8. The Army Air Corps, established in 1926, continued to exist after the Army Air Forces was created in June 1941, but all of its operations were absorbed by the Army Air Forces when the Office of Chief of the Air Corps was dissolved in March 1942. Neither the Army Air Corps nor the Army Air Forces were officially disestablished until the modern U.S. Air Force achieved its current status as a separate branch of the military by act of Congress, September 18, 1947.

9. The first General Equivalency Diploma or General Educational Development (GED) test was developed in 1942, chiefly due to the large number of Americans who dropped out of high school to join the military or the civilian work force in defense-related factories during World War II. Its purpose was to promote further education for all Americans whose studies were interrupted by the war.

CHAPTER 18: THE NAVAL RESEARCH LABORATORY

October 1942–July 1943 Time Line

October 9: First U.S. 100-bomber attack on German-occupied Europe. *Total U.S. Army Air Force bombing missions over Europe in 1942: 27.*

October 11–12: The Battle of Cape Esperance, near Guadalcanal, Solomon Islands. *U.S. Navy and Marines sink four Japanese destroyers.*

October 12: President Roosevelt announces plans for "the teen-age draft." *Prior minimum age for compulsory military service was twenty.*

October 15: Physicist J. Robert Oppenheimer is asked to head the Manhattan Project.

October 23: The Battle of El Alamein, Egypt. *U.S. planes support British tanks in the first major Allied offensive in North Africa.*

October 26–27: The Battle of Santa Cruz, near Guadalcanal, Solomon Islands. Hornet (CV-8), *fourth and last large U.S. aircraft carrier ever lost in combat, is sunk.*

November 8: Operation Torch, first U.S. ground offensive of WWII against German and Italian forces, begins. *American tanks and troops join British in desert warfare in North Africa.*

November 11: German and Italian forces invade Vichy France.

November 12–15: The Naval Battle of Guadalcanal is another major defeat for Japan. *U.S. land and carrier-based planes sank seven Japanese troopships.*

November 13: Draft age for all American males is lowered to eighteen.

November 13: The Sullivan brothers die on the same U.S. warship. *All five brothers were aboard the light cruiser* Juneau (CL-52) *when it sank in the naval Battle of Guadalcanal.*

November 16: Los Alamos, New Mexico, is chosen site for Manhattan Project research.

December 4: First U.S. bombing attack on Italian mainland during World War II. *U.S. Army Air Force strikes Italy's fleet in Naples harbor.*

December 16: Nazis order Gypsies (now known as Roma) to Auschwitz. *About 80 percent of Europe's Gypsies died in this and other concentration camps during the war.*

December 17: Holocaust facts are revealed to British House of Commons. *British foreign secretary announces mass execution of European Jews by Nazis.*

December 31: Aircraft carrier *Essex* (CV-9) is commissioned into the U.S. Navy.

1943

January 14–24: The Casablanca Conference: Roosevelt and Churchill meet in Morocco. *Roosevelt says Germany's "unconditional surrender" is required to end the war in Europe.*

January 27: First U.S. Army Air Force bombing mission to Germany. *Primary target for 91 heavy bombers is port city Wilhelmshaven.*

February 1: 442nd Regimental Combat Team is authorized by U.S. Army. *Most of these soldiers were volunteers from Japanese American internment camps in the United States.*

February 2: Hitler's first major battlefield defeat of World War II. *At Stalingrad, the German Sixth Army surrendered to the Soviet Red Army.*

February 6: U.S. military declares Guadalcanal secure. *Surviving Japanese troops evacuate to other islands in the Solomons.*

February 13: U.S. Marine Corps accepts women for combat support duties.

About 18,500 American women volunteered as Marines during World War II.

February 17: Aircraft carrier *Lexington* (CV-16) is commissioned. *It was named in honor of the* Lexington *(CV-2) that sank in the Battle of the Coral Sea.*

February 18: U.S. warships shell beaches of Japanese-occupied Attu, Aleutian Islands, Alaska.

February 27: First attempt to slow or stop Nazi research on nuclear weapons. *Allies bomb German heavy water factory in Norway.*

March 2–5: Battle of Bismarck Sea. *U.S. and Australian forces sink twelve ships en route to Japanese-occupied Lae, New Guinea.*

March 13: Crematorium II opens at Auschwitz-Birkenau concentration camp. *Nazis can now burn bodies of about 8,000 gas-chamber victims per day.*

March 15: U.S. Navy subdivides into numbered fleets. *Even-numbered Fleets are in the Atlantic; odd numbers are in the Pacific.*

March 26: Battle of Komandorski Islands: U.S. warships defeat Japanese Navy in Alaskan waters. *This was the only World War II naval battle in which no planes or submarines were involved.*

March 29: U.S. government begins rationing meat, butter, and cheese to American civilians.

April 15: Aircraft carrier *Yorktown* (CV-10) is commissioned into U.S. Navy. *Total American carriers of all sizes added during World War II: 98. Japan built 12.*

April 18: Death of Admiral Yamamoto, Commander in Chief, Imperial Japanese Navy. *His plane was shot down by U.S. Army Air Force fighter planes over the Solomon Islands.*

April 19-May 16: First major civilian resistance to the Holocaust: Warsaw ghetto uprising. *About 60,000 Polish Jews were killed or captured by heavily armed Nazi troops.*

May 11–30: The Battle of Attu: a U.S. Army victory over Japanese occupation forces in Alaska. *This was the only major land battle of World War II fought in North America.*

May 13: End of the war in North Africa. *About 250,000 German and Italian soldiers are now Allied prisoners of war.*

May 22: The Battle of the Atlantic ends: Germany suspends U-boat attacks on Allied vessels. *By this date, Allied warships had sunk about three-quarters of all German submarines in the North Atlantic.*

May 29: "Rosie the Riveter" appears on the cover of U.S. magazine *Saturday Evening Post. The Norman Rockwell painting symbolizes all women factory workers during World War II.*

June 9: George H. W. Bush becomes the youngest pilot in the U.S. Navy. *The future forty-first president of the United States graduated from flight school days before his nineteenth birthday.*

Historical Notes

1. The Naval Research Laboratory, founded in 1923, was the first modern research institution created within the U.S. Navy. The first modern radar to be installed on a U.S. Navy ship (battleship *New York* [BB-34] 1938) was invented and designed at this facility located near the Pentagon in the southwest quadrant of Washington, D.C.

2. Primarily to save tire rubber for military use, owners of "nonessential" civilian vehicles in seventeen states could purchase only three gallons of gas per week, beginning in May 1942. Gas rationing went into effect in all states on December 1, 1942.

3. About 59,000 women joined the U.S. Army Nurse Corps during World War II; 201 died from enemy action or accidents. Another 150,000 women served as WAACs (Women's Auxiliary Army Corps) or the later WACs (Women's Army Corps). Nursing was one of the few combat-support duties for which neither WAACs nor WACs were normally trained or used.

4. The liquid thermal diffusion method to obtain enriched uranium for nuclear weapons was invented at the Naval Research Laboratory in 1942 by American physicist Philip Abelson (1913–2004). The code name given to all secret research in this field during World War II was the "Manhattan Engineering District," also known as the "Manhattan Project." It required approximately 600,000 American workers and 2.2 billion dollars to build the three atomic bombs that exploded in 1945.

5. Because of disastrous accidents on dirigibles such as *Hindenburg,* the U.S. Navy discarded the rigid airship in favor of the less dangerous nonrigid airship variation, commonly called "blimps." Blimps were typically used to spot enemy submarines approaching U.S. coastal

cities. (In 2004, the U.S. Army revealed that blimps are again being developed for military surveillance purposes.)

6. Bernard R. Hubbard (1888–1962), a Jesuit priest and geology professor at Santa Clara University, was internationally famous for his films and lectures from his expeditions to Alaska. Father Hubbard advised the U.S. military in its efforts to defeat Japanese troops who occupied the Aleutians Islands Attu and Kiska.

7. The Aleutian Islands had been a combat zone since Japanese carrier planes bombed the U.S. base at Dutch Harbor in June 1942. Few Americans were aware of Japan's subsequent invasion and occupation of the Aleutian Islands, due to the general policy of secrecy pertaining to most U.S. military operations in Alaska.

8. Many U.S. military flights to, from, and within the Aleutian Islands were canceled or aborted because of adverse weather conditions, frequently characterized as among the worst in the world. The season of almost daily fog in this region of the North Pacific begins in June.

9. The Jewish-American violinist Yehudi Menuhin (1916–1999), one of the world's leading classical musicians of the twentieth century, gave hundreds of concerts for Allied troops during World War II. After the war, he gave a series of free concerts for Holocaust survivors at the liberated Nazi concentration camp Bergen-Belsen.

10. Free long-distance calls and other services for military personnel at USO clubs were paid for by a $33 million fund-raising campaign, headed by Prescott Bush, father of the forty-first president, George H. W. Bush. About 1.5 million Americans volunteered for USO work during World War II.

CHAPTER 19: COLD BAY

July Through December 1943 Time Line

July 5: The Battle of Kursk, largest tank battle in history, begins in Russia. *This six-week battle involved 6,000 German and Soviet tanks, 4,000 planes, 2 million men.*

July 6: Battle of Kula Gulf: Seven U.S. warships engage ten Japanese destroyers en route to the Solomons.

July 10: Allies invade Sicily: U.S. and Britain begin landing 160,000 troops on Italian soil.

July 10: First U.S. bombing raid on Japanese territory from an Alaskan air base. *Eight medium bombers from Attu attacked Japan's Kurile Islands.*

July 19: Allied planes drop 800,000 warning leaflets on Rome, bomb military targets near the city.

July 25: Italy's fascist dictator Benito Mussolini is deposed and arrested.

August 2: *PT-109*, a U.S. Navy patrol torpedo boat, sinks in the Solomon Islands. *The captain was future thirty-fifth president of the United States, John F. Kennedy (1917–1963).*

August 19: The Quebec Agreement. *American, British, and Canadian scientists agree to work together on atomic bomb research.*

September 8: Allies announce Italian government's surrender; Nazis still occupy northern Italy.

September 11: German forces occupy Rome.

September 12: German commandos rescue Mussolini. *Hitler later appoints Mussolini to govern German-occupied northern Italy.*

September 12: Japanese-occupied Salamaua, New Guinea, falls to Allied ground forces.

September 22: Last U.S. bombing mission over North Africa during World War II.

September 29: New Italian Prime Minister Pietro Badoglio signs armistice with Allies.

October 5–6: Six-carrier U.S. task force attacks Japanese-occupied Wake Island.

October 10: Chiang Kai-shek (1887–1975) is sworn in as President of China.

October 13: New civilian government in Italy joins Allies, declares war on Germany.

November 22: Chiang Kai-shek meets British Prime Minister and U.S. President. *They agree to an Allied invasion of Japanese-occupied Burma.*

November 28: First Big Three conference: Roosevelt, Churchill, and Stalin meet in Teheran, Iran. *They discuss plans for Allied invasion of German-occupied Europe.*

November 29: U.S. carrier *Hornet* (CV-12) is commissioned.

It was named in honor of Hornet *(CV-8) that sank in the 1942 Battle of Santa Cruz.*

December 4: Six-carrier U.S. task force attacks Kwajalein and Wotje atolls, Marshall Islands.

December 10: German bombers attack U.S. air bases in England.

December 12: U.S. fighter planes defend Hengyang, China, from major Japanese bomber attack.

December 24: U.S. Army Gen. Eisenhower is named to command all Allied forces in Europe.

Historical Notes

1. Harbor security was one of many Coast Guard duties as part of the Navy during World War II. Coast Guard crews operated 802 cutters— ships longer than sixty-five feet—plus 351 Navy and 288 Army vessels. They sank eleven enemy submarines during the war. (Total World War II U.S. Coast Guard personnel: 231,000 men; 10,000 women.)

2. Aleuts are Native Alaskans, indigenous to both the Aleutian Peninsula and Aleutian Islands. Some Aleuts refer to themselves as Unangan, which translates to "the real people" or "we the people." (Population of King Cove in 2005: 723.)

3. After World War II, much of this region was set aside as the Izembek National Wildlife Refuge. It now preserves the natural habitat of migratory birds, caribou, and grizzly bears on the Aleutian Peninsula.

4. Quonset huts, named for their production facility near Quonset, Rhode Island, were developed for the U.S. Navy during World War II. The original model of this prefabricated structure was 16 by 36 feet. Total Quonset huts acquired by the Navy use during the war: 153,200. (After the war, many Quonset huts were sold for $1,000 each to civilians as homes, barns, and classrooms.)

5. In May 1943, about 15,000 U.S. Army troops landed on Japanese-occupied Attu. All but 29 of the 2,379 Japanese soldiers on Attu were found dead after a series of suicidal charges. Total U.S. casualties on Attu were 549 killed, 1,148 wounded, 2,100 noncombat illnesses and injuries. This percentage of American casualties for a single battle was second only to Iwo Jima during World War II.

6. Many Aleuts were killed or captured by Japanese invasion forces on the island of Attu in June 1942. At least thirty-nine Aleuts from the small village on Attu were taken back to Japan as prisoners of war.

7. At the tip of Alaska's Aleutian Peninsula in early July, the sun does not drop below the horizon. Although sunset occurs at approximately 8:30 P.M. and sunrise comes at 3:15 A.M., the night hours in between are characterized as "bright twilight."

8. Cold Bay, originally a Navy air field in 1942, became a Naval Auxiliary Air Facility in 1943, housing about 500 personnel. The Army's nearby Fort Randall, designed for 3,500, grew to nearly 5,000 during the summer of 1943. By the end of that year, U.S. and Canadian forces at these and other bases in the Aleutians totaled about 144,000.

9. Of the 130 Japanese submarines destroyed or lost during World War II, only fourteen were confirmed sunk or damaged beyond repair by bombs from any type of Allied aircraft.

10. A major attack on the estimated 10,000 Japanese soldiers who occupied Kiska began with offshore bombardment from sixteen U.S. warships, supported by Army Air Force bombers and fighter planes, August 2, 1943. On the nearby islands of Amchitka and Adak, 34,000 U.S. and Canadian troops were training for the amphibious assault to follow.

11. In 1943, bombers dropped about 60,000 "kiri leaflets" on Japanese troops in the Aleutian Islands. These leaflets were deliberately designed to resemble a leaf from the paulownia tree. In classical Japanese literature, a single falling leaf from the paulownia tree is a symbol of great misfortune or death.

12. U.S. and Canadian troops landed unopposed on Kiska, August 15, 1943. Japanese postwar records indicate their entire occupation force of 7,800 was evacuated from Kiska by submarines and surface ships under cover of fog by July 28. (All Allied casualties on Kiska—twenty-eight killed, fifty-five wounded—were caused by accidents or friendly fire.)

13. The unusual weather conditions in the Aleutian Islands, including year-round fog and frequent williwaws, are caused by their location in the North Pacific, where the warmer Japan Current intersects with the much colder waters of the Bering Sea.

14. The heaviest single-day loss of B-17 bombers and crews in 1943 occurred at Regensburg and Schweinfurt, Germany. On August 17, 60 out of 315 planes were shot down. Another 60 (out of 230) were shot down over the same target on October 14, 1943. These losses brought an end to all daylight bombing over Germany for several weeks.

15. Beginning on November 19, 1943, about 17,000 Marines landed on beaches at Tarawa and Betio, Gilbert Islands. All but 146 of the 4,500 Japanese occupying force died in the four-day battle that followed. Total Marine casualties: 980 dead; 2,050 wounded. Navy ground casualties were chiefly medical corpsmen: 29 killed, 51 wounded. (An additional 323 Navy casualties occurred on the landing transport ships.)

16. Although Japan did continue sporadic air and sea attacks on Adak, Kiska, and Attu for the remainder of the war, there were no further attempts to occupy any portion of Alaska after the Japanese troops were evacuated from Kiska in July 1943.

17. Hideki Tojo (1884–1948) was the Japanese Army General who served as Premier and virtual dictator of Japan from 1941 to 1944. After the war, he was tried and executed in Tokyo for crimes against humanity.

18. *Algonquin* (YAG-29/CG-4/RC), a 205-foot U.S. Coast Guard cutter, was built in 1897 and served in European waters during World War I. It was decommissioned in 1930 and sold to a Washington State company in 1931. *Algonguin* was often in Alaskan waters with a civilian captain and crew during World War II.

CHAPTER 20: KODIAK

January Through December 1944 Time Line

January 4: U.S. Army Air Force begins Operation Carpetbagger. *Planes drop supplies to the Underground, Nazi resistance forces in German-occupied Europe.*

January 6: Soviet Armies advance into German-occupied section of Poland.

January 22-May 24: Battle of Anzio, the Allied invasion of German-occupied southern Italy. *U.S. casualties are 5,200 killed or missing in action, 11,000 wounded.*

January 27: Siege of Leningrad ends. *Soviet forces defeat German troops who had surrounded this city for two years.*

January 31-Feb 3: Battle of Kwajalein, Marshall Islands, is a U.S. victory. *About 200 of the 5,000 Japanese forces chose surrender over death in combat.*

February 17–18: Nine U.S. aircraft carriers strike Japanese air and naval base Truk, Caroline Islands.

February 18: Manhattan Project is revealed to selected members of U.S. Congress.

February 20: First U.S. 1,000-bomber attack on Germany.

March 3: Italy's remaining warships are divided among U.S., British, and Soviet navies.

March 6: First major daylight bombing raid on Berlin. *Sixty-nine of 658 U.S. heavy bombers were shot down.*

March 17: First U.S. bombing raid on Vienna, Austria. *About 200 B-24 Liberator heavy bombers attacked this Nazi-controlled city.*

March 19: German forces occupy Hungary.

April 22: First large-scale U.S. amphibious invasion of New Guinea. *Eighty thousand Americans storm the beaches near Japanese-occupied Hollandia.*

May 3: End of meat rationing for American civilians. *Coupons are no longer needed to buy most grades of meat in the United States.*

May 15: Nazis begin deporting 380,000 Jews from Hungary to Auschwitz.

May 17: First major U.S. ground offensive in Asia during World War II. *Merrill's Marauders capture a large air base in Japanese-occupied Burma.*

June 3: Manhattan Project scientists visit the Naval Research Laboratory, Washington, D.C. *They acquire designs for uranium enrichment plant at Oak Ridge, Tennessee.*

June 4: German-occupied Rome falls to the Allies. *Roman civilians celebrate in the streets and cheer for U.S. and British soldiers.*

June 6: D-Day, first day of the Battle of Normandy, the Allied ground offensive in Europe. *Largest amphibious invasion in history begins on beaches of German-occupied France.*

June 12: Fifteen U.S. aircraft carriers attack Japan's bases in the Marianas Islands.

June 13: Germany launches its first V-1 rocket attack on London.

June 15-July 8: The Battle of Saipan: U.S. Marines have 2,000 casualties on the first day. *Of the 30,000 Japanese forces on Saipan, all but 1,000 died in combat or committed suicide.*

June 15: First major bombing raid on Japan during World War II comes from air bases in China. *Forty-seven American B-29 Superfortresses struck factories at Yawata, Japan.*

June 15–16: First U.S. aircraft carrier strike on Japan's Bonin and Volcano Islands.

June 19–20: Battle of Philippine Sea, also known as the Great Marianas Turkey Shoot. *U.S. carrier pilots shot down about 350—all but 35—of Japan's remaining carrier planes.*

June 19: *Shokaku* is sunk in the Philippine Sea by torpedoes from U.S. submarine *Cavalla* (SS-244). *Of the six Japanese carriers that attacked Pearl Harbor, this was the fifth to go down.*

June 22: President Roosevelt signs the Readjustment Act of 1944.*The G.I. Bill, funds jobs, housing, education for anticipated return of military veterans at war's end.*

July 3: Soviet air and ground forces defeat Germans at Minsk, Belarus.

July 7: Death of Adm. Nagumo by suicide on the island of Saipan. *Nagumo commanded the Japanese carrier task force at both Pearl Harbor and Midway.*

July 17: First use of napalm in history of human warfare, near St. Lo, France. *U.S. fighter planes dropped this jellied form of gasoline on a German-held fuel depot.*

July 18: Japanese Army Gen. Tojo resigns as Premier after the fall of Saipan.

July 20: Adolf Hitler survives an assassination attempt by German generals.

July 21: Guam, Marianas Islands, is liberated by the U.S. Army and Marines.

July 24: First Nazi concentration camp liberated by Allied forces during World War II is Majdanek, Poland. *It was discovered by the Soviet Army advancing from the east.*

August 1: Last entry in Anne Frank's diary, three days before her capture by the Gestapo. *Nazi police discovered the Frank family's secret annex in Amsterdam.*

August 25: Liberation of Paris ends the Battle of Normandy. *Allied armies continue east through German-occupied Holland and Belgium.*

September 2: Future U.S. President's torpedo plane is shot down over Japan's Bonin Islands. *Carrier pilot Lt. (j.g.) George H. W. Bush was rescued by submarine* Finback (SS-230).

September 3: Brussels, Belgium, is liberated by Allied armies.

September 6: Independence (CVL-22) becomes the first designated "night carrier" to operate with a U.S. task force. *The crew was specially trained for night launches and recoveries.*

September 8: First German V-2 rocket attack on London.

September 9: First U.S. carrier plane strikes on Japanese-occupied Philippine Islands.

September 12: First U.S. Army ground forces enter Germany.

September 23: U.S. battleship *West Virginia* (BB-48) returns to service with the Pacific Fleet. *This was the last ship repaired from damage during the attack on Pearl Harbor.*

October 4: First—and last—U.S. Navy carrier operation of World War II in the North Atlantic. *Planes from* Ranger (CV-4) *sank five German ships.*

October 10: First U.S. carrier strikes on Japan's Okinawa and Ryukyu Islands.

October 12: First U.S. carrier strike on Japanese-occupied Formosa (Taiwan).

October 14: Allied armies liberate German-occupied Athens, Greece.

October 14: Field Marshal Erwin Rommel, accused by Hitler of treason, commits suicide.

October 19: U.S. Navy announces WAVES will accept African American women.

October 20–21: First major U.S. amphibious invasion of Japanese-occupied Philippines begins.

October 21: First German city captured by Allied armies is Aachen.

October 23–25: Largest naval battle in history: Battle of Leyte Gulf, Philippines. *A force of 216 American and 2 Australian warships engage and defeat 64 Japanese warships.*

October 24: First U.S. Navy ship sunk by Japanese kamikaze attack during World War II. *The escort carrier* St. Lo (CVE-63) *went down during the Battle of Leyte Gulf.*

October 25: Last surviving carrier of the six that attacked Pearl Harbor is destroyed. Zuikaku *was one of twenty-eight Japanese warships that sank during the Battle of Leyte Gulf.*

November 7: Franklin D. Roosevelt is elected to his fourth term in office. *The Republican challenger was Thomas E. Dewey.*

November 24: First major U.S. bombing raid on Tokyo. *The assault by 111 B-29s was launched from newly captured Japanese bases in the Marianas Islands.*

November 25: Himmler orders gas chambers at Auschwitz destroyed.

December 14: U.S. Navy creates new rank of Fleet Admiral (five stars).

December 15: U.S. Army Air Force bandleader Glenn Miller is reported missing, presumed dead. *He was en route to Paris when his plane vanished over the English Channel.*

December 16–27: Battle of the Bulge, Ardennes Forest, Belgium. *Hitler's last major offensive in Europe is defeated by the advancing Allied armies.*

December 17: Japanese Americans are permitted to return to their homes on the West Coast. *In 1988, 60,000 internment camp survivors were awarded $20,000 each in reparations.*

December 18: Typhoon in the South Pacific sinks three U.S. destroyers, damages twenty-one other warships.

Historical Notes

1. Kodiak, largest island in the Gulf of Alaska, became the U.S. Navy's main headquarters in Alaska during World War II. The base and naval air station were designed to accommodate about 11,500 officers and enlisted personnel.

2. Japanese submarine *I-180* was sunk by the U.S. destroyer escort *Gilmore* (DE-18) off the coast of Kodiak, April 26, 1944. The last Japanese warship confirmed sunk in Alaskan waters was the frigate (similar to a destroyer) *Ishigaki* by the submarine *Herring* (SS-233), May 31, 1944. (Fifty-five percent of all Japanese ships lost during World War II were destroyed by U.S. submarines.)

3. About 7,000 professional entertainers performed at USO camp shows on American military bases during World War II. Bob Hope was one of many major celebrities who supported the troops in this way. His first overseas USO tour was to Kodiak and other bases in Alaska, September 1942. (Total USO camp shows, 1941–1947: 428,521.)

4. At this time in 1944, there were 430,000 commissioned officers and officer candidates in the U.S. Navy (including Marines and Coast Guard). Total Navy officers and enlisted personnel had increased to 3.5 million, compared to the less than 200,000 prior to World War II.

5. "Jim Crow" was the title of a nineteenth-century minstrel show song. Beginning in the 1880s, Jim Crow laws were passed to enforce segregation of African Americans from other Americans in both public and private areas, including housing, education, transportation, employment, and even marriage. Although Jim Crow laws were more numerous in southern states, the majority of U.S. states had such laws until the 1960s.

6. The U.S. Navy began training African Americans for all specialties in April 1942. By early 1944, about 6 percent of all Navy enlisted personnel were African Americans. (By 1945, the Navy's official policy was to "accept no theories of racial differences in inborn ability.")

7. "Joint use of facilities" (such as barracks and mess halls) was "desirable," according to Navy policy during World War II, "particularly where the ratio of 'Negro' to 'white' personnel is not high." President Truman ordered an end to all racial segregation in all branches of the U.S. military in 1948.

8. June 6, 1944, was the first day (D-Day) of the long-planned Allied invasion of German-occupied France. Although most of the 156,000 Allied troops who landed by air and sea on that date were American, British, and Canadian, others came from Australia, New Zealand, and the German-occupied countries Belgium, Czechoslovakia, France, Greece, Holland, Norway, and Poland. U.S. casualties on June 6, 1944: 3,393 killed or missing in action; 3,814 wounded.

9. The Battle of Normandy continued from D-Day to August 25, 1944. During that time, about one million additional Allied troops crossed the English Channel to fight the German forces that had occupied France since mid-1940. Total casualties—killed/missing in action/wounded—for U.S. ground forces during the Battle of Normandy: 125,847.

10. The transfer of warplanes to the Soviet Air Force during World War II began in Alaska in 1942. From 1943 to 1945, 7,835 American planes (chiefly fighters and light or medium bombers) were flown out of Alaska by Soviet pilots. In August of 1944 alone, the United States transferred 403 warplanes to the USSR at Kodiak and other bases in Alaska. (Total U.S. planes given to Great Britain, the USSR, China, and other allies during the war: 43,021.)

11. At peak strength in 1944–1945, the USSR had about 12,500,000 serving in all branches of their military. Total Russian military personnel killed or missing in action during World War II is estimated to be 7,500,000.

12. After conferring with Adm. Nimitz and Gen. MacArthur at Pearl Harbor, President Roosevelt traveled to Alaska, arriving on the heavy

cruiser *Baltimore* (CA-68) in Kodiak's harbor on August 7, 1944. He had lunch at Fort Greely—an Army base on Kodiak—went fishing, and departed on the same ship, bound for Washington State, seven hours later.

13. The Soldier Voting Act of 1942 which *required* all states to permit service members to vote via absentee ballot was amended in 1944 to *recommend* such procedures. U.S. military personnel were not *guaranteed* absentee registration and voting rights by all states until Congress passed the Overseas Citizens Voting Rights Act of 1975.

14. Of the 144,000 U.S. and Canadian military personnel in Alaska in mid-1943, all but about 50,000 were transferred elsewhere by the end of 1944.

CHAPTER 21: VICTORY DAYS

January 1, Through August 28, 1945 Time Line

January 17: Soviet Army captures German-occupied Warsaw.

January 20: Roosevelt is inaugurated to his fourth term as President.

January 27: Soviet Army liberates Auschwitz-Birkenau concentration camps, Poland. *They discover hair, clothing, other remains of about 1.5 million victims.*

February 4–11: Yalta Conference: Roosevelt, Churchill, Stalin plan Europe's postwar future.

February 13–14: Allied bombing raids on Dresden, Germany, cause a major firestorm.

February 19–March 26: The Battle of Iwo Jima, largest of Japan's Volcano Islands. *From this base, U.S. fighter planes will have the range to escort heavy bomber missions to Tokyo.*

February 23: U.S. Marines capture Mount Suribachi on Iwo Jima and raise the American flag.

February 23: Allies liberate Manila, Philippines, from Japanese occupation.

March 9–10: Firestorms break out in Tokyo after U.S. bombing raids. *Approximately 100,000 Japanese civilians died in the fires; about one million were made homeless.*

March 26: British and U.S. aircraft carriers join for preinvasion strikes on Okinawa.

April 1–June 22, 1945: The Battle of Okinawa. *U.S. Army and Marines invade and conquer the largest of Japan's Ryukyu Islands.*

April 4: U.S. Third Army liberates Nazi concentration camp at Ohrdruf, Germany.

April 7: Last major naval battle of World War II, East China Sea. *U.S. carrier planes sank Japan's Yamato, world's largest battleship.*

April 11: U.S. Third Army liberates Buchenwald, Germany, finds 21,000 survivors. *This Nazi concentration camp held about 240,000 prior to and during World War II.*

April 12: President Roosevelt dies of brain hemorrhage/stroke. *Vice President Harry S Truman is now President of the United States.*

April 13: President Truman is informed of the Manhattan Project's existence. *Details of the project were revealed to him on April 25.*

April 13: Vienna falls to advancing Soviet ground forces.

April 15: British and Canadian soldiers liberate Bergen-Belsen, Germany, and find 10,000 bodies. *Anne Frank died of typhus in this concentration camp, two to four weeks before its liberation.*

April 25: U.S. and Soviet armies meet as Allies at Germany's Elbe River.

April 27: U.S. Target Committee considers seventeen Japanese sites for future atomic bomb attack.

April 28: Death of Mussolini: Italians capture and kill the former fascist dictator of Italy.

April 29: U.S. Seventh Army liberates concentration camp Dachau, Germany. *Soldiers discover evidence of Nazi torture and cruel medical experiments.*

April 30: Death of Hitler: Nazi leader commits suicide in underground bomb shelter, Berlin.

May 2: Soviet Army captures Berlin; German forces in Italy surrender to the Allies.

May 4: German Armies in Holland, Denmark, and northwest Germany surrender to Allies.

May 5: United States announces 400,000 Americans will remain in Germany as an occupation force.

May 7: All remaining German military forces surrender to Allies. *Documents were signed at Allied headquarters, Rheims, France.*

May 8: President Truman announces V-E Day, end of World War II in Europe.

May 25: United States sets November 1 as D-day for invasion of Kyushu, southernmost of Japan's four main islands. *Total warships (carriers, subs, battleships, cruisers, destroyers) in the U.S. Navy at this time: 1,161*

June 26: Delegates from fifty countries sign the United Nations Charter in San Francisco. *The United Nations will replace the prewar League of Nations.*

July 1: U.S., British, and French troops enter Berlin.

July 9: U.S. Gen. Douglas MacArthur announces liberation of the Philippines.

July 10: Fourteen U.S. aircraft carriers begin preinvasion strikes on Japan's home islands. *Total U.S. Navy planes of all types at this time: 40,417 (versus the prewar, mid-1941 total of 3,406).*

July 13: Italy declares war on Japan.

July 16: World's first successful test explosion of an atomic bomb. *In the Alamagordo desert, near the Manhattan Project laboratory, Los Alamos, New Mexico.*

July 16: Cruiser *Indianpolis* (CA 35) departs United States with two disassembled atomic bombs. *Destination is the U.S. air base on Tinian, Marianas Islands.*

July 17–August 2: The Potsdam Conference in Germany, last summit meeting of World War II. *The United States, Great Britain, and China issue unconditional surrender ultimatum to Japan.*

July 24–28: U.S. carrier planes attack remaining Japanese warships in the Inland Sea. *They sank 2 carriers, 3 battleships, 5 cruisers, 1 destroyer, 1 submarine.*

July 26: New British Prime Minister is Clement Atlee.

Churchill's Conservative party lost its majority in Parliament.

July 27: Japanese military leaders reject Allies' demand for unconditional surrender. *Japan's civilian officials leaders were not consulted.*

July 30: Japanese submarine sinks cruiser *Indianapolis* in the Philippine Sea. *Only 316 of 1,199 crew members survived.*

July 30: President Truman consents to use of atomic bombs against Japan.

August 1: U.S. bombers drop one million leaflets on thirty-five Japanese cities, including Hiroshima. *Leaflets warn civilians to evacuate those cities "immediately."*

August 5: Japanese Army officials receive news from Tokyo University. *Japanese research on the principles of nuclear fission for weapons is under way.*

August 6: First use of a nuclear weapon, dropped by a U.S. B-29 bomber. *Industrial city Hiroshima, Honshu Island, housed Japanese Army troops and supply depots.*

August 6: Last U.S. warship lost during World War II, submarine *Bullhead* (SS-332).

August 8: Soviet Union declares war on Japan and invades Japanese-occupied Manchuria the next day.

August 9: U.S. plane drops an atomic bomb on Nagasaki, Kyushu Island.

August 10: Japan's civilian leaders deliver surrender message to Allies.

August 14: President Truman announces Japan has surrendered to Allies. *Japanese Army officers tried to destroy the emperor's prerecorded radio message of surrender.*

August 15: President Truman orders two V-J Day holidays for American workers. *Japanese radio broadcasts Emperor Hirohito's surrender message to his country.*

August 16: Japan's Prince Norukiko Higashi-Kuni forms a new civilian government.

August 28: First U.S. military occupation forces arrive in Japan by air and sea.

Historical Notes

1. San Diego was known as the "Port of Navy Wives" during World War II. The city's civilian population doubled—to nearly 400,000—largely due to the sudden increase in military dependents. By 1945, the Navy was training about 90,000 recruits per year at the Naval Training Center in San Diego.

2. With nearly 10 percent of the U.S. population drafted or volunteering for military service during World War II, the nation's civilian unemployment dropped to a record low of 1.2 percent in 1944.

3. The Naval Training Center at Gulfport, Mississippi, was the largest of several U.S. Navy facilities in Mississippi during World War II. (After the war, it became a center for a Naval Construction Battalion, also known as Seabees.)

4. In late 1942, delegates from nine German-occupied countries reported to the United Nations that at least 3.4 million people had died in Nazi concentration camps. The civilian press gave little coverage to these well-documented reports until American journalists accompanied Allied armies through Germany in the spring of 1945. Edward R. Murrow's radio description of Buchenwald aired April 15, 1945; Margaret Bourke-White's photos of corpses and survivors from the Holocaust appeared in *Life* magazine, May 7, 1945.

5. After losing most of their remaining carrier pilots in the Battle of the Philippine Sea, the Japanese military resorted to the Special Attack Force, commonly known as "suicide planes" or "kamikazes," during the Battle of Leyte Gulf, October 1944. The civilian press did not reveal this new enemy tactic until late April 1945. (Total kamikaze missions, October 1944–August 1945: 2,940. They sank 34 U.S. ships and damaged 288.)

6. Of the 20–23,000 Japanese forces on Iwo Jima, fewer than 200 were found alive after a six-week battle with about 30,000 U.S. Marines. Total Marines killed in action or died shortly thereafter from wounds received on Iwo Jima: 5,521. Another 3,114 Marines were "invalided from service"—discharged due to severity of their injuries. The Japanese troops' refusal to surrender in this and all other battles may have stemmed from a certain tradition within the Shinto faith: that the soul of one who dies in military combat becomes a *kami*—a Shinto spirit—to be worshipped at the Yasukuni Shrine in Tokyo, Japan.

7. The Battle of Okinawa, April 1–June 22, 1945, was the largest amphibious invasion of the war in the Pacific. Approximately 150,000 air, land, and sea forces began the assault, followed by about 150,000 more in subsequent days and weeks. Total Americans killed on Okinawa: 12,281. Estimated Japanese military and civilian deaths on that island: 160,000.

8. U.S. military strategists scheduled the first amphibious invasion of Japan's home islands for November 1, 1945. It was estimated that a total of 1.5 million U.S. forces would be required to conquer and secure the heavily populated and defended island of Kyushu.

9. In wartime the Merchant Marine, the nation's commercial ships and the sailors who operate them, becomes an auxiliary to the U.S. Navy. Pass Christian, Mississippi, was one of three locations for training the 243,000 sailors in the Merchant Marine during World War II.

10. Alarm clocks were one of many items that most Americans could not buy during World War II. Other consumer goods that were either un-

available or in short supply included cars, refrigerators, washing machines, bedsprings, typewriters, bicycles, and hairpins.

11. The Smyth Report, a general explanation of the Manhattan Project's research and development of the world's first nuclear weapons was released to the American civilian press August 12, 1945, after two major Japanese cities had been destroyed by atomic bombs.

12. The Japanese Army's headquarters on Honshu was located in the city of Hiroshima, with an estimated troop strength of 25,000. Earliest Japanese estimates of both civilian and military deaths from this first use of an atomic bomb in warfare: 71,000 dead, 68,000 injured. (At least 40,000 were killed and 60,000 injured when the second atomic bomb was dropped on the city of Nagasaki three days later.)

13. Eniwetok, an atoll in the Marshall Islands, was captured by U.S. forces in 1944. It became a test site for U.S. atomic bombs in 1947. The first thermonuclear (hydrogen) bomb was test-exploded on Eniwetok in 1952. The island was not declared safe for human habitation until 1980.

14. Most of the nearly 3.5 million Navy officers and enlisted personnel who were on active duty in 1945 accepted discharge within five years of the end of World War II. By 1950, total U.S. Navy personnel dropped to about 380,000.

EPILOGUE

1. After World War II, about 500,000 American military personnel served varying periods of deployment to Japan as part of the occupation forces under the command of General of the Army Douglas MacArthur. During the seven years of postwar occupation (1945–1952), Japan received U.S. grants and loans of $2.2 billion (in 1945 dollars) for reconstruction, demilitarization, and democratization. The 1951 peace treaty that restored Japan's status as an independent, self-governing nation went into effect on April 28, 1952.

2. The CAA—Civil Aeronautics Authority—created in 1938 to regulate civilian air traffic in the United States, split into two federal agencies in 1940: the CAB—Civil Aeronautics Board—and the CAA—Civil Aeronautics Administration. The FAA, Federal Aviation Administration, absorbed the functions of both in 1958.

3. From 1946 to 1964, nearly 80 million children were born in the United States. This sudden population growth, the postwar baby boom, is com-

monly believed to have resulted from the roughly 16 million young Americans who came home, married, and started families after they were discharged from military service at the end of World War II.

4. The United States recorded 292,131 military personnel killed during World War II, broken down by branch of service as follows: Army and Army Air Force, 234,874; Navy, 36,950; Marines, 19,733; Coast Guard, 574. (The Merchant Marine reported 5,662 deaths, 4,780 missing, presumed dead.)

5. Anyone who has been exposed to events that threatened death or serious harm may exhibit symptoms of the anxiety disorder known as posttraumatic stress disorder. The most common symptoms of PTSD are a desire to avoid being reminded of the event, flashbacks, and nightmares.

6. Shortly after its founding in 1958, the Pearl Harbor Survivors Association estimated 70,000 American military veterans qualified for membership. In April 2008, this national organization's membership was 4,923. Of the total 16,112,566 Americans who served in the U.S. armed forces during World War II, 2.5 million are estimated to be living in September 2008.

7. On September 11, 2001, at nearly the same time of day as the attack on Pearl Harbor in 1941, nineteen terrorists hijacked four American commercial jets and deliberately crashed them, killing themselves, 238 passengers and crews. The plane that crashed into the Pentagon, Washington D.C., killed an additional 125 people; the two that crashed into the World Trade Center buildings in New York City killed at least 2,630. This attack, often referred to as "9/11," began the War on Terrorism, 2001–present.

8. The museum built over *Arizona* (BB-39) at Pearl Harbor lists the names of the 1,177 crew members who died on that ship during the Japanese carrier planes' attack on December 7, 1941. In 1980, the U.S. Navy turned the operation of this museum over to the National Park Service, which now offers tours from the visitor center on shore.

9. Japan reported 1,140,420 military personnel killed during World War II. Japanese civilian deaths have been variously estimated from 700,000 to 10 million. Worldwide, the total number killed during World War II is estimated at 54,770,000, of whom about 38,573,000 were civilians. World War II was the first war that caused more civilian deaths than military.

BIBLIOGRAPHY

GENERAL PRINT RESOURCES

Ambrose, Stephen. *American Heritage New History of World War II*. New York: Viking, 1997.

Chambers, John Whiteclay, II, and Fred Anderson, eds. *The Oxford Companion to American Military History*. New York: Oxford University Press, 1999.

Craven, Wesley Frank, and James Lea Cate, eds. *Army Air Forces in World War II*. Washington, DC: Office of Air Force History, 1983.

Boyne, Walter J. *Clash of Titans: World War II at Sea*. New York: Simon & Schuster, 1995.

Bradley, John H. *The Second World War: Asia and the Pacific*. West Point, NY: Square One, 2002.

Carter, Kit C. and Robert Mueller. *The Army Air Forces in World War II: Combat Chronology, 1941–1945*. Washington, DC: Center for Air Force History, 1991.

Dunnigan, James F., and Albert A. Nofi. *Dirty Little Secrets: Military Information You're Not Supposed to Know*. New York: Morrow, 1990.

Ellis, John. *World War II: A Statistical Survey; The Essential Facts and Figures for All the Combatants*. New York: Facts on File, 1995.

Fahey, James C. *The Ships and Aircraft of the United States Fleet*. Victory Edition. New York: Ships and Aircraft, 1945.

Hoyt, Edwin P. *How They Won the War in the Pacific: Nimitz and His Admirals*. Guilford, CT: Globe Pequot/Lyons, 2002.

Ireland, Bernard, and Eric Grove. *Jane's War at Sea: 1897–1997*. New York: HarperCollins, 1997.

Kenney, George C. *General Kenney Reports: A Personal History of the Pacific War*. Washington, DC: Office of Air Force History / U.S. Air Force, 1987.

Morison, Samuel Eliot. *History of United States Naval Operations in World War II*. 15 vols. Edison, NJ: Castle Books, 2001. (A later edition of the set's first publication in 1947.)

Morrison, Wilbur H. *Above and Beyond: 1941–1945*. New York: St. Martin's Press, 1983.

Sweetman, Jack. *American Naval History: An Illustrated Chronology of the U.S. Navy and Marine Corps, 1775–Present*. 3rd ed. Annapolis: Naval Institute Press, 2002.

World at War: 1939–1945. Pleasantville, NY: Reader's Digest, 1999.

World War II: A Fiftieth Anniversary History by the Writers and Photographers of the Associated Press. New York: Henry Holt, 1989.

ADDITIONAL PRINT RESOURCES FOR SPECIFIC TOPICS, BY CHAPTER

Chapter 1: The Tree Army

Baker, William J. *Jesse Owens: An American Life*. New York: Free Press, 1986.

Burg, David F. *The Great Depression*. New York: Facts on File, 1996.

Essin, Emmett M. *Shavetails and Bell Sharps: The History of the U.S. Army Mule*. Lincoln: University of Nebraska Press, 1997.

Kaltenborn, H. V. *Fifty Fabulous Years: A Personal Review*. G. P. Putnam's Sons: New York, 1950.

Rich, Doris L. *Amelia Earhart: A Biography*. Washington, DC: Smithsonian Institution Press, 1989.

Waldman, Carl. *Encyclopedia of Native American Tribes*. New York: Facts on File, 1999.

Woog, Adam. *Roosevelt and the New Deal*. San Diego: Lucent, 1998.

Chapter 3: Basic Training

Bluejackets' Manual: 1939. 9th ed. Annapolis: United States Naval Institute, 1939.

Bluejackets' Manual: 1946. 13th ed. Annapolis: United States Naval Institute, 1946.

Camacho, Mary E. *Cradle of the Navy: The History of Naval Training Center San Diego, 1923–1997*. N.P.: Jostens Publishing Company, n.d. (Comprised of photos and articles from the base newspaper.)

Canfield, Bruce. "100 Years of the '03 Springfield." *American Rifleman: Official Journal of the National Rifle Association of America*. March 2003, vol. 151, no. 3, pp. 42–45.

Chapter 5: Radio School

Zmijewsky, Steve, et al. *The Complete Films of John Wayne*. New York: Carol Publishing Group, 1990.

Chapter 8: The Attack on Pearl Harbor

Cohen, Stan. *East Wind Rain: A Pictorial History of the Pearl Harbor Attack*. Missoula, MT: Pictorial Histories Publishing Co., 1990.

Delgado, James P. *Pearl Harbor Recalled: New Images of the Day of Infamy*. Annapolis: Naval Institute Press, 1991.

Ireland, Bernard. *Jane's Battleships of the 20th Century*. New York: HarperCollins, 1996.

Lord, Walter. *Day of Infamy*. New York: Holt, 1957.

Slackman, Michael. *Target Pearl Harbor*. Honolulu: University of Hawaii Press and Arizona Memorial Association, 1990.

Weintraub, Stanley. *Long Day's Journey into War: December 7, 1941*. New York: Dutton, 1991.

Chapter 9: Aftershocks

Young, Stephen Bower. *Trapped at Pearl Harbor: Escape from Battleship Oklahoma*. Croton-on-Hudson, NY: North River Press; Annapolis: Naval Institute Press, 1991.

Chapter 10: The Submarine

Gray, Edwyn. *Submarine Warriors*. Novato, CA: Presidio Press, 1988.

Roscoe, Theodore. *United States Submarine Operations in World War II*. Annapolis: United States Naval Institute, 1949.

Submarine Veterans of World War II: A History of the Veterans of the United States Naval Submarine Fleet. Dallas: Taylor Publishing / Military Publications, 1986.

Wilson, John S. *The Story of the Great Bands: 1936–1945*. N.P.: Readers Digest Association, 1980.

Chapter 11: The Aircraft Carrier

Angelucci, Enzo. *The American Fighter*. New York: Orion, 1995.

Grossnick, Roy A. *Dictionary of American Naval Aviation Squadrons*, vol. 1. Washington, DC: Naval Historical Center, 1995.

Reynolds, Clark G. *The Carrier War*. Alexandria, VA: Time-Life Books, 1982.

Sherman, Frederick C. *Combat Command: The American Aircraft Carriers in the Pacific War*. With a preface by William F. Halsey. New York: Dutton, 1950.

Stafford, Edward Peary. *The Big E: The Story of the USS Enterprise*. Foreword by Arthur W. Radford. New York: Random House, 1962.

Wooldridge, E. T., ed. *Carrier Warfare in the Pacific: An Oral History Collection*. Foreword by John B. Connally. Washington: Smithsonian Institution Press, 1993.

Chapter 12: The Battle of the Coral Sea

Johnston, Stanley. *Queen of the Flat-Tops: The USS Lexington and the Coral Sea Battle*. New York: Ballantine, 1970. First published 1942 by Dutton.

Chapter 13: The Battle of Midway

Lord, Walter. *Incredible Victory*. New York: Simon & Schuster / Pocket Books, 1968.

Chapter 15: Rescued at Sea

Ballard, Robert D. *Return to Midway*. Toronto: Madison Press, 1999.

Chapter 16: The Summer of '42

Frank, Anne. *Anne Frank: The Diary of a Young Girl*. New York: Pocket Books, 1965. First published 1952 by Doubleday.

Kallen, Stuart A. *World War II: The War at Home*. San Diego: Lucent, 2000.

Chapter 17: First Leave

Whitfield, R. V. "Return to Treasure Island." *All Hands: The Bureau of Naval Personnel Career Publication*. February 1967, pp. 16–18.

Chapter 18: The Naval Research Laboratory

Groves, Leslie. *Now It Can Be Told: The Story of the Manhattan Project*. New York: Harper, 1962.

Chapter 19: Cold Bay

Alaska at War, 1941–1945: The Forgotten War Remembered. Papers from the Alaska at War Symposium, Anchorage, Alaska, November 11–13, 1993. Edited by Fern Chandonnet. Anchorage: Alaska at War Committee, 1995.

Capture of Attu, The: Tales of World War II in Alaska, As Told by the Men Who Fought There. Foreword by Terrence Cole. Edmonds, WA: Alaska Northwest Publishing Co., 1984.

Cohen, Stan. *The Forgotten War: A Pictorial History of World War II in Alaska and Northwestern Canada*. Missoula, MT: Pictorial Histories, 1981.

Donovan, Robert J. *PT-109: John F. Kennedy in World War II*. New York: McGraw-Hill, 1961.

Rigge, Simon. *War in the Outposts*. Alexandria, VA: Time-Life Books, 1980.

Chapter 20: Kodiak

Coffey, Frank. *Always Home: 50 years of the USO—the Official Photographic History*. Special foreword by Bob Hope. Washington, DC: Brassey's, 1991.

Nalty, Bernard C. *With Courage: The U.S. Army Air Forces in World War II*. Washington, DC: Air Force History and Museums Program, 1994.

Russell, Richard A. *Project Hula: Secret Soviet-American Cooperation in the War Against Japan*. U.S. Navy in the Modern World Series, No. 4. Washington, DC: Naval Historical Center / US Government Printing Office, 1997.

Smith, Blake W. *Warplanes to Alaska*. Surrey, BC: Hancock House, 1998.